continued from the

of overcrowded schools and parks, air and water pollution, endless traffic jams, and shortages of water.

The authors describe how this has come about. They carefully examine the arguments in favor of rapid growth and expose the fallacies of conservatism and of our religious attitudes on the question of birth control. Finally, they propose ways in which our unstable growth may be voluntarily stemmed before nature intervenes with a higher death rate, or coercive measures, abhorrent to our cultural and moral values, become inevitable.

LINCOLN DAY was born in Iowa in 1928. After attending the public schools of Colorado, he received his B.A. degree at Yale and his M.A. and Ph.D. degrees at Columbia. He has been a United Nations statistician and has taught sociology at Mt. Holyoke College, Princeton, and Columbia. On leave from his post as a Research Associate at Columbia's Bureau of Applied Social Research, Dr. Day is currently a Visiting Fellow in Demography at the Australian National University.

ALICE DAY, a New Yorker, attended the Brearley School in New York, and received her B.A. from Smith College and her M.A. from Columbia, where she met her husband. She has done research at the Bureau of Applied Social Research at Columbia and at the American Institute of Public Opinion and has taught sociology at Mt. Holyoke and the University of Massachusetts. The Days have two children.

Too
Many
Americans

Too
Many
Americans

Lincoln H. Day
and
Alice Taylor Day

HOUGHTON MIFFLIN COMPANY BOSTON
The Riverside Press

24008

To Thomas and Caroline

Preface

THE PURPOSE of this book is to challenge, and present an alternative to, the widespread notion that Americans can afford to be complacent—even enthusiastic—about their present high rate of population increase. The need for such a book was impressed upon us by the scores of letters received in response to an article by one of us on the American birth rate.[1] The overwhelming preponderance of these letters indicated confusion and misinformation about the facts both of world population growth in general and of American population growth in particular. Sometimes this stemmed from a distorted time perspective—failure to distinguish between immediate and long-range consequences of growth, for instance—at other times from ignorance, and at still others from misunderstanding of the issues involved. Overall was the inability, or unwillingness, to consider the meaning of American population growth in broad, general perspective, rather than merely in terms of its impact on particular individuals or groups. The idea that population growth in the United States might affect the welfare of people elsewhere in the world was entirely lacking.

The same failings occur in the treatment accorded this subject in the press, television and radio, and in letters to newspapers. Growth rates in the United States are rarely even alluded to. Americans seem almost to regard their country as immune from any difficulties associated with numerical increase, and themselves as in no way responsible—despite their own high birth rate—for contributing to the difficulties of providing for the world's people.

In this book we enumerate the reasons why early attainment of population stability in the United States would be in the best interests of Americans, and we discuss how, given the predominant values of American culture, this goal might best be achieved. Since attitudes toward population policy must inevitably rest on a blend of information and values, we include a general discussion of those religious and secular beliefs and values that seem most influential in shaping American attitudes toward family building and population control. We also discuss the relevance and irrelevance, merits and demerits, of the arguments against cessation of population growth in the United States. Almost any suggestion that population growth should be checked is likely to be countered vigorously by appeal to one or another of the four such arguments we discuss here.

We have many intellectual debts. Those of longest standing are to our teachers: especially Professors Charles H. Page (now of Princeton University), and the late Gladys Bryson of Smith College, and Professors Stephen W. Reed, James G. Leyburn (now of Washington and Lee University), and the late Raymond Kennedy of Yale. During post-graduate study at Columbia our thinking was greatly influenced by Professors Kingsley Davis (now of the University of California, Berkeley) and Robert S. Lynd.

At various stages of this work we have gained much from the thoughtful comments and questions of such friends as W. D. Borrie, Harold K. Douthit, Jr., Constance Dulles Weems, Robert M. Northrop, and Curtis and Elaine Smith.

But we are especially indebted to two other friends, A. J. Jaffe and Leslie W. Dunbar, both of whom read large portions of the manuscript in its initial form. Whatever merit this book may have owes much to their learned and searching criticisms.

Finally, we must acknowledge our debt to Erik Wensberg,

former editor of the *Columbia University Forum,* for his very helpful suggestions concerning the article from which all this started.

Though each of these persons has contributed much to our thinking, no one of them can be held directly accountable for the particular direction it has taken in this book.

L.H.D.

A.T.D.

Contents

Preface   vii

Introduction   1

PART I. THE MEANING OF POPULATION GROWTH
IN THE UNITED STATES

1. American Population Growth in the World Context   11
2. Too Many or Too Few: The Idea of the Optimum   35
3. Population Growth and the American Way of Life   45

PART II. FACTORS SHAPING THE ATTITUDES OF AMERICANS
TOWARD THEIR POPULATION GROWTH

4. Religion   77
5. Attitudes and Values   103

PART III. THE ARGUMENTS AGAINST A STABLE POPULATION
—AND WHY THEY ARE INVALID

6. The Economic Argument   133
7. The "Scientific" Argument   155
8. The Military Argument   173
9. The "Selective Control" Argument   189

PART IV. CONCLUSION

10. Achieving a Stable Population in the United States   219

Notes   249
Selected Bibliography and Suggested Readings   269
Index of Names   279
Index of Subjects   287

Too
Many
Americans

Introduction

Perhaps we should begin with an apology—an apology for writing a book on population that does not focus on the hungry, crowded majority of the world's people, but seeks instead to describe the meaning of population growth among that mere five or six percent who inhabit the richest country in the world. There is little dispute today about the relevance of population growth to poverty in the economically underdeveloped regions of the world. But a like appreciation for the relation between such growth and a people's well-being in the more affluent countries is, with few exceptions,[1] conspicuously lacking. In particular, Americans—who are, after all, nearly 190 million people—need to be made aware of the facts of their current population growth and of the implications of this growth for their own and their children's welfare. And they need to know, also, that the size of their population is relevant to the fate of people elsewhere in the world.

The United States is currently experiencing one of the most rapid rates of sustained population growth in the history of man; and this at a time when population in the world as a whole is itself increasing at an unprecedented rate. In the midst of this "explosion" Americans seem to regard their own numerical increase with indulgent complacency: unaware of the consequences of this growth, unconcerned about the fact of it, and desirous, in many instances, of having more children than did their parents. At the same time, there is, in the United

States, extensive control over the two determinants of population growth—mortality and natality. Death rates are among the lowest in the world, and the knowledge of how to prevent conception is nearly universal.[2] We possess, in short, the means of controlling our growth. We need not be victimized by it.

With the average American couple having fewer than three children, the present situation in this country is a dramatic illustration of a new and tremendously significant fact: no longer is the large family a requisite of population increase. The low mortality rates of today permit a rapid, sustained population growth when average family size is of only moderate dimensions. For anyone concerned with attaining population stability by voluntary means, this raises two important problems: first, the moderate size of the average family impedes public awareness of growth and widely diffuses responsibility for it, and second, with the typical family no larger than it is, any further reduction in average family size can hardly come without entailing for many a heavy personal sacrifice.

If we in America are to attain population stability without an increase in mortality, our birth rate must ultimately be reduced to a figure some 40 percent lower than it now is.

In every continent, man is increasing rapidly. Until some 150 years ago, human populations, like those of the animals, were highly responsive to nature's capacity to provide. The birth rate fluctuated only slightly, tending to remain at a consistently high level. But not so the death rate. Without migration, shortages in food, water, or other essentials led inevitably to higher mortality. Today this is no longer the case. The balance of nature has been upset. By learning to control death, man has deprived nature of her means to maintain the stability of human populations. Thus, a new stability is called for, one in which control over the number of births is extensive enough to balance the lowered incidence of death.

Control over births is already widely used and accepted in

industrialized countries, but justification for this practice is almost exclusively in terms of specifically individual goals. Though certain ancient and primitive peoples attempted to regulate their populations, the notion that we may need to control the growth of our whole species is new and alien to traditional ideas about man's place in the universe. The principle of a whole society's responsibility for stabilizing its numbers continues to be evaded. Certainly this is true in the United States. Americans are, on the whole, poorly informed and little concerned about their population growth. One reason for this may be that the little discussion there is of population is focused almost exclusively on the growing pains of the underdeveloped countries—with the implication that our own growth is of no moment either to us or to anyone else. It may also be that a rich country can meet, more readily than a poor one, the extra costs that population growth entails. We in the United States, for instance, can afford to alleviate, if only in the short run, many of the deleterious consequences of population density before the discomfort and inconvenience they cause become acute. As a result, there is a very real danger that efforts to halt population growth here and in other industrialized countries will at best be ineffectual until we, the affluent minority, experience at firsthand the penalties such growth already visits on a majority of the world's people. Then, too, our religious climate has undoubtedly inhibited the circulation of ideas about population growth and control, as much by the fear it creates of open controversy between religious groups as by active religious opposition to the principle of population control itself.

Americans are adding substantially to the current burgeoning of world population. Since World War II, the American population has been growing at a rate almost as high as during the last decade of the nineteenth century—and this with total numbers nearly three times as large. Our growth rate of 2.1

GROWTH OF UNITED STATES POPULATION
1790-1980

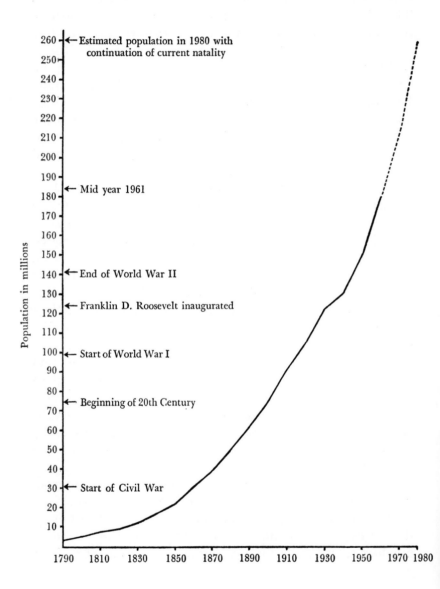

percent added a yearly average of 1,300,000 in the 1890's, but a rate that has averaged 1.8 percent since the end of World War II has been adding more than 2,800,000 to our population *each year,* a number about equal to the population of the whole San Francisco–Oakland urban area, and nearly half a million larger than the entire Boston metropolitan area. Less than one hundred years at this rate and our number would be one billion—over a third of the present population of the entire world.

Now much can be done at this point with the compound interest formula: 365 years at present rates and our country would have the population density of New York City; 772 years and it would be so dense as to give each person an average of only one square foot, and so forth. It has become almost a game among demographers to see who can think up the more grotesque example. Professor Charles Westoff of New York University offers the following to describe world trends: "If the current rate of world population growth had prevailed since the beginning of the Christian era, the world would now contain 90 billion times 10 to the 12th power or 90 billion times a trillion persons—a number," he adds, "which staggers the imagination." But the calculation that Professor Westoff modestly says appeals to him the most is the following, computed by Professor Ansley Coale of Princeton: "In about 6,500 years, if current growth continues, the descendants of the present world population would form a solid sphere of live bodies expanding with a radial velocity that, neglecting relativity, would equal the velocity of light."[3]

The compound interest formula easily lends itself to the production of shocking statistics. (What was that figure about the number of years it would take at their current rate of growth before scientific journals smothered us all?) Obviously, there is no necessary connection between mathematical possibilities and human realities. Population does not follow some ineluctable logic all its own. What happens to population is the result of what happens over the whole range of human experience: our living standards, the organization of our families, our aspirations, and our fears.

The extrapolation of present trends merely shows what would happen—in a numerical sense only—if these trends were to continue. But since the nature and rate of population growth will itself serve to change the social setting, such extrapolations do little more than offer a fairly adequate picture of the immediate future, while making abundantly clear the fact that population growth will—indeed *must*—eventually cease. Long before our numbers reached the stage represented by these extreme projections, levels of living would necessarily have dropped so low in response to the pressure of continued growth as to produce a substantially higher death rate. This would be tantamount to returning to pre-industrial conditions of life, with poorer nutrition, less adequate medical and public health care, substandard housing, and inferior schooling.

Back in 1944, Professor Frank Notestein of Princeton, speaking specifically of population growth in the underdeveloped countries, concluded that "unless there are drastic changes, sooner or later there must come a point at which continued increase forces down living levels, so that mortality will begin to rise."[4] Today, nineteen years (and an additional 650 million people) later, the situation is even more desperate. Production has already fallen behind population growth in many parts of the world. At a rate such as this, increases in mortality can be only a matter of time. What these extreme projections show better than anything else is that man himself must assume responsibility for stabilizing human numbers by limiting births, else that stability will come about, instead, through a higher incidence of death.

The decisions we Americans make about population control today will greatly determine the kind of society we live in tomorrow. Even if population growth does not at times appear to have very great importance for our short-run welfare, the point at which it is halted will have great consequences for succeeding generations. Their level of living, in a material sense, and the degree of freedom and dignity possible to them, will depend on the point at which stability is achieved.

A United States with 200 million inhabitants in 1980 would be a substantially different United States from one with 250 million. A United States with one billion inhabitants in the year 2058 would be substantially different from a United States that had achieved population stability at a figure one-fourth as large. The size and character of a population, its rate of growth or decline, act as forces changing and shaping social conditions. Such differences in the population size of the United States would indicate differences in family life, in economic conditions, in opportunities for the individual, and in values. They would also represent differences in the tendency to perpetuate certain ways and change others.

The question we Americans must ask is this: How large are we going to let our population become before it stops growing, and what will be the conditions of life—in terms of diet, housing, work, play, security, freedom, and personal liberty— once this growth has ceased? How much, that is, will we have to sacrifice—materially, ethically, politically, aesthetically—here, and in the rest of the world, before population growth is halted? And there is another question, too: By what means will numerical stability be achieved, and, once achieved, maintained? Will that means be a higher death rate, or will it be a lower birth rate?

Part I

The Meaning
of Population Growth
in the United States

I

American Population Growth
in the World Context

By the middle of the seventeenth century the population of the world had grown to some 500 million. Depending on which calculation you accept for the length of time man has been on earth, it may have taken as few as 1000 or as many as 10,000 centuries to reach that number. But in only *three* additional centuries, from the middle of the seventeenth to the middle of the twentieth, world population increased a total of *six* times!

Were present rates to continue, a mere forty more years would see the addition of three billion more people to double the present population of the world. The next doubling, coming but forty years later, would add six billion to bring the total up to twelve billion by the year 2040—a rather far remove from that 500 million at the time of the first European colonization of America.

To this remarkable expansion of human numbers, the United States has been a leading contributor. Rapid population increase has been a prominent feature of American life since before the founding of the Republic. The components of American growth have undergone considerable change, however. Today's set of factors, though an outgrowth of earlier patterns, is without precedent.

In the past our high rate of growth was sustained by a combination of large-scale immigration and large-sized families. What sustains it today is a combination of four demographic conditions, each of which has become more pronounced in the period since World War II: low death rates, a clustering of family size in the two- to four-children range, nearly universal marriage, and a generally early age at marriage. Migration now figures but little in the total, while the large family of six or more children occurs only rarely.

Only three processes determine the size of any population: natality, mortality, migration. It is these which also determine its age and sex composition. Natality is measured by the birth rate: the number of live births in a given year per 1000 population; mortality by the death rate: the number of deaths in a given year per 1000 population; and migration by the excess of immigrants over emigrants in a given year per 1000 population. Every condition affecting the number of people in a given area, or their age and sex composition, must operate through one or the other of these three variables. It must either raise or lower the birth rate, raise or lower the death rate, increase or decrease immigration and emigration. There is no other way. (On a world scale, of course, only natality and mortality need be considered, since migration to and from the earth is nonexistent, and, as we shall see in Chapter 7, can be expected to remain nonexistent.)

Two facts stand out prominently in the demographic history of the United States: first, our unique position as a receiver of immigrants; second, our continuously high rate of growth from natural increase — that is, from an excess of births over deaths. Except for the 400,000 descendants[1] of the various Indian tribes, ours is a nation of immigrants, their children, grandchildren, and great-grandchildren. Immigration quotas, established for the most part after World War I, and entrance restrictions, imposed ostensibly for security reasons, have changed this to a degree. But even with the restrictions currently in force, the number of people moving to this country has continued to be substantial by comparison with the experience of other countries.[2] In fact, although they added *proportionately* little to our population growth, the number of immigrants to the

United States over the past decade was as great as during the Irish famines of the 1840's.[3]

Nevertheless, despite the influx of more than a million immigrants during each of the peak years, it is probable that natural increase has added more to our growth than immigration in every year of our history.[4] Even during the decade of the 1840's, when the Irish potato famine brought a sudden doubling of immigrants, only a fourth of the increase in numbers came from net immigration; while in 1900–1910, the peak decade of immigration to this country, the gain from natural increase exceeded that from migration by some 85 percent.[5] Thus, from a purely demographic standpoint, the excess of births over deaths has been of far greater importance in determining the size of our population than has the addition of persons through immigration. This gain from natural increase has, moreover, surpassed that of any of the western European countries— countries whose levels of economic and social development are most comparable to ours.

Migration

Yet, the fact of immigration, the distribution and heterogeneity of the migrants, have surely been among the most important determinants of our way of life and the character of our institutions. Except for the importation of African slaves and a few Chinese laborers, the peopling of the United States was part of a general growth and expansion of European peoples that in less than three centuries had increased their number by nearly 700 million, and raised their proportion of the world's population from 19 to 39 percent.[6]

Altogether, some 38 million had actually immigrated by 1930,[7] of whom 370,000 to 400,000 were Africans imported as slaves.[8] There was a reverse movement, of course, but it tended to be small by comparison, averaging, as nearly as we can tell from not too reliable statistics, about 30 percent of the number immigrating.[9] It seems probable that most of these latter were foreign-born returning to their countries of origin. Apart from the rather numerous departures during the Colonial period, the rate of emigration was at its highest in the Depression years of 1931–1936, when there was actually a net loss through migration of some 239,000 persons.[10]

By 1870, one out of three white Americans was either an immigrant or the son or daughter of an immigrant. Rising to 37 percent by 1890, this proportion reached a peak of 39 percent in 1910.[11] But by 1950, it had dropped to 22 percent.[12] Of all the regions of the country, only the South failed to participate to any great extent in this peculiarly American experience.

The immigration experienced by the United States was unique in the history of the world. No other country before or since has received so many people in so short a time. No other migratory stream has been fed by so many traversing such great distances. In a very real sense it was the unique result of a unique combination of circumstances: demographic and economic conditions in Europe, an amount of political freedom for purposes of geographical movement unknown since the fall of Rome, vastly improved communications, a large and relatively unsettled land rich in resources, and—particularly after the introduction of the steamboat—unprecedently swift, inexpensive, and reliable ocean transport. Such a fortuitous combination can hardly occur again. Free migration and free entry on this scale no longer seems possible. Such vast numbers of people may still migrate, but it is most unlikely that any country will receive them except under duress. If migration of this magnitude occurs in the world as it is now constituted, it can hardly come otherwise than as the result of war or the threat of war. It will not be a peaceful movement. The number of potential migrants far exceeds the number of places for them.

When migration is proposed as a solution to drain surplus population from critical areas, it might be well to remember our own history. The peak year of immigration to this country was 1907. In that year the number who entered as immigrants was not quite 1.3 million—a number less than one-fourth the current yearly addition to the population of India.

Natural Increase

As early as 1798, in the first edition of his celebrated "Essay on Population," Thomas R. Malthus claimed that the population of the United States was increasing at a rate "probably without parallel in history." Whether or not, as he also claimed, it had over the preceding century and a half been doubling itself every twenty-five years,[13] natural increase in the United States has most certainly been consistently high. This has been the result more of a higher birth rate than of a particularly low death rate, however. In fact, duration of life in the United States has tended to be somewhat shorter than in northern and western Europe, though it is still long by world standards.[14]

The American birth rate has been consistently higher than that in northern and western Europe, right up to the present time. Some 125 years ago, the birth rate was about 32 in England and Wales, 28 in France, and 31 in Sweden.[15] But during the same period in the United States, with a roughly equal proportion of women in the childbearing ages, it was some 55 per 1000 population,[16] a figure roughly approximating, and even somewhat in excess of, that in many of today's underdeveloped areas. The demographer Alfred J. Lotka has estimated that American population increase between 1790 and 1820 required an average of as many as 8.3 births per mother.[17] Had it not been for the excessive mortality of the early nineteenth century, American population growth, with natality rates of this magnitude, would have reached levels comparable to those extant today in many countries where natality is correspondingly high, but where the application of modern medicine and public health practices has made possible some measure of control over death.

After beginning at this high level, American natality declined fairly steadily throughout the last three-quarters of the nineteenth century and the first third of the twentieth. By 1850, it was about two-thirds of the level of a generation earlier, half that level by 1900, and a mere third of it by 1940. A graphic way of illustrating this gradual decline is by the "net reproduction rate," a measure defined as the extent to which the average woman will reproduce herself during her period of childbearing. It is calculated by relating the number of female births to the number of women of reproductive age. A net reproduction rate of 1.0 means that the women being studied are exactly reproducing themselves. One of 1.2 means an *increase* of twenty percent in a generation, one of .9, a *decrease* of ten percent in a generation. Though of but limited value as a predictor of future population size (the purpose for which it was originally devised), the net reproduction rate is an excellent indicator of what the birth rates current at any one time would mean if continued.

On the basis of Lotka's estimates for the period, it appears that net reproduction in the United States between 1790 and 1820 was at a rate of approximately 3.9, that is, 1000 women at that time bore an average of 3900 daughters. By 1905–1910, this rate had declined to 1.34, while for the period 1933–1939 (excepting the year 1938), it was actually below replacement levels, reaching an all-time low in 1933 of .956, that is, of 956 daughters per 1000 women.[18] Had natality not begun to increase after 1939, this rate of reproduction, in combination with the then current levels of mortality and migration, would ultimately have produced an actual decline in total numbers.

Yet even during these years when net reproduction was so low, natality in the United States continued to exceed that in northern and western Europe. Talk of "race suicide" took on a

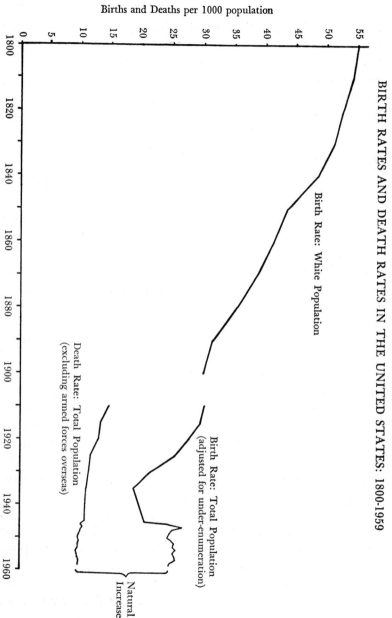

BIRTH RATES AND DEATH RATES IN THE UNITED STATES: 1800-1959

Births and Deaths per 1000 population

Birth Rate: White Population

Birth Rate: Total Population
(adjusted for under-enumeration)

Death Rate: Total Population
(excluding armed forces overseas)

Natural
Increase

shrill note of urgency in countries like Germany, where the net reproduction rate fell to .698 in 1933, and England and Wales, where it was .773 the same year. In France, with a history of natality control going back at least 150 years, it dropped to .870, actually producing a slight decrease in total population,[19] while Austria touched bottom with a rate of only .67 in 1933.[20]

The Period since World War II

The beginning of World War II saw an end to this period of decline, so far as western European populations were concerned. In those countries not actually invaded, population grew at a faster rate during the war than it had during the depression which preceded it. But it was with the end of the war that population growth in western Europe and the English-speaking countries overseas really surged ahead. By this time extensive population increases were also occurring in much of Asia and Latin America. In the industrial countries, however, this growth was based on increased natality, not, as elsewhere in the world, on decreased mortality.

During this postwar period, the birth rates of most of the industrial countries reached their peaks in 1947 and 1948, and then descended subsequently to levels more nearly approximating what was necessary for stability or merely slow growth. Birth rates did not, however, drop far in the "newer" countries —the United States, Canada, Australia, and New Zealand. The birth rate in the United States, in fact, remained quite consistently at a figure higher than it had been for the previous forty-two years. At first, it appeared that this high American rate was but a short-run fluctuation, for there was considerable evidence to suggest that it was this high because women who had postponed their childbearing, during the Depression of the 1930's and the war period of the 1940's, were making up for lost time by having their children in rapid succession.[21] But by the 1950's it was becoming increasingly evident that the downward trend of the birth rate had not only ended, but given way to a period of substantial increase. Some making up had occurred, to be sure. But the high natality rates were continuing as younger women began to have their families—women too young for their childbearing to have been affected by either the Depression or the war.

Though increase since World War II has been extensive, it has not meant a return to the large families of two and three generations ago. Whereas declines in the proportion of higher-order births (fifth births and over) accounted for more than half of the difference in family size between women born in 1892 and women born in 1909 (the latter being the group bearing the smallest average number of children), fully 70 percent of the increase in the average number of children born to women completing their families today has come, instead, in the second-, third-, and fourth-order births.[22]

Thus, this dramatic and quite unexpected upturn in birth rates represents more than a mere reversal of earlier downward trends. It represents a change in the American family and in its patterns of childbearing. The proportion of couples having families of six or more children has been declining for a long time. But over the past two decades there has been a change at the other end of the family-size spectrum, as well—a movement away from both childlessness and the one-child family. The chart on page 20 highlights these parallel developments.

Women born in 1910—those in our chart[23] whose childbearing was most likely to have been affected by the Depression and World War II—had the highest proportion remaining childless or bearing but one child. The percentage in the childless or one-child category fluctuated from 31 percent for those turning 45 in 1920 (that is, born in 1875), up to 40 for those reaching their forty-fifth birthdays in 1955 (that is, born in 1910). The percentage bearing five children also fluctuated,

FAMILY SIZE BECOMES MORE HOMOGENEOUS

PROPORTIONS WITH SPECIFIED NUMBERS
OF CHILDREN EVER BORN

Native White Women Born in Selected Years

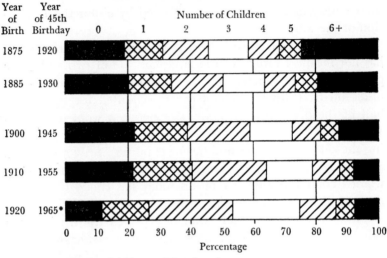

*Number of children partially estimated

although to a much lesser extent. But the proportion bearing six or more children shows a considerable downward trend; while the proportion bearing two to four children shows as steady a trend in the opposite direction. What we are witnessing is a general narrowing of the range of family size—a departure from both the large family of six or more children and the small family of no children or but one child.

Our current population growth has been augmented by two other postwar trends: a steady increase since the 1930's in the proportion of Americans who marry, and a rising proportion of early marriages. We were always one of the "marryingest" of European peoples, even when our sex ratio was out of balance because of the greater proportion of men among the immigrants. But today, the proportion of us who marry is higher than that for any other people of European stock. Nearly 95 percent of all adult Americans can expect to be married sometime during their lives; this is some seven percentage points higher than among the British, and a full twenty-five percentage points higher than among the Irish.[24] Nor has this increase in the proportion marrying been accompanied by any increase in the proportion remaining childless or having but one child. In fact, as we have already pointed out, these proportions are lower today than they were a generation ago. That they are is probably at least partly a consequence of the generally younger age at marriage, for, as with family size, there has been a considerable narrowing of the range in age at first marriage. The proportion of American women marrying after age twenty-four, for instance, remained about the same (approximately 50 percent) between 1890 and 1940. But by 1951, only about a third of those who married did so after age twenty-four,[25] while today only about a tenth wait that long.[26] Since the ability to conceive seems to decline gradually to about age thirty and then more rapidly thereafter, this trend toward early marriage means that a substantially higher proportion of American women are now married during the ages when they are best able to conceive, and that for this reason there may be less involuntary sterility (and possibly *more* involuntary conception).

The results of these changes in the patterns of American marriage and family-building are these: a higher birth rate, a slightly larger number of children per family than in the 1930's, and a rapidly growing population.

Distribution

Already numerous, and growing rapidly, Americans are at the same time highly concentrated in urban areas and becoming more so each year. Four-tenths of the population already lived in urban areas when America entered the twentieth century. By the eve of World War II, urbanites were 57 percent of the total. Today, they are 70 percent, with over a third of our total population living in the largest centers of more than 1,000,000.[27]

Results of the 1960 census show these trends to have accelerated in the decade 1950–1960. The total urban proportion went up 13 percent. But this represents the sum of different trends. The number of urbanites living in the larger metropolitan areas (1,000,000 and over) increased 25 percent, while that in the metropolitan areas, but outside the central cities, increased 49 percent. During the same period the number in rural areas declined by 1 percent.[28] Some four-fifths of the population increase predicted for the next four decades is expected to come in the form of additional people in these metropolitan areas.

A substantial portion of American population densities are now as high as, or higher than, those in many of the most densely populated countries of the world. No American state has yet attained the density of the Netherlands (the most densely settled country in the world), with its average of 906 persons per square mile; but Rhode Island, with 812 persons per square mile in 1960, and New Jersey, with 806, both exceed Belgium, whose 773 persons per square mile make it the second most densely settled country in the world. Other relationships are shown in Table 1.

In the great metropolitan centers the densities are, of course, even higher. And already two-thirds of our population lives in these conurbations, with the proportion expected to reach some three-fourths by the end of the century.[29] Moreover, with our greater spread in the form of suburbanization and our extensive use of the automobile, a given density with us Americans means a far more intensive use of total land area than is

Table 1

PERSONS PER SQUARE MILE: 1960

State or Country	*Density*
Netherlands	906
Rhode Island	**812**
New Jersey	**806**
Belgium	773
Massachusetts	**654**
Japan	650
Republic of Korea	637
United Kingdom	554
Federal Republic of Germany	551
Connecticut	**522**
Italy	422
Ceylon	379
New York	**350**
Haiti	323
India	320
Maryland	**314**
Denmark	274
Pennsylvania	**252**
Delaware	**225**
Austria	218
France	212

Source: U.S. Bureau of the Census, *Statistical Abstract of the United States: 1961,* Tables 6, 212, and 1238, pp. 10, 161, and 919–20.

the case elsewhere. The result is a correspondingly lesser amount of available open space.

As we have become more urbanized, agriculture has employed an ever smaller proportion of the work force. That proportion was 38 percent in 1900. But by 1940, though involving about the same number of workers, it was down to only 17 percent; while by 1960, it had undergone an absolute decline of 3,817,000 persons from the 1940 figure in the process of dropping to but 8.3 percent.[30]

Such a shift toward city living and urban-centered occupations not only denotes a change in our way of life, it also creates new needs—such as those for more urban services, government, and regional planning—and it intensifies old ones—for open space, for recreational areas, for simply, on occasion, getting away from other people. That much of present-day urbanization is in the form of suburbs does little to obviate these needs. In fact, it often engenders additional problems of its own. Increasing 49 percent between 1950 and 1960, the growth in suburban areas accounted for two-thirds of the national increase during that decade.[31] Yet in its usual form of houses "splattered . . . all over the countryside in a rigid pattern of equal size lots" the suburb does little more than create a temporary illusion of more rural living while all too often fouling "the very amenities people moved outward to seek."[32] As we shall see in Chapter 3, these trends in the distribution of our population aggravate problems we already face as a consequence of population growth itself.

The United States and the Rest of the World

The present demographic situation in the United States is a departure not only from this country's own past experience, but from the experience of other countries, as well. In today's world of suddenly expanding populations, when annual rates of natural increase have reached as high as 3.5 percent in some countries, the United States' rate of 1.5 percent may appear comparatively modest. But in no country with a similar level of economic development has the birth rate remained so high and for such a long period of time.

Historically, declines in both natality and mortality have been associated with the process of industrialization.* After World War II, however, as we have seen, there was a partial deviation from this pattern in the fact that birth rates in most of the older industrialized countries went up a bit from the low levels reached in the prewar years. But the high level of births in the United States represents the most substantial deviation of all. As the table on page 26 shows, postwar trends in our patterns of marriage and childbearing have produced a rate of natural increase that has (with the exception of the first postwar years in Japan) consistently exceeded that of other industrial countries.[33]

In the first group of countries to become industrialized, population changes followed what appeared to be a regular pattern of three stages: from the historical condition of relatively high birth and death rates, through a transitional stage of continued high birth rates and declining death rates, to the unprecedented condition of low birth and low death rates. Why the birth rate should have declined in an industrializing society admits of no single explanation. Improvements in contraception in these

---

* By "industrialization" is meant far more than simply the changeover to power-driven machinery in manufacture, important as this is. Industrialization is characterized also by high levels of productivity in all fields of economic endeavor—in agriculture and mining as much as in manufacturing. In an industrialized country, moreover, the average worker is highly capitalized (in terms of schooling and social services as well as in plant and equipment) and he is highly specialized. In such a country most workers are employed outside of agriculture and most of the people live in cities. Finally, the average material level of living is far higher in the industrialized than it is in the non-industrialized countries.

Table 2

RATE OF NATURAL INCREASE
(Annual Excess of Births over Deaths per 1000 Population)

Selected Industrialized Countries

Year	United States	United Kingdom	France	West Germany	Sweden	Japan	World (estimated)
1947	15.7	8.3	8.2	4.9	8.1	19.7	—
1953	15.0	4.5	5.8	4.5	5.7	12.6	16.2
1959	14.7	5.2	7.1	6.8	4.6	10.1	—

Birth Rate
(Annual Number of Births per 1000 Population)

Year	United States	United Kingdom	France	West Germany	Sweden	Japan	World (estimated)
1947	25.8	20.7	21.4	16.5	18.9	34.3	—
1953	24.6	15.9	18.9	15.5	15.4	21.5	34.5
1959	24.1	16.9	18.4	17.6	14.1	17.5	—

Sources: Calculated from United Nations, *Demographic Yearbook 1956*, Tables 1, 20, and 23, and *Demographic Yearbook 1960*, Tables 13 and 15.

countries appear to have coincided with a number of social changes which served to intensify what must already have become a widespread desire for control over the frequency and timing of childbearing. As the Royal Commission on Population reports of this development in England,

> The explanation lies . . . in the profound changes that were taking place in the outlook and ways of living of the people during the 19th century. The main features of these changes are well-known. They include the decay of small scale family handicrafts and the rise of large scale industry and factory organization; the loss of security and growth of competitive

individualism; the relative decline in agriculture and rise in importance of industry and commerce, and the associated shift of population from rural to urban areas; the growing prestige of science, which disturbed traditional religious beliefs; the development of popular education; higher standards of living; the growth of humanitarianism, and the emancipation of women. All these and other changes are closely inter-related; they present a complex web, rather than a chain, of cause and effect; . . .[34]

To lower the death rate, on the other hand, required no particular change in outlook. Every society has sought control over death; but it is only in recent history that early death has ceased to be a commonplace for any of the world's people. The process of industrialization produced changes in ways of living —better diets, better clothing, purer water, the paving of streets, new methods of sanitation. It is these that first brought about substantial savings in life, often quite without the knowledge of those who were most directly affected. Eventually, industrialization also made available, through the development of scientific medicine and public health administration, the means by which savings in life could be consciously achieved, as well.

The tremendous population increase over the last three centuries is actually one of the most remarkable achievements of man, representing as it does a decrease in mortality that rests on the steady accumulation of the knowledge and skill necessary to save human life. Famine and disease still take their toll, even in countries with extensive control over mortality, but nowhere in the industrialized world is the frequency and severity of these killers comparable to what it was formerly—or to what it is now in the underdeveloped countries.

Many of these underdeveloped countries have made great strides in the direction of controlling mortality, but they are still a long way from achieving the extensive control over it to be found in industrialized areas. It is probable that in these underdeveloped countries no child reaches adulthood without a close, personal experience of death—the death of a parent, a sibling, or a friend. The contrast between this kind of experience and that of the typical American teenager is the contrast between the possibilities of the twentieth century and the realities of every century that preceded it.

In the transitional period, during which the birth rate remained at or near its former high level while the death rate declined, the excess of births over deaths led to rapid population increases. It was population increases of this period that made possible the mass migration of Europeans to the Americas. To explain why declines in the birth rate should have lagged behind those in the death rate we must look to social, not biological, conditions. A society with only limited control over mortality—and that means all societies before the Industrial Revolution—had to depend for its survival on a great many births to counteract the large losses to death. In such societies a high birth rate was maintained by a number of beliefs and practices (the need for sons to support one in old age or to carry on the family name, for example) which seldom had any specifically demographic rationale. Gradually evolved for other purposes (religious or economic, for instance), they had the unanticipated consequence of also supporting high natality. The changes that came with the Industrial Revolution weakened many of these older beliefs and incentives without, however, removing them completely or weakening them all. The result was that in every country in which births came under a measure of control, this control came ordinarily not only later than that over deaths,[35] but also originally because individual couples acted in opposition to a substantial body of public opinion.*

---

* For example, social differences in natality are known to have existed in the United States as early as 1800. Yet, when three generations later the national birth rate began to decline rapidly, laws against the dissemination of information on contraception were passed by the Federal government and by nearly every state of the Union; and every religious group that took a stand on the issue defined control over birth as immoral.

Demographers originally thought that *every* country, as it became industrialized, would undergo this three-stage "demographic transition" from high to low vital rates. But the recent upturn of birth rates in the United States and (though to a much lesser extent) in various European countries, represents a departure from the condition of numerical stability that it was assumed would be the third and final stage of this transition. It shows that the demographic transition model, as first defined, must be used with caution even when applied to those Western countries on the basis of whose earlier population changes it was formulated.

We suggest, however, that this model is still applicable—if redefined. The essence of the demographic transition was not so much change in the rates themselves as it was the extension of control to those vital processes that determine the level of the rates: conception and parturition, with respect to natality; the maintenance of health and the curing of disease, with respect to mortality. It is the transition to *control*—not necessarily a shift from high to low vital rates—that constitutes the essential element of the demographic transition.

To show how the present position of the United States compares with that of other countries, we can divide the world into three categories corresponding to the three stages of the demographic transition model, as redefined. This would find most of native Africa and large portions of the Near East and Asia at Stage I: where there is little or no control over either births or deaths. At Stage III, where the transition is essentially complete, would be most of Europe, Canada, the United States, Australia, New Zealand, Japan, and possibly Argentina, Uruguay, and the USSR. All the rest would be at Stage II: having begun to control mortality while retaining their traditional patterns of relatively little control over natality.

The differences in living standards between the peoples of the countries at Stages I and II and those at Stage III are probably greater than the differences that have separated any other contemporaneous peoples since the beginning of time. Most of the former live much as did their ancestors for centuries before them; but the way of life of those who have achieved control over their vital processes is vastly different from that anywhere in the world only two centuries ago. Illiteracy, low levels of living, low productivity, little urbanization—and hunger— characterize the countries at Stages I and II. Relative population stability, where it exists in these countries, is maintained by the wasteful, enervating means of a high birth rate counteracting a high death rate. In countries that have not yet begun the transition, infant and child mortality is extremely high. As many as two out of five (or possibly even four) babies die without reaching their fifth birthdays. By contrast, this figure is about one out of 34 in the United States. Other differences are shown in Table 3, page 32.

With the outstanding exception of the United States and the Soviet Union, most of today's unprecedented population increase is coming from the countries at Stage II—Ceylon, India, Indonesia, Latin America, and possibly China. If present trends continue, those at Stage I will commence the transition to control over mortality within the next decade or two, thus swelling the volume still further.

It is understandable that Americans should attach but little importance to the annual portion of world population growth originating with them. With but six percent of the world's people and a growth rate (including that from migration) approximately equal to that of the world as a whole, they account for only six percent of the annual growth in world population. The Indian subcontinent (India plus Pakistan) alone accounts for twice that much. But let us look at the American figure more closely. This six percent of the world's increase is being added at a time of unprecedented population growth. In absolute terms, it amounts to a net increase of nearly 3,000,000 people annually. And these are additions to a people with the highest material level of living in the world—a people who consume roughly half of the world's annual production of nonrenewable resources. In other words, from the standpoint of the relevance of population to depletion of the resources necessary to improve levels of living throughout the world (and from the standpoint of its relevance to the supplies of capital that must be invested to attain these improvements) we Americans could be said to account not for one-sixteenth but for something closer to *one-half* of the world's annual increase.

Important as the overpopulation—or threatened overpopulation—of much of the rest of the world may be, when it comes to depletion of the world's natural resources, it takes a lot of Asians or Africans or Latin Americans at *their* material levels of living to consume as much as one American at *his*. Any precise statistical comparison is impossible, yet it may not be far wrong to say that each year the average American consumes in natural resources as much as do twenty-five or thirty Indians. When we remember that because of a much greater life expectancy the American has more than twice as many years of consuming ahead of him, the bracing yearly addition of 4,250,-000 American babies takes on importance far beyond our own borders. So long as our population and material levels of living rise, the demand for goods and services requiring the exploitation of these resources will accelerate, and thus raise their price for people elsewhere in the world to whom they represent a necessity and not a luxury. As present supplies of these resources are used up, the costs of furnishing raw materials necessary to the maintenance of the industrial system are bound to rise. More money will have to be spent to discover and develop substitutes. The greater the depletion, the greater the costs.

We know that part of the new nationalism in Asia, Africa,

Table 3
SOME QUANTITATIVE DIFFERENCES BETWEEN INDUSTRIALIZED AND NON-INDUSTRIALIZED COUNTRIES DURING THE 1950's

	Industrialized Countries					Non-Industrialized Countries					
	U.S.A.	United Kingdom	Sweden	Australia	Japan	Egypt	Guatemala	Mexico	Venezuela	Ceylon	India
Birth rate	25	16	14	23	18	37	49	45	45	36	39
Death rate	10	12	10	9	8	23	21	13	10	11	20
Death rate among infants under 1 year of age	27	23	16	21	35	238	104	81	66*	68*	97*
Average number of years of life remaining at age 0	70	71	72	70	67	39**	39	39**	—	60	32**
Percentage of adult male population engaged in agriculture	9ᵃ	6	25ᵇ	16ᵇ	33ᵇ	63**	—	56ᶜ	46	51**	70
Percentage of total population living in cities of 100,000 or more inhabitants	51ᵃ	51ᵈ	24	56	37	22**	10	15	39	5	7
Percentage of adults with no schooling	2	—	—	—	7	—	71	43	45	—	—
Per capita annual income in U.S. dollarsᶠ	1950	830	1060	930	190	90	—	200	570ᶻ	100	50
Per capita consumption of energy from inanimate sources (kilograms of coal equivalent)	7640	4741	2971	3644	869	248	140	755	2550ᵉ	88	137
Average daily caloric food intake per capita	3100	3300	2910	3200	2240	2570	—	2380	2270	2110	1890
Percentage average daily per capita consumption of food (in calories) of animal origin	41	38	41	42	7	11	—	13	15	4	6
Average daily per capita consumption of protein (grams)	93	87	82	91	68	75	—	64	59	43	50

Sources: Except where otherwise noted, all figures obtained from United Nations, *Demographic Yearbook* for 1956 (Tables 12 and 18), 1957 (Tables 3 and 5), and 1959 (Tables 9, 25, 28, and 32); and from United Nations, *Statistical Yearbook* for 1959 (Tables 1, 129, 131, and 167).

NOTES TO TABLE 3:

— Comparable figure unavailable
* Unreliable. Rate too low
** Pre–1950 figure
a Source: U.S. Bureau of the Census
b Source: United Nations, *FAO Production Yearbook*, vol. 13, 1959, p. 22
c Both sexes combined
d England and Wales only
e Figure is high because of extensive refinery operations that employ few workers and affect native levels of living only very slightly.
f Computed from data in Paul Studenski, *The Income of Nations*, N.Y., New York University Press, 1958, pp. 508–510. Figures are based on national income at factor cost.
g Great inequities in distributions mean that the vast majority of the population have incomes far lower than this.

and the Near East expresses the desire of other peoples to live better. Understandable as this is, it can only worsen the situation. Even without improvement in their levels of living, rapid population increases in these countries will place ever-mounting demands on the world's resources. To the extent that these peoples attain the higher levels to which they aspire, the supply of raw materials will be depleted just that much faster. That fraction of the world's population living in the United States cannot for long continue to consume such a disproportionately large share of the world's resources.

Consider how we must appear to these people. On one hand is our rapid population increase (in the face of wide dissemination of the means of birth control). On the other is the world's highest rate of consumption of natural resources. The more we grow, the greater the amount we will be obliged to spend just on the needs of our own population; and the less will we be willing—or able—to contribute to the development of the poorer countries. A double standard is implicit in our attitudes —*our* population increase is justifiable because we can afford it; *theirs* a calamity because they cannot. Yet, we deny them technical assistance to halt their crippling population growth, and extend financial assistance in amounts far from adequate to the task of improving their economies. If only on selfish grounds, we should heed the words of a man like India's Commissioner General for Economic Affairs, who has warned: "It is simply not possible for small oases of prosperity to continue to exist amidst vast deserts of poverty without engendering storms that might engulf those oases."[36]

For any nation to exult in its own population growth at a time when all signs point to increasing difficulties in providing for the world's people as a whole would seem in bad taste. But for a nation with our incomparable wealth and living levels, with our opportunities for leading world opinion, with our hopes of attracting the support of the overcrowded, poverty-ridden peoples of the world, to uphold a double standard of population growth is surely insensitive and undiplomatic in the extreme.

Too Many or Too Few: The Idea
of the Optimum

WHILE THERE MAY BE a certain novelty in the recognition that population growth in one country can affect the welfare of people in another, the relationship of population size to the welfare of one's own group has concerned men in all ages and in all kinds of societies. The theories they have advanced about this relationship and the measures they have adopted to influence it have reflected their values, their knowledge of the available alternatives, and the conditions of their times.

Any claim that a country's population is too large or too small implies some idea of an optimum size, and some standard by which to measure deviation from it. It also implies the existence of goals, the attainment of which is thought to be affected by the number of people. Were this not so, no one would concern himself with population as a factor in his country's well-being. He would be content to look no further than to, say, politics, or religion, or technology.

"First among the materials required by the statesman is population: he will consider what should be the number and character of the citizens, and then what should be the size and character of the country. Most persons think that a state in order to be happy ought to be large; but even if they are right, they have no idea what is a large and what a small state." So claimed Aristotle, twenty-three centuries ago, as he argued the case for the city-state versus the empire. "To the size of states there is a limit," he continued, "as there is to other things, plants, animals, implements; for none of these retain their natural power when they are too large or too small, but they either wholly lose their nature, or are spoiled." Aristotle's definition of optimum size stems directly from his values concerning the ideal form of government for his ideal form of society, the democratic city-state: ". . . the best limit of the population of a state is the largest number which suffices for the purposes of life and can be taken in at a single view."[1]

The same kind of question was explored, less self-consciously perhaps, by a small group of people whose society contrasted sharply with Aristotle's highly civilized Athens. These were the 1300 inhabitants of the Polynesian island, Tikopia. When the New Zealand anthropologist, Raymond Firth, visited them in 1928–1929, he found a people with an articulated policy of population control designed for the expressed purpose of helping them achieve certain of their tribal goals. Whereas with Aristotle and his disciples the criteria applied to population size were primarily political, those used by the Tikopia were primarily economic.

"In this small but flourishing community [writes Firth], there is conscious recognition of the need for correlating the size of population with that of the available land. Consequently it is from this point of view that limitation of families is mainly practised."[2] In one tribe the principle of family limitation was even incorporated into a ritual address recited annually: "Heads of families were formally exhorted to limit the numbers of their children by *coitus interruptus,* and the reason given was the prevention of theft and other social disorder."

A Tikopian gave his view of the need for family limitation in this way: "Families by Tikopia custom are made corresponding to orchards in the woods. If children are produced in plenty, then they go and steal because their orchards are few. So families in our land are not made large in truth; they are made small. If the family groups are large and they go and steal, they eat from the orchards, and if this goes on they kill each other."

Defining the Optimum Size

There is no exact formula for determining optimum population. One man's optimum may be another's overpopulation; and not even the demographer has an ultimate way of determining which is right. We are uncertain, for instance, how to measure the relationship between population and any particular condition that we choose to define as desirable. We know in general, but we do not know in great enough detail to say, for example, that country X would be 8 percent better off with two million fewer inhabitants, country Y 3 percent better off with 250,000 more. Nearly anyone who has studied conditions in India, Egypt, or Java will assure you that the country suffers from overpopulation. But he will not, except in the very broadest terms, detail the numerical extent of this overpopulation without first making a number of assumptions about all the other variables which interact with population to, say, increase agricultural production, or lower the incidence of maternal death. "Other things being equal," we usually say; but, unfortunately, "other things" do not remain "equal." Since they do not, the importance of population to any particular combination of variables cannot be precisely determined.

As direct measurement of these conditions is impossible, the only recourse is to seek an approximation by substituting some *quantifiable* measure: for example, per capita income as an indicator of the level of living, infant mortality and expectation of life at birth as indicators of general health, average number of years of schooling, homicide and suicide rates, and the per capita number of museums, libraries, and theaters as indicators of the quality of life. It is a moot question, however, as to whether the measure used approximates so closely the condition it is taken to represent that a given fluctuation in the one can be presumed to represent a change of equal magnitude in the other. Can it be assumed, that is, that a per capita annual income of $1000 in one society means that its people are twice as well off as those of another where per capita annual income is only half that much—or, for that matter, that they are *any* better off? Complete reliability in a substitute measure of this sort can only be approached, never attained.

Any search for an optimum population size is confounded further by the two facts of social change and cultural difference. It is these that make it so difficult to generalize about optimum population conditions for more than one time period or for more than one culture. What is said about the relationship between population and certain conditions for any one time may be quite inappropriate for another. At the time of Columbus what is now the territory of the United States supported hardly more than a million people, and because of the harsh conditions of life in many areas may have seemed to some tribes to be overpopulated even then. Yet, four and one half centuries later, under remarkably different cultural conditions, it supports 180 times as many—and at a material level of living incomparably higher than that of the early aboriginal inhabitants. And there are some who claim the country could benefit with even more people.

However perplexing to the determination of optimum population size may be the facts of social change, or the difficulties of assessing the relationship between population and various social conditions, the most difficult question facing those who wish to speak in terms of "ideal" population size is still this: What are the criteria of "ideal"? Those of the militarist who defines national strength in terms of the numbers to be unleashed against The Enemy? Those of the churchman to whom additional numbers represent souls for eternal salvation (or damnation)? Those of the businessman who views babies as potential consumers of his product? Those of the wildlife fancier observing the progressive extinction of species? Those of the misanthrope?

There is no dearth of such criteria or of quantifiable measures to indicate the degree to which the desired state of affairs has been attained. But each of these is to some extent a product of, and relevant to, a particular cultural setting. Since people differ in their views concerning such fundamental matters as the value placed on material goods, the desirability of saving for posterity, and the definition of "the good life," the criteria of an optimum population and the techniques by which to measure movement in the direction of this "optimum" are always to some degree "culture-bound."

The Economic Criterion

Of all the criteria brought to bear on the idea of optimum population, the economic is probably the most explicit and the most widely used. It is certainly the criterion underlying most current discussion of under- or overpopulation, as these terms are applied to conditions in both the United States and the underdeveloped countries. Briefly, the economic criterion defines the optimum population as the one in which any change in numbers will be accompanied by a reduction in per capita income. If the number of people in a given area is below this level of economic optimum, that area is said to be "*under*-populated"; if above, it is considered to be "*over*populated."

A country defined by this criterion as "underpopulated," and completely dependent upon its own labor supply for support (i.e., when income is not supplemented by gifts or grants from abroad), is one in which that statistical construct, the average man, lives less well than he would if the country's population were larger. He may still live very well, however. Labelling his country as "underpopulated" simply means that the presence of more people would raise levels of living even further—other things being equal, of course.

In the extreme case of underpopulation, there would not be enough workers to permit the construction or operation of such perquisites of a "higher" level of living as railroads, steamships, airplanes, telephones, radios, TV, and movies. More importantly, there might be too few people to permit the specialization necessary for a high level of productivity and, hence, of consumption; and too few, also, to permit development of the mass market necessary to the full utilization of the economies of large-scale production. The smaller the potential market for a product, the less the need for increasing its production through greater specialization, either of workers or of equipment. The result is workers producing less than they could if working on a larger scale—and, ultimately, a lower per capita rate of consumption.

On the basis of the economic criterion alone, there are a number of countries that might be described as currently underpopulated: Canada, Australia, New Zealand, and Argentina, for example. With present resources and larger populations (other things being equal) each of these countries might be expected to have higher production per capita. But since they can accomplish this end in other ways—through greater capitalization or national specialization in combination with international trade, for instance—it is doubtful that they will need for long to pursue with much vigor any policy of extensive and rapid population growth. As many of the world's smaller populations—the Dutch, Belgians, Danes, Swiss, Finns, Norwegians, and Luxembourgers, among others—have already demonstrated, a high level of living can be attained by producing more than is needed of some things (taking advantage in this production of the economies offered by specialization and large-scale operation) to trade with other countries for what is not produced.

But of far greater importance today is economic "*over*population," a condition besetting some three-fifths to two-thirds of the world's people. At its extreme a crop failure means famine, not merely a small rise in prices; poverty and malnutrition are endemic. For the vast majority, life is a never-ending scramble for the bare necessities. In the overpopulated countries any reduction in numbers would immediately increase the amount of goods and other essentials available for those who remained. So much of the total social product must be expended simply for subsistence that there is little if any left over for investment in those enterprises that, given time to develop, could lead to an improvement in living conditions.[3]

However convenient it may be as a descriptive device, use of the economic criterion to compare relative economic positions is open to considerable criticism. Ordinarily, the use of the economic criterion implies that an increase in gross national product (the GNP of a country divided by its population gives us a figure approximately equal to per capita income) will necessarily lead to a general improvement in levels of living. Actually, of course, there is no assurance that this will happen. It is not at all uncommon for a particular political or economic structure to maintain such inequality of incomes as to permit even declines in living conditions for the great majority of the population in the face of increases in per capita (i.e., average) income. Current conditions in much of Latin America, or those in the Soviet Union of a generation or two ago, or in England of the first half of the nineteenth century, illustrate this possibility. If a millionaire moves into your town, his presence raises the *average* income of its residents—but you and your neighbors will still have to meet your bills out of the same size paychecks. Should he gain control over the town's industries, he could conceivably raise output, and his profits along with it, without ever sharing the proceeds with his workers or fellow townspeople.

A Sense of the Future

The economic criterion may be the closest we have yet come to a concrete measure of the quality of life. Certainly it is an extremely useful one. It is also the most fully developed—in the sense that numerous quantifiable measures have been adapted to it. Yet it is by no means the last word on population size. We should beware of making an end of what is merely a means: is it a higher per capita income itself we seek, or an improvement in the quality of life?

Per capita income in the United States has never been higher. It will doubtless continue to rise for a while longer, even in the face of substantial population increases. But does that mean we will necessarily be living better? Whatever the first appearances, there is no necessary connection between higher incomes and higher levels of living—even with an adjustment for inflation. Like that census occupational category ("Professional, Technical, and Kindred Workers") that unites professors and prostitutes, the computation of gross national product gives equal status to such disparate entities as race tracks and hospitals, steel mills and chewing gum—with no mention whatever of Mom's apple pie or anything else manufactured and distributed outside the market system. When the housewife of two decades ago canned peaches for her family, neither the production nor the consumption of those peaches entered into the calculation of an economic indicator. Today she does the same thing in a cannery and the result—such is the magic of national accounting—is a higher per capita income and a palpably inferior diet. The reckoning of per capita income counts in the house in suburbia, the second car, power mower, and backyard cook-out; the proliferation of roads, the outcropping of motels, bowling alleys, driving ranges, gas stations, and short-order emporia. But it takes off nothing for fatigue and loss of time endured in the lengthening commutation to work, the pollution of air and water, and the ever-receding countryside.

The economic criterion of optimum population would seem, in fact, to have progressively less utility as one moved from countries of low income to those of high. It is currently best suited to the analysis of conditions in the non-industrialized countries. Where per capita annual income is no greater than a few hundred American dollars an increment of even a dollar or two may represent a real gain in well-being. But where that income is already substantial, as in the United States where it now borders on $2,000 a year, it is not so much the level itself that denotes well-being as it is the directions in which resources are allocated. Without this qualification, increases in per capita income in the richer countries can themselves connote only a quantitative change; they have no necessary implication for the general quality of life.

When viewing the relation of any population—our own included—to a people's welfare, the question to be asked is this: Would the continuance of present population trends be a major factor in checking improvements in the quality of life, or tend to jeopardize the possibilities of such improvements in the future?[4] Estimating the effect of these trends on per capita incomes alone would not be enough. The definitive answer would have to consider the whole human condition, and not just a part of it.

The world's greatest need, C. P. Snow has written, is "an appetite for the future . . . All healthy societies are ready to sacrifice the existential moment for their children's future and for children after those. The sense of the future is behind all good policies. Unless we have it, we can give nothing either wise or decent to the world."[5] We need right now this "appetite for the future" with respect to our population growth. To support an increase of another 180 million—the number we can expect in but 44 more years at current rates—this country will have to undergo changes in the conditions of life nearly as radical as those that have occurred since Columbus. But unlike those earlier changes, which generally raised the level of living, those that will be called for in the future—with the huge increments in human numbers that constitute our population increases of today—can hardly escape having the opposite effect in a number of very important ways. Population is becoming—in fact, it has already become—a substantial burden for many aspects of our present way of life. We make no claim that Americans in the future would be unable to make some kind of adjustment to less. But the larger our population grows, the further from our present way of life, and the more difficult of attainment, must any adjustment be.

3

Population Growth
and the American
Way of Life

THOUGH THE CONSEQUENCES of our present rate of growth can be expected to fall most harshly on persons as yet unborn, there is still ample reason for Americans already alive to hope for population stability in the very near future. The deleterious effects of rapid growth on our conditions of life are already considerable. These we are experiencing right now. Yet, half of us can expect to live long enough to enter the twenty-first century when, if present rates continue, we will number 385 million and the difficulties attending population growth will have been increased and magnified by the fact of *two* Americans for every *one* here now.

If population growth in the poorer countries operates to keep people so impoverished that life itself is placed in jeopardy, its most widespread consequence in the more affluent is as a depressant on certain of the personal freedoms and pleasures achieved by mankind upon liberation from extreme want. When the statesmen of Asia, Africa, Latin America talk of overpopulation, they must of necessity talk in terms of economic development and the provision of bare essentials. But when we speak of overpopulation in an affluent country like the United States, it can be in terms of the quality of life.

Numerical stability must come, and soon, if we Americans are to maintain and extend a high quality of life. It is not that we are threatened by a condition of "standing room only."

Quite obviously, we are a long way from being extinguished as a people by the burden of sheer numbers. Nor, for a while at least, does our population growth present us with the prospect of becoming inadequately fed or of losing possession of the world's highest material level of living. What we stand to lose —and what to some extent we have already lost—is to be reckoned essentially in *qualitative* terms.

Often in combination with the paraphernalia of a high material level of living, population growth in the United States has already meant increasing control from external sources, less flexibility permitted individual behavior, greater centralization in government, crowded schools and recreation areas, vanishing countryside, air and water pollution, endless traffic jams, and a steady loss in time, solitude, and peace of mind.

Such deterioration cannot, of course, be attributed entirely to population growth. It is rapid growth superimposed upon our American way of life that makes inevitable these declines in quality.

We have been able during the last hundred years [wrote a prescient observer of his native England in the period immediately following World War II], to maintain a population of from thirty to forty million in an area appropriate to eight or nine, by contriving so to confine and canalize the many that the few were able to remain unaware of their existence. We penned them in towns; we gave them wages so low that they had no resources wherewith to escape from the towns, and we gave them holidays so few . . . that even if they had had the resources, they would not have had the time. In the years to come . . . there will be holidays for all, extending for at least a fortnight; they will be staggered holidays and they will be holidays with pay. A cheap car . . . will be made available for these newly-enfranchised millions, with the result that for the first time we shall experience to the full the effects of maintaining forty odd millions in a country designed for a quarter of that population . . .[1]

As Joad observes, how a people experiences population growth will be mediated very largely through its cultural practices and standards. Population increase does not lead to crowded schools in a country of low educational levels. But when the median length of schooling approaches 12 years, as it does today in the United States, rapid growth means teacher shortages, split sessions, and a decreasing adequacy of school facilities. A 20 percent increase over a decade brings with it no corresponding increase in traffic jams, no overcrowding of vacation spots, no loss of land to roads and municipal facilities if only a few own cars, or live in suburbs, or have vacations. But with more than 340 automobiles per 1000 population, a housing ratio of less than one person to a room and the single family dwelling unit the national norm;[2] with a probable majority of the work force enjoying an annual paid vacation, and with a third of the population required by the distribution of employment opportunities (if nothing else) to live in urban concentrations of more than a million people,[3] rapid population growth makes ever more difficult the task of maintaining those levels already achieved and, when continued, must eventually lead to their very deterioration. Of course, urbanization, industrialization, or rising material levels of living (a per capita increase in the number of automobiles, for example) can have corrosive effects on the quality of life even when a population is small or remains stable. The traffic congestion now spreading over many parts of Europe is certainly the legacy of a postwar rise in affluence. But when the size of a population is rising simultaneously with its material standards and expectations, the difficulties are compounded and the blight spread over a wider area.

As we observed in Chapter 2, declines in quality are ultimately to be defined in terms of values. Data on the increasing difficulty of coping with the problems occasioned by population growth can simply offer clues to the existence and magnitude of these declines, and a foretaste of what is in store should population growth continue.

Some profess to see in our numerical increase a source of aberrant forms of behavior: crime, juvenile delinquency, mental illness, racial antagonisms.[4] But the evidence for this seems tenuous, at most. Any growth in numbers might be expected to produce a higher incidence of deviant behavior, if only because there will be more people to commit crimes (and to have crimes committed against them), more to become mentally ill, and so on. But this does not mean that population growth is necessarily causally related to these conditions; that it increases their *rate* or heightens their *severity*. Because of the difficulty of isolating it as a variable, the effect of density on individual and social well-being has been the subject of little more than claims and counterclaims. Some recent experiments have shown high density to result in profoundly pathological behavior among rats.[5] But whether this is analogous to the human situation, is as yet little more than a hypothesis.

The case for arresting American population growth need not depend on such tenuous claims, however. There are numerous examples of the deleterious effects of rapid growth on our conditions of life which are at once more concrete and more obviously related in a causal fashion to our growth in numbers. It is to examples of such cases that we now turn. These we discuss under separate headings only to facilitate description. Actually, considerable overlap exists between them. Rising economic costs and an increase in external controls, for example, are germane in some measure to each.

Space and Recreation

> Each year the gap between the active demand and the opportunities for outdoor recreation grows wider, and the gap between potential demand and opportunity wider still.[6]

We Americans have a strong tradition of love of natural beauty, open space, and outdoor recreation. This is attested to by the establishment of our national parks and forests and the rapidly expanding recreational use being made of them (from 61 million visits in 1950 to 151 million less than a decade later); the popularity of vacations—or just picnics—in scenic areas (more than 259 million visits to state parks in 1960); the growth of the pleasure boat and skiing business;* the more than 20 million fishing and 15 million hunting licenses sold annually.[7]

To be sure, the outdoors has no monopoly over the sources of recreation and aesthetic satisfaction. But would any deny its importance? The availability of *both* indoor and outdoor satisfactions would seem an essential element of the "good life" for a majority of Americans. But preservation of the latter, because of its very nature, will require far more effort and imaginative planning than has up to now been expended on it. It will also be immeasurably advanced by an early cessation of population growth.

Our need as a people for parks, wilderness areas, beaches, and other recreational and restorative areas has never been greater. The combination of population increase, higher incomes, shorter working hours, and ever greater concentration in ever larger metropolitan centers has resulted in a demand for these kinds of facilities far exceeding that which existed when we were a less numerous, less materially affluent, less urban people. Recreational use of public lands has more than trebled since the end of World War II, and it is still increasing.[8] More of these facilities, if not absolutely essential from the standpoint of physical survival, are certainly essential from the standpoint of the quality of life. Population growth, with its attendant increase in population density, makes the ready accessibility of space and recreational facilities ever more necessary while at the same time making it ever more difficult to attain.

In sheer acreage the United States is plentifully endowed

* The number of outboard motors alone increased from 2.8 million in 1950 to more than 6.1 million in 1961.

with the land and water area to meet current needs. But little of it is very accessible. The South and North Central regions of the country, each with about 30 percent of the population, have but 12 percent of the recreational acreage of the forty-eight contiguous states. The Northeast, with one-quarter of it, has only 4 percent.[9] And it is in the Northeast that open lands like farming and grazing areas are also in shortest supply.

Estimates of future increases in population, coupled with predictions on travel, leisure time, and income, forecast an increase in visits to our National Parks from 63 million in 1959 to 240 million by 1980, and well over 400 million by the year 2000.[10] Yet, facilities in most of them are already overburdened. Crowding and overuse have in some instances jeopardized and, in others, made it difficult to enjoy, the scenic and natural wonders which the establishment of these parks was to preserve and make forever available to the people of this country. This arises in part, of course, from higher levels of living—particularly the extension of paid vacations. But population increase *alone* would have brought the probable number of visitors up to the capacity of these parks by 1955, had the level of living risen no higher than it was in 1940. That material levels of living have increased at the same time as population merely adds to the problem.

Young sequoia trees in California's Sequoia and Yosemite National Parks, seeded from the oldest living things on earth, are becoming sick "because the great number of visitors is trampling the earth down so hard during visits that rain water is running off and not getting down to the roots.[11] Everglades National Park, Florida's best recreational area and a "world-famous wonderland of nature," has suffered the inroads of real estate speculators and is in considerable danger of suffering irreparable damage as "expanding Miami makes it desirable to drain more of the area adjacent to the park, and expanding markets for winter crops create an irrigation demand for the water which might otherwise be drained to the park."[12]

But these are the famous places, the places of national importance established by a national government for a nation's
people. As long as they have vacations and money, Americans
will flock to Yosemite, Yellowstone, the Great Smokies, and the
Everglades. A visit to one of these parks occurs once a decade,
or once a lifetime. What of the areas closer to home—the areas
for weekend and daily living? The increasing shortage of space
is probably for the majority of Americans the most obvious
consequence of population growth. Witness the traffic jams that
beset all our major cities and most of our smaller ones as well.
In some places this blight has afflicted us so long that it is now
an accepted part of urban life. But the traffic jam is spreading
to places where no one could have expected it ten or fifteen
years ago: Yellowstone National Park and the mountains west
of Denver, for example. While the increased mobility that has
come with the spread of the automobile has to some extent enlarged our recreational opportunities.

> the blessing is a mixed one, for the very apparatus that has
> made the outdoors more accessible has changed the nature of
> much of it. As people push outward, they push the country-
> side before them. "Non-residents not allowed" signs go up on
> county beaches, and what yesterday was a pleasant hour's drive
> to a picnic spot is now only a gruelling preliminary.[13]

And all too often the situation is little better on arrival. To
quote Lewis Mumford: Do we "increase the opportunities for
recreation when we turn a woodland into a parking lot, or an
ocean beach into a fishing net filled with squirming human
bodies?"[14] State park facilities in California were already 31
percent short of requirements four years ago.[15] In Colorado,
hand signals have been devised to prevent collisions between
skiers on certain of the state's once-spacious ski slopes, and there
has been talk of installing traffic lights at various locations in
the ski area at Winter Park.[16] Michigan, which calls itself the
"Water Wonderland," had to turn away 28,000 campers—one

in every five—for lack of space in 1958.[17] And this is but a minimum figure, for we have no way of knowing how many would-be campers the crowded facilities discouraged from even trying.

Overcrowded beaches, overcrowded campgrounds, overcrowded picnic spots; recreation areas established with an eye to needs a decade hence filled to capacity within but weeks of their opening: such conditions are general throughout most of this country and are the daily lot of the vast majority of our people. The locale varies; but whether it is Indiana Dunes State Park in Indiana, Rooster Rock State Park in Oregon,[18] or Anthony Wayne Recreation Area in New York,[19] the frustration is the same, the decline in the quality of life just as real.

And then there are the cities and towns that run together, connected by a gum of suburbia and "highway culture": a picnic or walk in the open country within easy motoring distance of home has become a virtual impossibility for a near-majority of our citizens. Once-green countryside is being bulldozed under at the rate of 1.1 million acres a year—three thousand acres a day; and, as William H. Whyte, Jr. has noted, "It is not merely that the countryside is ever receding; in the great expansion of the metropolitan areas the subdivisions of one city are beginning to meet up with the subdivisions of another."[20] The product of this expansion is some 15 super-cities. The great majority of Americans live in one or another of them. Nearly every American has to contend with them. They range from comparatively small ones like Fort Worth–Dallas, or Colorado Springs–Denver–Cheyenne, up to the largest of them all, the Atlantic Region, which extends northward to Maine, westward to Buffalo, and southward to Portsmouth, Virginia.[21] There are patches of green here and there, of course, but the split levels, the shopping centers, the billboards, drive-ins, highways are rapidly taking over; and they give every indication of continuing to do so as our population grows apace.

Economic Costs

> The explosive combination of multiplying possessions and multiplying people is causing an ever larger portion of our high level of living to be used to escape from the consequences of congestion.[22]

An accompaniment of our growing population and its increasing density, cases of higher real costs for the maintenance of the standards Americans regard as minimal can be multiplied over and over. Air and water purification, traffic control, urban renewal, the acquisition and processing of natural resources, provision of social services, upkeep and preservation of parks and recreational areas, protection and conservation of wildlife all offer numerous examples. It costs us more simply to hold onto the standards of life we have already attained, let alone to achieve any improvement. That so many of these standards, outward signs of our quality of life, have already had to be lowered as a consequence of population pressure is evidence that the cost is more than merely monetary.

As our population grows and becomes more urbanized we must spend more on nearly every kind of public service—partly because of the increased demand these added numbers represent, and partly because of the increased competition they produce for scarce land and materials:

> Westchester's present contests with industry include residents' fights to prevent General Motors factories from absorbing Kingsland Point Park at North Tarrytown, a $9,000,000 hotel from rising in a semi-residential area of White Plains and the Guardian Life Insurance Company from building among homes on North Avenue, New Rochelle.[23]

Housing, schools, roads, industries all compete with one another and with parks and recreational areas for an increasingly limited supply of land in areas of high population density. Industry competes with community for water and drainage facilities. Airlines compete with airlines, and with community interests, for space around airports. Some localities, becoming conscious of the health hazards in air pollution, are even moving to restrict industrial use of the atmosphere as an avenue for the elimination of wastes.

The economic costs of transportation and communication have also risen in response to our population growth. Sunday afternoon traffic jams are seldom costly, at least in economic terms. But those in the middle of the week are. In all our larger urban areas road and air traffic seems already to be running into increasing costs from traffic density.[24] Motor trucks average less than six miles an hour in New York traffic today, as against eleven for horse-drawn trucks in 1910.[25] The cost of traffic jams, according to estimates by business and automotive groups, is $5 billion yearly.[26] And as only the most recent in a long series of appropriations to this end, our Federal government has allocated some $41 billion for the construction of an additional 41,000 miles of highway (and note how much that is per mile), an extension of roads which, upon completion, will cover as much area as there is in the whole state of Rhode Island.[27]

But it is probably with recreation that the economic effects of competing demands arising from population and urbanization are at their most obvious. The Department of the Interior estimates that its proposed acquisition of a badly needed 4.6 million acres for national parks and forests will run as high as $250 million a year for a period of ten years.* The Outdoor Recreation Resources Review Commission, noting that "all

---

*It is said that the size of this sum has prevented adoption of the program (see Nona B. Brown, "Park Plan for Tomorrow," *New York Times*, July 30, 1961, p. XX); but since it represents less than $14 per person for the whole ten years, and but 1/190th of the military budget for a *single* year, perhaps the real problem is that this figure is so low as to be completely intelligible. As Parkinson notes in discussing his "Law of Triviality": "The time spent on any item of the agenda will be in inverse proportion to the sum involved." (C. Northcote Parkinson, *Parkinson's Law*. Boston. Houghton Mifflin, 1957, chap. 3).

levels of government must provide continuing and adequate funds for outdoor recreation," warns that "in most cases, this will require a substantial increase over present levels."[28]

But if these higher economic costs come in the main from the spread of urbanization that accompanies our population growth, there are others that originate in the fact of numerical increase itself. Population growth may once have been essential for economic prosperity in the United States, but it can hardly be considered so any longer. When a man's strength was an important source of energy, and per capita consumption was at a low level, a growing population in a sparsely settled land was indeed an important factor in creating a high level of material living. The more people, the more energy, the greater the possible division of labor, the greater the potential market for goods.

It is different today. The combination of an increasing population and a generally rising level of consumption has revealed limitations in the supply of raw materials and increased the costs of developing them. All minerals and most of the sources of energy in current use are *non-renewable*. It took millions of years to create them. They represent capital. As we use them up we are using capital, not income. Though the outlook is not altogether bleak, rising demand has, even in the case of certain *renewable* resources, produced some serious and costly shortages. One of these is in water. Despite extensive efforts at development and conservation of this resource, our continued growth in numbers, combined with our rising level of living, has placed steadily mounting demands upon it. As the Rienows have noted:

> More than a thousand cities and towns [in the United States] already have been forced to curtail their water service. Near Chicago, where artesian wells flowed under their own pressure a hundred years ago, new wells must go down 2000 feet to

reach the water table. Dallas is already pumping the salt-tainted Red River into its main, and New York faces the likelihood that eventually it will have to purify the polluted Hudson to slake its growing thirst. In Mississippi, wells are now 400 feet deeper, on the average, than they were only ten years ago. Denver, eager for new industry, has been turning away manufacturers whose production processes involve a heavy use of water.[29]

Even if our population ceased to grow, we could expect rising costs for many of the raw materials essential to our way of life, first, because of higher production costs attending depletion of the more readily accessible supplies and, second, because of greater competition for these materials from other countries as a result of their own population increases and efforts to raise their levels of living. Since our population is not stable, but is, instead, growing rapidly, there is added to these two sources of higher costs a third—an annual addition of some three million people to that population with the world's highest rate of material consumption.[30]

In a private or mixed economy one can expect higher prices to spur development of new techniques for reclaiming scrap, encourage more extensive exploration, and bring into production marginal, low-yield deposits. A mining geologist and businessman like McLaughlin may assure us that these approaches will postpone "beyond the foreseeable historic future . . . the evil date of drastic scarcities,[31] but not even he would claim it can be done without substantial increases in real costs.

Pollution

The world's cleanest people . . . bathe with scented fats and drink a factory's slime. Of course, our water company cleans up the liquid for us—this same liquid in which not even hardy carp can live—by putting chemicals in it to kill other chemicals from upstream. The water is not, of course, cleaned up again before it is put back in the river, it is re-enriched.[32]

And the river? Well, it is not fit to swim in, there is a good chance that water fowl meet the same fate as the fish, and that it is pretty ugly and evil smelling. It is also likely to be something of a health hazard. In recent years outbreaks of infectious hepatitis have been traced to pollution of streams in Oregon and Utah; outbreaks of paralytic polio in New Jersey have been found by public health experts to be correlated with the prevalence of open sewers; polluted water has caused a typhoid epidemic in Keene, New Hampshire,[33] and infection in clams dug off New York and New Jersey. On the opening day of the 1961 swimming season, the New York City Department of Health listed four of the city's beaches as safe for bathing, six as marginal where bathing is permissible in dry weather but dangerous in wet, and four (the largest) as so polluted that the Department does not even bother to test them.[34]

Our water supply contains an ever increasing "dividend" of insecticides, herbicides, detergents, solvents, dyes, petroleum wastes, synthetic compounds, radioactive wastes, waste materials from canneries, hospitals, and slaughter houses, human wastes, myriads of germs and viruses, corrosive chemicals.[35] The rate at which we pollute our water rises with every increase in our material level of living. Yet, increasing urbanization makes us ever more dependent on these same sources of water for satisfaction of both recreational and utilitarian needs. As our population increases, the effect of these forces is intensified.

The same three factors that in combination pollute our water lead also in combination to pollution of the air: population growth, greater concentration, higher material levels of living. The heaviest contributors to air pollution in the United States are automobiles (in pulverized rubber and asphalt, as well as gases), industrial plants, households, and municipal installations, in that order.[36] If our population becomes still larger and more concentrated, minimum health standards will necessitate resort to costly control devices and far more stringent restrictions on both public and private use of the atmosphere.

In February, 1961, New York was smothered under one of the worst snowstorms in its history—bad enough for the mayor to order all nonessential vehicles off the streets for a week. During that week the pollution rate from carbon monoxide dropped two-thirds from the rate for the previous month, despite the fact that temperature inversions for five of the ban's six days would normally have resulted in extremely high pollution readings.[37] That it remained as high as it did gives some clue to the amount of pollution New York receives from localities where the ban was not in effect. That it dropped as low as it did suggests what can be accomplished by one kind of stringent control.

But just as the battle against water pollution has so far met with few successes,* so also has the battle against air pollution.

"We pledge . . . Federal authority," the Republicans cautiously and laconically wrote in their 1960 national platform, "to identify, after appropriate hearings, air pollution problems and to recommend proposed solutions." That was all. Candidate Kennedy's Conference on Urban Affairs showed a certain awareness of the problem and its origins in noting, "The air we breathe is fouled by exhaust fumes, industrial smoke and furnaces, creating a menace to public health. The problem

* A touching example was supplied by President Dwight Eisenhower who on February 23, 1960, vetoed a bill that would have authorized $900 million (1/417 of the then gross national income) for a 10-year Federal grants-in-aid program to help municipalities build sewage treatment works. With pollution in some measure affecting every river and nearly every stream in the country, with all but seven states having at least a part of their borders defined by a body of water, and with even these seven sharing several rivers with their neighbors, the President held that "water pollution is a uniquely local blight."

grows more critical as our population increases." But its conclusion hardly outdistanced that of the Republicans: "We must act to conquer these hazards and purify our air and water, our two most precious natural resources."[38]

The haze of polluted air that surrounds our cities is readily visible to anyone flying near them. On occasion it is also visible to those less airborne. Nor is this true only of the larger cities. A New York State report on air pollution in 1958 found that only one of the state's forty communities with a population of 25,000 or more had air pollution so slight that it could be termed "negligible." Among the smaller cities, either major or minor air pollution affected approximately 60 percent of those of 5000 to 25,000 population, and one-third of those with fewer than 5000.[39] Whether or not they see it, those on the ground most certainly sense it—in smarting eyes, burning throats, headaches, dirty eyeglasses, shirts that require laundering after but a few hours' wear. But the problem is more than one of mere discomfort and dirt. There is growing evidence that contaminated air may actually initiate disease. What happened in Donora, Pennsylvania (1950 population: 12,000), is most instructive. In October, 1948, that city was beset by a thermal inversion (i.e., a layer of warm air at a high altitude trapping a layer of cold air—and its pollutants—at the ground). By the third day, 5910 persons were reported ill. More than 60 percent of the inhabitants aged 65 and over were affected, almost half of these seriously so. Twenty persons died, 17 of them on the last day of the smog. Four years later, a week-long smog in London accounted for an estimated 4000–5000 additional deaths. Yet, in neither disaster was any single smog component present in a higher concentration than usual, a finding which

> points to the ugly conclusion that the same smog breathed by everyone a day or two at a time without immediate or apparent

ill effect may be highly injurious to substantial numbers of people when it is breathed continuously for only a few days more.

Even more disquieting is the subsequent experience of those involved in the Donora disaster. Before the episode residents of Donora appeared to have the same health status as people in the rest of the country. In the first nine years thereafter, however, those who became ill and recovered showed a higher mortality and incidence of illness than those who were present but unaffected at the time of the smog.

And, most important,

those Donora residents who had no history of heart disease prior to the dark days of 1948 but became ill in this period of smog have had a higher subsequent illness rate.[40]

As long as the volume of wastes is related to the combination of material levels of living and population size, an increase in either of these will be accompanied by increases in costs, and in the need for controls. To the extent that future Americans will be able to live at levels as high as those current today, the already serious problem of pollution can hardly help becoming at once more hazardous to health and more burdensome to control.

Social Services

Problems of immediacy always have the advantage of attracting notice—those that lie in the future fare poorly in the competition for attention and money.[41]

Continuous, rapid population growth threatens the quality of life from yet another direction: the provision of social services. Many an American community already faces difficulties in providing such services as schooling, public transportation, roads, courts, housing, prisons, libraries, and nursing homes as a consequence of its rapidly expanding population. Inevitably, it seems, the supply and quality of social services must fall behind the greater demand generated by numerical increase.

There are three reasons for this. First is the difficulty of estimating future needs and appropriating for them. Though present requirements can often be determined with a fair measure of accuracy, the calculation of future demand is necessarily a much less certain undertaking. For one thing, fashions and attitudes change. So also do the size and distribution of the incomes with which a society's members can act on their beliefs or pursue the dictates of fashion. Twenty years ago, who could have reasonably predicted the present vogue in outdoor recreation, the extensive participation in costly sports like skiing and boating? Professor Charles Westoff predicts an increase in the mental hospital population over the next 20 years, not only because, as he says, "in its simplest terms, more people mean more patients," but because "people will become more educated about mental health and more sensitized to its importance."[42] Given a general prediction like this, the problem is then to translate it into concrete estimates of the additional facilities and personnel that will be required—a difficult task even under conditions of population stability, but one made all the more difficult by population increase. Faced with such uncertainty on the one hand, and with appropriations that often involve thousands or even millions of dollars on the other, the easiest course is to play it "safe" with the public's money and appropriate with a view primarily to meeting present demand—with a fraction occasionally added to cover marginal increases in the future.

A second source of lag between need and provision of service (once a decision has been reached about the character of the need and an appropriation been made for it) lies in the time it takes to train the necessary personnel and to construct the necessary facilities.

> There is now a shortage of physicians. There has been no increase in the last ten years in numbers of graduating doctors. We have been able to hold the line only by the importation of foreign doctors. Seventeen per cent of physicians entering practice in the United States last year received their training abroad.
> In 1959 there were 5,000 vacancies in hospital staff residencies.
> The situation is worsening. By 1970 there will be 33,000,000 more of us . . .[43]

Here we see clearly illustrated the consequences of a lack of population stability. For the demographic determinants of this shortage of physicians arise not only in the rapid increase in population since World War II, but also in the sharp decline in the birth rate during the depression of the 1930's. Had the birth rate either not risen in the postwar period, or else not fallen during the 1930's, there would have been no doctor shortage (other things being equal). But, as it was, the two worst things that could happen so far as the provision of physicians is concerned did, in fact, take place: a rapid and sustained *increase* in the birth rate followed upon a rapid and temporary *decline* in such a way as to maximize the demand for physicians at precisely the time when their number had been depleted through changes in age structure brought about by the earlier decline in fertility. Those nonexistent physicians of the 1950's and today were simply not born. Thus, we see the need not only for a ceiling on our numbers, but also for a minimal fluctuation in the number of births around that figure necessary to maintain the population: in short, population *stability* in the fullest sense.

Were we willing to mobilize our energies and resources to that purpose, a year or two might suffice to end *for the present* the shortage of hospital facilities arising from our growth in numbers. But under current professional standards it takes some ten years of college and postgraduate training to produce a physician. Thus, the number of new entrants to the medical profession in 1973 will have to have started training this year; the number of new entrants in 1972, last year; the number of new entrants in 1971, two years ago, and so forth. Thus, even if our population ceased growing tomorrow, we would have a decreasing ratio of physicians to patients for at least another decade. The training of other health personnel—nurses and technicians, for example—takes less time, but recruitment into these fields has also lagged far behind our growth in population. In part, as in the case with physicians, this is occasioned by changes in the age structure. But there is with these latter groups a further force in the fact of the relative inferiority of their salaries, working conditions, and professional responsibilities. In the absence of drastic changes in these, recruitment to these occupations seems likely to continue to lag behind that into their less essential competitors. In the meantime, further increases in our numbers steadily aggravate the shortage. The eventual coming-of-age of the "baby boom" generation will bring some relief. But the alleviation can be only partial because of the continuation of high birth rates since the peak of the "boom."

What has been said of health personnel can also be said in varying degrees of other skilled service personnel: teachers, social workers, parole and probation officers, for example.

Finally, population growth in the United States produces a deterioration in our social services because of the fact that a certain amount of overuse must precede any enlargement of facilities or staff. We do not add, say, 124 cubic feet to the local schoolhouse and one-fifteenth of a teacher to its faculty for every additional pupil. Relying on the private automobile to provide mass transportation may appear at first to be an exception—one more commuter: one more automobile. And unquestionably, the automobile does allow for an immediate adjustment of carrying capacity to the number of people to be moved. But to be an effective means of transportation it requires other goods and services—roads and traffic control, for instance—the expansion of which is subject to the same kinds of difficulties that we have observed to be the case with other social services and to which, moreover, there are definite geographic limitations.

Depreciation may be quite considerable before a community's efforts can be mustered to expand an overloaded service. How much pressure has to be generated before something is done will depend on a number of things: the nature of the service involved (roads seem to fare better than most other community services—certainly better than schools or parks), the financial position and predominant values of the community, its political leadership, etc. But there will always be a delay of some extent between the decline in quality of service that arises from its overuse and the awareness of the need to expand it.

Educational facilities in particular have been adversely affected by this kind of delay in construction of plant and expansion of personnel. Here, for an example, are some figures on the situation in densely populated, highly urbanized New Jersey, a state whose school population increased by 62 percent in the decade 1950–1960:[44]

> With a record enrollment of 1,090,000 pupils, 36,000 more than last September; a record 48,000 teachers, 2000 more than a year ago, and forty-three new schools, the classroom shortage and the number of children on half sessions will still be far more pronounced than it was in 1950.
>
> In addition, the number of teachers with substandard licenses will be nearly 7000, or 14 per cent of the total, in comparison to 2600, or 8.4 per cent of the total, in 1952. . . .
>
> Meanwhile, taxes for the 573 school districts will have reached a record of $468,000,000, an increase of $195,000,000 since 1956

and their total debt will surpass $744,000,000 in comparison with $365,000,000 in 1955. . . .

The more than 57,000 pupils expected to attend school on a half-session basis will be nearly ten times as many as in 1950. . . . And the pupils with substandard teachers will exceed 48,000 in comparison to 31,218 in 1955. . . .

"Worst of all," the report stresses, "provisional and emergency teachers frequently must learn on the job, often at the expense of their pupils."[45]

A decade earlier, the Economics Committee of the Royal Commission on Population had concluded:

A rapidly increasing child population makes it constantly necessary to build new schools in order to prevent overcrowding and a lowering of standards; and if the educational standards aimed at are comparatively high, the annual amount of school-building thus required may be very considerable. *This makes it very difficult to reconcile high educational standards with a high birth-rate.*[46] (Italics added)

Nor are such conditions confined to schooling. This sort of thing can be found throughout the social services: in housing, sanitation, police and fire protection. Even the administration of justice is affected:

Personal injury cases in most of the nation's state courts are subject to more than a year's delay before reaching trial, the Institute of Judicial Administration reported yesterday. . . .

The longest delays, it said, were in courts in counties with the largest populations.

In counties of more than 750,000 persons the average delay was 22.6 months; in those of 500,000 to 750,000, the delay was 14.5 months; and in those of less than 500,000, the delay was 6.9 months.[47]

The provision of social services for a growing population must of necessity be a never-ending race against the threat of declining standards. A constant upwards adjustment must be made to avoid falling behind. Facilities conceived to meet future needs may well be rendered obsolete by population increases between the blueprint stage and the time they are ready for use. Moreover, because of the difficulties of assessing future needs and of incorporating them into concrete programs, there is an understandable reluctance to undertake any long-range plans—the only kind that could be expected to measure up to the task. Thus the present administration in Washington is looking only a decade or two ahead in its plans for coping with the needs of Americans for additional housing, schooling, mass transport, recreational facilities. About what is to happen then, the planners are conspicuously reticent. Yet, the most optimistic assessment is that, even if executed, these programs could succeed in little more than keeping pace with our growth in numbers. Without a concomitant cessation of this growth, any long-range improvement can hardly even be hoped for.

Freedom

One of the major pressures that give rise to the need for increasing numbers of laws, more elaborate organization, and more centralized government is increase of population. . . . In the future we can expect that the greater the population density of an industrial society becomes, the more elaborate will be its organizational structure and the more regimented will be its people.[48]

[C]ontinuation of population growth is likely to intensify various social and economic problems, solutions to which will be sought largely through state intervention. Should this come to pass, the economy would become less flexible and the freedom of individuals to do as they please would tend to become highly circumscribed. In this event the stork would have managed to do what the followers of Marx had found themselves unable to do for all they tried—fasten fetters on mankind.[49]

If freedom for the individual can be defined as the "oppor-tunity to achieve his goals without external restraints,"[50] the average American is at once more free and less free today than formerly. His freedom has been increased by the general im-provement in his economic position, by his greater amount of education and training, his higher productivity, his gain in power through the extension of collective bargaining. It has been decreased by his country's involvement in a "cold war," and by the increasing size and urbanization of the American population.

Under present conditions the Cold War is probably the great-est single threat to those freedoms that distinguish a democratic from a non-democratic society: freedom of speech, thought, assembly; the right to oppose; the right to a fair trial; the right to privacy; the right to travel freely. What is threatened by the growth and concentration of population, however, are those more mundane freedoms which, for all their lack of dramatic content and emotional appeal, still figure prominently in our daily lives.

With growing numbers, life becomes more complex. There develops a wider range and frequency of interpersonal contact, and a greater competition for scarce resources like space, raw materials, air, water, and social services. At the same time, the need is intensified for fire and police protection, sanitation, traffic and pollution control, zoning, building codes, custodial care for the mentally and physically dependent—services that are far less essential to the functioning of smaller or less densely settled populations, and which, though capable of being handled by more individual means when a population is small, require increasingly collective action when it is large and growing. In combination, these social changes lead to an ever greater need for external control over the individual, for a narrowing of the range of his unregulated behavior. For as the complexity of life increases, there must be a corresponding increase in the organization of human activities to assure, first, the necessary minimum predictability in social relations and, second, the required efficiency in the use and distribution of scarce resources.

Were our numbers to double, many of what are today but trifling restrictions would necessarily be hardened into onerous constraints. This would be part of the price we would have to pay to achieve the efficiency in the use of land area and other resources, and in the provision of social services, that these numbers would make necessary.

Some of the means to this control over the individual are already in use. Others are being strongly urged. Though speed laws, traffic signals, stop signs are not especially burdensome, pollution ordinances, building codes, and zoning restrictions often are; and we can expect them to become even more so as further population growth brings about a necessary extension of their range. In urban areas, zoning is now so commonplace as to be generally tolerated—if not invariably welcomed. But opposition to zoning in rural areas, a form of control likely to become increasingly necessary with continued growth, will undoubtedly be more strenuous. Proposals made at a zoning symposium at the 1960 meeting of the American Association for the Advancement of Science suggest the possible shape of such controls in the near future: establishment of public corporations to buy land and hold it until conditions warrant its resale for the most desirable use; extension of the size of present government landholdings to include the most important areas for agriculture, watersheds, greenbelts, and recreation; a requirement that suburban developers exhaust the acreage unsuited to agriculture before being allowed to loose their power shovels on farm land.[51]

In the longer run, of course, even more stringent controls would have to be imposed. To the extent that land could be allowed to remain privately owned in a United States with double or triple its present numbers, its use would have to be further and further circumscribed. Eventually, there could be no such thing as a "family farm" or a "place in the country"— or, under still greater pressure of numbers, even a backyard— whose owner could be allowed the luxury of determining for himself how he wanted to use it, whether to use it for growing flowers instead of for the production of food or minerals. In these more extreme conditions, the right of eminent domain would become little more than a museum piece; the idea that a man's home was his castle, something of a wry joke.

Continual population growth will require ever greater efficiency in our use of recreational areas, too. Ultimately, of course, a growing population would force the transfer of all such areas to the production of food and minerals, or to the provision of sites for housing or transportation facilities. But even in the very near future there is a strong possibility that pressure on these facilities will become so great that access to them will have to be considerably limited. As one observer has noted,

> It may be argued with some logic that those who plan to visit parks during the peak hours of use must expect to find facilities crowded, sometimes be required to make advance reservations, perhaps pay an admission fee, and at times be turned away.[52]

And when it comes to mass transportation the need for extensive controls is already blatantly obvious in most of our metropolitan areas, even with population no larger than it is now. The question presents itself with growing urgency: how much longer can the individual be allowed to exercise freedom of choice in the mode of transportation he will take to work or shopping? A source of pleasure and freedom on the open road, the private automobile was never suited to mass commutation. No matter how well organized the car pools, automobiles can move people at a rate but one-seventh that for buses, and only one-twentieth that for rail facilities.[53] In view of relationships like these, it seems certain that as cities strive to adjust to their growing populations, the freedom of movement afforded the individual by the private automobile will eventually have to give way to more efficient means of mass transport.

The submerging of individual interests to cope with the difficulties attending growth will also be duplicated at other levels of the society. Whatever the action taken to meet population pressures, if it is to be effective it will have to apply to more than a single community. More centralization is inescapable. Necessitated by the combination of our way of life and our rapid growth in numbers, local autonomy will increasingly have to defer to regional approaches: regional planning, regional zoning, regional public corporations to manage and operate. Of the 192 metropolitan centers in this country, 23 straddle more than one state, and among these are some of the largest: New York, Philadelphia, Chicago, St. Louis, Cincinnati, Washington. The 1467 distinct political entities in the Greater New York Metropolitan Area,[54] for example, each with its own power to tax and spend, plan and zone, are no instrument by which to combat air and water pollution, plan for transportation facilities and sewage disposal, and secure a sufficiency of park and agricultural lands. Such governmental splintering, however useful still for some purposes, simply cannot meet all the needs of today's metropolis. The very existence of separate communities becomes steadily more anachronistic in the face of urban sprawl and population growth. Localities run into one another and struggle to provide for ever greater numbers spread over an ever greater area. Our population growth and our concentration in urban centers have made an absolute necessity the creation of special governmental units with broad powers to plan and administer over a wide geographical area.

At the same time that population growth forces a decline in the degree of flexibility allowed the individual it widens the gulf between him and his government.* To be sure, such a gulf has no necessary bearing on either the efficiency of government agencies or the quality of their personnel. Nevertheless, the individual under these circumstances will have increasingly less influence both on decision-making and on administration. In 1900, the average Congressman represented 190,000 people. By 1960 this number had risen to 410,000. Letters received by Congressmen concerning any particular issue are now so voluminous that if they have any influence at all it is—to judge from the statements of politicians themselves—to be reckoned in terms of quantity rather than content: "My mail is running four to one in favor." In Australia, with one-eighteenth as many people as the United States, an ordinary citizen (not just an officer of the American Medical Association or an oil millionaire) can submit a question to his representative and actually have it brought up and discussed in Parliamentary session.

No wonder, then, that in the United States those who perceive their interests particularly at stake must resort to lobbying to receive a hearing. On his own, the individual citizen has hardly a chance. Yet with lobbying, because of its very nature, some groups will have far greater access to and influence over legislators and executives than will others. It is the well-financed, well-organized lobbyists for business, veterans, doctors, the military, farmers, and labor unions whose efforts meet most frequently with success. Compared with these powerhouses, the civil libertarians, conservationists, consumers representatives, or peace groups are but 90-pound weaklings. As a Stanford University political scientist has pointed out:

> [F]ormulation of policy requires more knowledge than choosing among alternatives which others have formulated. As a result, influencers need more information about the policy

---

* Government is only one source of external control, of course. Religious bodies, corporations, labor unions, educational institutions, among others, are also important agencies of control. But since government is more directly affected by population growth, we limit ourselves to discussing only that agency.

areas they operate in than even the most well-informed voters; hence their data costs are higher. . . .

Naturally, the men who stand most to gain from exerting influence in a policy area are the ones who can best afford the expense of becoming expert about it. Their potential returns from influence are high enough to justify a large investment of information. In almost every policy area, those who stand the most to gain are the men who earn their income there. This is true because most men earn their incomes in one area but spend them in many; hence the area of earnings is much more vital to them than any one area of spending. . . .

. . . Clearly, the cost of acquiring information and communicating opinions to government determines the structure of political influence. Only those who can afford to bear this cost are in a position to be influential.

A striking example of this fact is the failure of consumers-at-large to exercise any cogent influence over government decisions affecting them. For instance, legislators are notorious for writing tariff laws which favor a few producers in each field at the expense of thousands of consumers. . . .[55]

If the ordinary citizen must speak with a group voice to be heard, there is still no assurance that the group to which he attaches himself will actually represent *him*. In fact, the larger and more durable the group, the more certain is it that the sounds it makes will be representative of the interests of its leaders—men who, as the Swiss sociologist, Robert Michels, pointed out two generations ago, are, by their very positions in the organizational structure of the group, increasingly removed from the way of life and thought of its members.[56]

So, with a large and increasing population, the individual finds his day-to-day existence ever more circumscribed: he must do certain things that he would not otherwise do and limit or refrain altogether from doing certain things that he would otherwise do. At the same time, again partly as a consequence of population growth, his chances of having a say at either the

decision-making or administrative stages of this control are
necessarily reduced. Yet, should he seek to gain a voice by
joining with others who supposedly share his views, he is more
than likely to find himself blocked, first, by the differences in
the distribution of power as between petitioning groups and,
second, by the system of leadership within the group itself.

The deleterious effects of population growth are all alike in
one important respect: they do not arrive suddenly. With
no dramatic warning of their onset, they creep upon their
victims so slowly it is hard to tell when the attack began. Because these costs—monetary, social, and personal—do not come
all at once, it is possible that man, with his nearly infinite
powers of adjustment, may for a time grow used to them in
much the same way that one grows used to a chronic ailment.
Yet, why (when it can be avoided) should we allow ourselves
to become victims of the chronic ailment—the lack of elbow
room, the air and water pollution, the destruction of wild life,
the ever greater restrictions on our freedom of action—just
because we might "grow used to it"? As John Stuart Mill wrote
more than a century ago:

> A population may be too crowded, though all be amply sup-
> plied with food and raiment. It is not good for man to be kept
> perforce at all times in the presence of his species. A world
> from which solitude is extirpated is a very poor ideal. Solitude,
> in the sense of being often alone, is essential to any depth of
> meditation or of character; and solitude in the presence of
> natural beauty and grandeur, is the cradle of thoughts and
> aspirations which are not only good for the individual, but
> which society could ill do without. Nor is there much satis-
> faction in contemplating the world with nothing left to the
> spontaneous activity of nature; with every rood of land brought
> into cultivation, which is capable of growing food for human
> beings; every flowery waste or natural pasture ploughed up, all

quadrupeds or birds which are not domesticated for man's use exterminated as his rivals for food, every hedgerow or superfluous tree rooted out, and scarcely a place left where a wild shrub or flower could grow without being eradicated as a weed in the name of improved agriculture.[57]

Part II

Factors Shaping
the Attitudes of Americans
Toward Their Population Growth

4
Religion

AMERICANS may mutter about traffic tie-ups, jammed recreational areas, new curbs on individual activities, the loss of scenic countryside to housing developments, roads, and billboards. They may long for the less cluttered, less hectic atmosphere of a scant ten or fifteen years ago. But when it comes to doing something about these conditions their usual reaction is one of apathy, even fatalism. Partly this may result from a feeling of impotence in the face of urbanization and population growth; partly it may be ignorance of the instrumental part played by population growth in contributing to these conditions. But it is undoubtedly a consequence also of the failure to think in terms of population control at all: a legacy of the religious climate and predominant value orientations prevailing in the United States today.

Aversion to the idea of controlling population is probably based most often on religious beliefs. Yet religious reasons are by no means always publicly acknowledged. Even Roman Catholics, the religious group most vocal in its opposition to the general principles of limiting population, will more often than not resort first to economic or scientific arguments to substantiate their position. Yet their ultimate argument—and, we would supose, that of many others—is religious. In essence, this springs from a fear that dire consequences will follow if man tampers with what is felt to be God's greatest mystery, the creation of life. Even many to whom family planning is quite

acceptable on the personal level will balk at the idea of intro-
ducing these same techniques on a wider scale—by, for instance,
giving technical advice about birth control to the peoples of
underdeveloped countries (even when their governments re-
quest it). Efforts to influence population trends on a mass scale
seem to constitute either too great an interference in God's
Design or too little faith in His Providence.

Population and its control have only recently emerged as
controversial public issues. It is only with the rise of the birth
control movement that mediaeval theological dogmas about
marriage and parenthood have ceased to be taken for granted.
Prior to the mid-19th century, neither knowledge of contraception, nor means to it were widely available. For the vast
majority the choice of whether or not to conceive simply did
not exist. Children were seen as an inevitable result of marital
relations—their number determined by the will of God.

From the standpoint of human survival, this lack of control
over conception was, as we have seen, an often necessary counterbalance to the high mortality characterizing the pre-industrial world. Early Judaic–Christian doctrines reflected this
preoccupation with the need for abundant births. And until
very recently, despite tremendous reductions in mortality, the
three major religions in the United States—Protestantism,
Roman Catholicism, Judaism—have tended to adhere to these
pro-natalist doctrines. In doing so, they have lagged behind
changes in public belief and behavior.

Social changes attending the Industrial Revolution in both
America and Europe created such pressures for the reduction
of family size that many couples were induced to break with
religious and social tradition in order to limit the number of
their children. In every country where this happened, private
acceptance of the principle of family limitation, demonstrated
most graphically by downward trends in the birth rate,[1] ante-
dated by many years—even generations—changes in the official
positions of the churches. In the United States, the general

trend toward a smaller size family seems to have started at least as far back as the mid-19th century,[2] and in certain instances as far back as the end of the 18th century.[3]

Declining rapidly from a high of about 55 per 1000 in the early 1800's, the crude birth rate of the white population in the United States reached a low of 18 per 1000 during the economically unstable years of the 1930's. Yet, in the Protestant churches, for example, there were no official statements in support of family limitation until but three decades ago, while the more significant pronouncements have come only within the last six years.[4]

On one thing the major religious faiths in the United States are now in agreement: they all approve of the limitation of births under at least some conditions. But there is wide divergence in their views on what these conditions are and on what constitute morally acceptable means. And there are still representatives of more orthodox persuasion from each of the three faiths who regard abstinence as the only moral method of family limitation.

The three faiths share a common pro-natalist heritage in the writings of the Old Testament: writings which were addressed to an innumerous people struggling to establish themselves in a relatively infertile, arid land, bordered in several directions by belligerent tribes at a time when warfare involved hand-to-hand combat. Under such conditions, the relation between population size and survival was abundantly clear. In Old Testament Jewish society the bearing of many children was considered a blessing; the childless marriage, a calamity; the preservation of family name through one's children, the only kind of immortality worth achieving.[5]

In the Old Testament are the two passages which form the customary support for the religious stand against the limitation of population and the use of birth control. Most frequently cited in opposition to the first is God's command in Genesis: "Be fruitful, and multiply, and replenish the earth," which

He addressed to the newly created Adam and Eve, at that time the sole inhabitants of an empty world. The same command was given a second time, following God's destruction of all His creation by the flood. On this latter occasion, it was directed to Noah and his family—eight persons in all—again, the sole human inhabitants of an otherwise empty world.

For the religious taboo against birth control the scriptural support is drawn from the story of Onan—also in the Book of Genesis. Onan refused to honor the ancient Jewish custom of the *levirate,* which required a man to marry his dead brother's widow in order to provide her with children and thus ensure the perpetuation of his brother's name.

> And Onan knew that the seed should not be his; and it came to pass, when he went in unto his brother's wife, that he spilled it on the ground, lest that he should give seed to his brother. And the thing which he did displeased the Lord; wherefore he slew him also.[6]

The only explicit Biblical reference to an act with contraceptive intent, this passage is interpreted by many theologians as indicating God's abhorrence of *coitus interruptus* in particular, and birth prevention in general. Some contemporary Jews and Protestants join with Catholics in adhering to this interpretation.

But there is another possible interpretation: Onan's punishment was not for his use of *coitus interruptus* with contraceptive intent, but for his refusal to fulfil his fraternal duty—"to raise up seed unto his brother," "to build up his brother's house." The rest of the story has been cited in support of this alternative interpretation: The widow, Tamar, still without child, is promised by her father-in-law, Judah, that he will give her as a husband his third son, Shelah. But Judah does not keep his promise. So Tamar disguises herself as a harlot and seduces Judah, obtaining his ring, cord, and staff in payment. When, three months later, Judah is informed that his daughter-in-law has played the harlot and is pregnant he orders her to be burned. But she sends the ring, cord, and staff to him with the message, "By the man, whose these are, am I with child." Judah acknowledges them saying, "She hath been more righteous than I; because that I gave her not to Shelah my son."[7]

Precisely which aspect of Onan's behavior was repulsive to the Lord obviously admits of no proof. But the controversy over interpretation is enlightening for the insight it gives into the kind of bases which have been adduced in support of religious opposition to family limitation. As the editor of the *Edinburgh Review* pointed out forty years ago, this story "portrays a system of ethics utterly at variance with the ordinary code of Christian ethics in European countries. Yet upon this story Christian theologians explicitly base their declared belief that the use of contraceptive devices is forbidden by God."[8]

While Old Testament references to marriage stress the procreative function, they nevertheless also contain numerous examples of conjugal devotion, thus suggesting that affection and companionship in marriage are to be valued as ends in themselves: Rebekah and Isaac, Rachel and Jacob, Ruth and Boaz. These are significant not only because it is unusual to find such an early appreciation for the independent role of woman as a companion to her husband, but also because they foreshadow changes in the theological doctrines relating to marriage and the family—changes that led eventually to the religious sanctioning of family limitation.

The Old Testament also contains ample evidence of affection for children and of appreciation for them as persons in their own right. From this source can be derived the importance that each of this country's three major faiths attaches to parental responsibility for the proper nurture of children— a responsibility which is also considered by each of the three to be one of the most morally defensible reasons for family limitation.

For Christians, an additional set of Biblical precepts relating

to marriage and the family is to be found in the teachings of
Jesus and the interpretation given these teachings by the
Apostle, Paul. These, however, are characterized by considerable ambivalence. Jesus gives a powerful affirmation to companionship in marriage by extending the Old Testament concept of husband and wife becoming one. When asked by the
Pharisees to comment on divorce, He replies,

> But from the beginning of the creation God made them male
> and female. For this cause shall a man leave his father and
> mother, and cleave to his wife; and they twain shall be one
> flesh: so then they are no more twain, but one flesh. What
> therefore God hath joined together, let not man put asun-
> der.[9]

The development of Christian doctrine concerning contraception has been profoundly affected by this concept. The gradual
acceptance of contraception by most of Protestantism may be
attributed in large measure to changes in theology that raised
the companionate function of marriage to a position equal with
the procreative.[10] It was this principle that the Anglican
bishops proclaimed at their church's 1958 Lambeth Conference:

> The Biblical revelation . . . does not limit the function of
> sexuality and the family to the reproductive purpose. Equally
> deep-rooted in Genesis is the reflection of a second factor—the
> need of man and woman for each other, to complement and
> fulfil each other and to establish a durable partnership against
> the loneliness and rigour of life. . . . This relationship of man
> and woman—of husband and wife—is rooted in God's creative
> purpose equally with the procreative function of sexuality. . . .
> [T]he procreation of children is not the only purpose of
> marriage. Husbands and wives owe to each other and to the
> depth and stability of their families the duty to express, in
> sexual intercourse, the love which they bear and mean to bear
> to each other.[11]

The evolution of Catholic doctrine has taken a different direction. Here the companionate functions are of secondary importance, with procreation still regarded as the primary end of marriage. Since the 1930's, however, Catholic theologians have been emphasizing these secondary, or companionate, ends of marriage to a much greater extent than previously in order to support their acceptance of the rhythm—or periodic abstinence—method of birth control. It is morally acceptable, they now argue, for a couple to enjoy sexual relations in the non-fertile period of the wife's cycle, for, writes Dr. Leo J. Latz in the standard Catholic manual on the rhythm method, "Sex, when used as intended by the Creator, preserves, deepens, and intensifies married love; it is love's expression and fulfilment; it confirms and strengthens the marital bond."[12]

But there is a negative element in Jesus' teachings about the family. This is suggested in His conviction that claims of the religious life have priority over those of the family:

> For I am come to set a man at variance against his father, and the daughter against her mother, and the daughter-in-law against her mother-in-law. And a man's foes shall be they of his own household. He that loveth father and mother more than me is not worthy of me: and he that loveth son or daughter more than me is not worthy of me. And he that taketh not his cross, and followeth after me, is not worthy of me.[13]

This preoccupation with the spiritual to the virtual rejection of family ties was carried even further by Paul. In his Epistles he is clearly ambivalent toward marriage and family life. For him, as for Jesus, the major concern was for the disciplined spiritual life dedicated to God. But with Paul the dominant tone is negative and misogynous. Marriage and family obligations are viewed almost completely as impediments to spiritual endeavor.

This negative element in Christian values and attitudes toward marriage and the family was furthered by the asceticism

of the early Church Fathers, and by the later modifications of
their teachings by Thomas Aquinas. Though serving in general
to perpetuate the high fertility bias of the Old Testament, the
teachings of these early Christians were based on something
other than merely the need to fulfil the Biblical injunction to
multiply. Essentially, they were the consequence of a puritan-
ical and ascetic attitude toward sex.

Asceticism in the writings of both Paul and Augustine took
the form of a profound distrust of the pleasureful element in sex.
Procreation thus became the only positive purpose of sexual
relations. The prevention of conception they condemned as
sinful and contrary to the Scriptures. Augustine declared that
"Intercourse, even with one's legitimate wife, is unlawful and
wicked where the conception of the offspring is prevented.
Onan, the son of Juda, (*sic*) did this and the Lord killed him
for it."[14]

The ambivalent attitudes of these early theologians toward
marriage and parenthood originated in their fear that sexual
behavior had detrimental effects on the spiritual life of man.
Celibacy they regarded as the holiest status; marriage they allowed mainly for its negative function of allaying the sin of
concupiscence. Said Jerome, "I do not detract from marriage
when I set virginity before it—wedded women may congratulate
themselves that they are next to virgins." And Thomas Aquinas
regretted that as a result of original sin conception could now
take place only at the cost of virginity.[15]

The objection of some opponents of birth control that contraception releases couples from the often painful consequences
of their sexual behavior (i.e. conception, pregnancy, childbirth,
and the responsibilities of childrearing) while allowing them to
enjoy its pleasures unimpaired, is certainly a derivative of this
early Christian ideal of asceticism:

> The pleasures associated with the use of sex are, as it were, a
> stimulus and a reward for willingness to accept the responsi-

bilities which are the consequent of human reproduction. To voluntarily seek or accept such pleasures in a manner which excludes the primary end of marriage, namely reproduction, is seriously sinful and places man in inimical relationship to God so long as he remains in an unrepentant state.[16]

On a more general level, the vague lingering feeling that even marital sex is somehow sinful seems also to be a legacy of this early asceticism. At the very least, this feeling has had the effect of inhibiting public discussion of family limitation and the relevance of such limitation to the alleviation of population pressure.

In neither Catholicism nor Protestantism is there complete uniformity of viewpoint concerning either the official teachings on marriage and the family or the application of these teachings to public policy. The diversity of thought and organization that characterizes Protestantism is widely recognized; but there is debate within Catholic ranks as well. It revolves around such matters as the conditions (both personal and social) that justify the regulation of conception, the amount of emphasis that should be placed on the responsibility of parents for the education of their children, the value that should be attached to the companionate aspects of marriage as ends in themselves independent of the primary end of procreation. These are the very areas in which we might expect to find a future liberalization of the Catholic Church's traditional stand on the population question. Indeed, it is in these areas that some change in the Roman Catholic concept of parenthood and related questions has already occurred.

Historically, the position of the Catholic Church has been to regard family limitation—for any reason and by any means other than complete abstinence—as a mortal sin. The doctrinal basis for this condemnation, apart from the Scriptures, is derived from Aquinas' writings on "natural law." Canon law states that the primary end of marriage is the procreation and education of children. To frustrate this end is a "sin against nature . . . which is shameful and intrinsically vicious."[17] This traditional Catholic view is based on two propositions: (1) Man can, by the use of his reason, discover God's purpose in the universe, and (2) God makes known His purpose through the physical arrangements of nature.[18] From these it is deduced that God intended sexual activity to be nature's means of perpetuating the species, a purpose not to be set aside by human whim.

Scientific verification of a "safe" period—a period in a woman's cycle during which conception cannot take place—prompted Catholic theologians to re-examine doctrines about the procreative ends of marriage and to place greater emphasis on the secondary ones, like love and companionship. The so-called safe period or "rhythm" method of contraception was first publicized in the United States in 1932. Since then, Catholic doctrine regarding family limitation has altered its focus with the church endorsing periodic continence (the rhythm method) as "nature's own" method of birth control. Catholic literature on contraception, which formerly emphasized the sinfulness of birth prevention and its harmful consequences, has shifted to a discussion of such practical questions as how to make The Rhythm work and how to use it effectively to limit family size. Since the evil consequences said to follow from birth control in general—e.g. that it removes the check on lust, encourages free love, contributes to economic stagnation by reducing population growth, or leads to race suicide—are equally applicable to control by a widespread use of the rhythm method, Catholic opposition to contraception has now come to rest primarily on the methods used. Regardless of the reasons for using them, all methods (the so-called "artificial" ones) which in any way—directly or indirectly—hinder or "frustrate" the possibility of conception as an outcome of the sex act are condemned as contrary to "natural law." This prohibition includes all chemicals or pills which inhibit ovulation or destroy the sperm and all mechanical devices or practices, such as *coitus interruptus,* which prevent the meeting of sperm and egg. Sterilization and abortion are condemned on other grounds, as they are also by most of the Protestant churches.

Conditions under which use of the rhythm method is morally acceptable are frequently reviewed in Catholic literature. Even the "natural" method, it seems, must be tempered by moral considerations. Pius XII touched briefly upon the nature of these conditions in his address to the Italian Union of Midwives, October, 1951: "[s]erious reasons, such as those found in the medical, eugenic, economic, and social indications can exempt [one] for a long time, perhaps, even for the whole duration of marriage, from this positive duty [i.e. to procreate]." He further emphasized this position a month later, in stating that "one may even hope . . . that science will succeed in providing this licit method with a sufficiently secure basis, and the most recent information seems to confirm such a hope."[19]

Though issued by the highest authority in the Church hierarchy, this pronouncement admits of a variety of interpretations. Thus we find publicly expressed differences among Catholics with a range as wide as that represented by the following:

> The family which courageously and even heroically rears a large number of children in an overpopulated area merits special praise for its virtue.[20]

Or, in contrast, this from a Jesuit demographer:

> An excessive rate of growth prevents orderly economic and social development. It presents problems with capital formation, with the creation of job opportunities, with the provision of adequate housing and living space in cities and so on.

It also has very serious impacts on education in the provision
of schools, teachers and facilities to educate people to live in
the new complex, technological civilization which is now
spreading to the underdeveloped areas . . .

I believe that we can look forward to eventual decline in
certain of these areas. *It is desirable that something reasonable
and morally acceptable is done to slow down rates of growth.*
(italics ours).[21]

The fact that under some conditions the Catholic Church
now condones the rhythm method of birth control is no reason
to conclude that Catholic doctrine is undergoing any evolution
toward the acceptance of contraception. Catholics may publicly
disagree about certain of the implications of parenthood for
today's population growth, but they still stand firmly united
in their opposition to all means of control they define as "artificial." It was in order to reaffirm this position, perhaps to con-
solidate wavering Catholic opinion, and to halt the illusion that
"artificial birth prevention is gradually becoming acceptable
even in the Catholic Church," that the American Catholic
Bishops issued their ringing statement, "Explosion or Backfire,"
on November 26, 1959. Closely following publication of the
Draper Report, the report of President Eisenhower's committee
to study the United States military assistance program, which
recommended that the United States foreign aid program include the giving of birth control information to countries re-
questing it, the Bishops' statement declared that American
Catholics would not support "any public assistance, either at
home or abroad, to promote artificial birth prevention, abortion or sterilization, whether through direct aid or by means of
international organizations." Apparently wishing to leave no
doubt as to where they stood on the matter, the Bishops went
on to declare: "United States Catholics believe that the promotion of artificial birth prevention is a morally, humanly, psychologically and politically disastrous approach to the population problem."

And here the matter rests. Even Father Gibbons, previously quoted as favoring a reduction in the rate of world population growth—especially in the underdeveloped countries—has reached this point of no retreat:

> ... artificial contraception by devices, chemicals, and so forth is morally wrong, and seriously so. The reason is not that it limits the number of babies born into the world—remaining single does that too—but because it vitiates the sex act as God and nature intended it should be performed. That is why we call such practices unnatural.
>
> *There is no possibility the Church will change her strong condemnation of this, whatever the problem may be.*[22] (Italics ours).

Thus, any program to curtail population growth that hopes to enlist Catholic cooperation must be prepared, at least for the time being, either to limit itself to those contraceptive methods approved by the Church, or to concentrate on indirect methods of reducing rates of growth, such as studying social and economic factors that might encourage declines in family size. Any attempt to argue, berate, inveigh against the doctrine will be self-defeating. The Catholic Church's position on parenthood rests on a system of ideas—logical within itself—which is impervious to attack, however logical, from another set of premises.

When it comes to the Protestant approach to birth control one finds no single systematic or widely authoritative formulation of a position. Individual Protestant churches have issued statements about their stands on marriage and family planning, but there are many that have yet to be heard from. This picture is now changing somewhat, though. Protestant churchmen are becoming increasingly concerned about population and seem gradually to be moving toward consensus. Ironically, the lead in this movement has been taken by that very denomination whose theology is closest to the doctrines of Thomas Aquinas—the Anglican communion. For some years, the Church of England has devoted more systematic attention to problems of marriage and family life than has any other Christian group, barring the Roman Catholic. After condemning "birth control" at both their 1908 and 1920 conferences, the Anglicans reversed this position in 1930, stating that where "there is a clearly felt moral obligation to limit or avoid parenthood complete abstinence is the 'primary and obvious method,' but that if there is a morally sound reason for avoiding abstinence, 'the conference agrees that other methods may be used, provided that this is done in the light of ... Christian principles.' "[23] By the time of its 1958 Lambeth Conference the Anglican Church had advanced significantly toward a more active approach to the population-parenthood problem. The report of Section V of this Conference, "The Family in Contemporary Society," has had a strong influence on the thinking of other Protestant groups. The following key statement from this report is representative of an emerging Protestant outlook:

> [S]ome form of family planning, particularly in those areas of rapidly growing population, is an urgent necessity. By "family planning" is meant an extension of the responsible use of science into the realm of procreation, within the permissible range of Christian ethics, in the immediate interest of the family and the more remote but no less real interest of society at large.[24]

Here in the United States, the National Council of Churches, a federation of 25 major Protestant bodies and eight Eastern Orthodox communions, on February 23, 1961, overwhelmingly approved the use of birth control methods for "responsible family planning." Though this is regarded as American Protestantism's first truly collective pronouncement in support of contraception, it should not be assumed to mean that unanimity concerning family planning has been achieved among non-Catholics. Not only are certain Protestant groups—generally, the more Fundamentalist—not members of the Council, but there is as yet no unanimity within the Council itself. Abstinence is still the only method of family limitation approved by the Orthodox communions, whose delegates refrained from voting in order to dissociate themselves from the pronouncement.[25]

The differences separating the Roman Catholic position on birth control from the position of those Protestant denominations that have declared themselves in support of it can be summarized in terms of three issues: (1) the criteria for determining the morality of birth control; (2) the definition of the primary ends of marriage; (3) the persons to whom religious doctrines apply.

Protestant theologians who support birth control claim no universal, objective criteria for judging the morality of its use. As the companionate function of marriage is of equal status with the procreative, the rightness or wrongness of the use of birth control in any given case depends upon the integrity of the individuals involved and the purity of their motives.[26] The means of preventing conception, provided they are medically sound and acceptable to both parties, are a matter of individual preference. The morality of birth control, according to Protestants, is more a function of the motives and goals shared by the husband and wife than of the methods they use. Protestant theologians maintain that there is no binding principle that can be universally applied. The choice of whether or not to prevent birth and the means to this end, must rest on individual conscience.

For Catholics, however, the primary end of marriage is procreation; the companionate relations between spouses, though important, are strictly secondary. In Catholic theology, these principles, based as they are on what Catholics believe to be God's immutable "natural law," are absolute, binding on all men everywhere, regardless of their personal or social conditions.

There would be no need to concern ourselves here with theological doctrines, however, were it not for the effect these seem
to have on both individual behavior and public policy in this
country. At the individual level is the fact that the behavior
of couples in planning their families, together with their attitudes toward family limitation in general, vary markedly along
religious lines. Recent research on a random sample of American couples divided into the three major religious groupings
and matched as closely as possible on six characteristics (occupation of husband, schooling of wife, income of husband, duration of marriage, metropolitan character of present residence,
and farm background) found that Catholic couples expected to
have 40 percent more children than either Protestant or Jewish
couples; that they were far less likely to express approval of
family limitation even by the general population (only 33 percent as against 96 percent of the Protestants and 97 percent of
the Jews); and that after an average of 8½ years of marriage
they were far less likely to have used a method of contraception
unacceptable under Catholic doctrine (15 percent as against 80
percent of the Protestants and 84 percent of the Jews).[27]

Fourteen years earlier (in 1941), a survey of native-white
couples in Indianapolis found that among those in which the
wife was 40-44 years of age (i.e., of essentially completed childbearing) Catholics had 25 percent more children than Protestants and almost 50 percent more children than Jews.[28] A
1933 study of Wisconsin urban couples, married between 1919
and 1930, found that in the first seven years of marriage the
natality rates of Catholic couples exceeded those of non-Catholic
couples in every occupational, residential, age, and duration of
marriage category.[29] The "common observation that Catholic
families, on the average, have more children than their non-
Catholic neighbors . . . has been confirmed in every competent
demographic study that contains information on religious differentials in [natality]."[30]

It used to be thought that these differentials were more the result of socio-economic differences (e.g., in income, schooling, occupation, extent of urbanization); and it was predicted that they would, like various other social differentials, decline in magnitude as the population became more homogeneous. Religious ideology tended to be minimized as a determinant of family size. Larger average family size among Catholics was assumed to be a temporary phenomenon which would disappear as Catholics attained positions in society similar to those of Protestants and Jews.

But more recent studies suggest that religion itself is an important determinant of American natality patterns. One such study[31] (the only one based on a nationwide sample) presents evidence that the Catholic family is not in fact undergoing those changes originally predicted for it. While the use of birth control tended to increase with economic and educational status among both Catholic and Protestant couples, the Catholic proportions were found to be always substantially lower than the Protestant at every income, educational, and occupational level. Indeed, as educational attainment rose, the gap between the two widened substantially. Among Catholic couples those with more schooling appeared to be most loyal to the doctrines of the Church, both in their attitudes toward the principle of family limitation itself and in their use of Church-approved methods. Further substantiation of the importance of religion was the fact that Catholic wives who attended church more frequently were found to be less likely than other Catholic wives to try to avoid conception. For Protestants the relationship was reversed: frequent church attendance was found to be associated with a *higher* proportion using contraceptive methods to plan their families.

In attempting to interpret this difference, the authors of the study suggest that "Catholics who attend church frequently are brought into contact with religious leaders and laymen who often express attitudes unfavorable to family limitation and especially to 'artificial birth control.' " In contrast, though the issue is much less likely to be discussed in Protestant churches, the discussions that do occur are apt to be favorable to the more effective means of family planning.

In general, a smaller proportion of the Catholics than of either the Protestants or Jews were found to have tried to prevent conception and of those who did, more had begun later in their marriages than was the case with either of the other two groups. Consequently, Catholics were much less likely than Protestants or Jews to have families in which each birth was planned. The proportion with completely planned natality was highest among Jews, with the proportion among Protestants falling between that for Jews and that for Catholics, although closer to the latter. The same relationship held for family size. While many more Catholic than Protestant wives—either completely or with reservations—disapproved of the general idea of family limitation (13 percent as against only one percent), the overwhelming majority of all wives interviewed approved of control under at least some conditions.

The widely-held assumption that Catholics have very large families because of uncontrolled natality and Protestants very small ones because of rational planning was not borne out. While Catholic-Protestant differences in the use of contraception were consistent and substantial, a majority (57 percent) of all the Catholic couples in the sample had used some method. Few Catholics said they wanted really large families: by the time the wife was 35–39 years of age, fully 85 percent of Catholic fecund couples (those for whom there was no evidence of inability to conceive) were users of some form of contraception. Yet, of *all* Catholics using some form of birth control (whether or not contraception) half were using the method endorsed by the church.* Moreover, the number of children Catholics

---

* This proportion going against Church doctrine is a minimum figure, for Catholic doctrine being what it is, there was probably some incentive for Catholic respondents to deny having gone against the precepts of the Church.

claimed they wanted and expected to have exceeded comparable figures for Protestants and Jews, even though the majority of Catholics did express a desire for a number within the range of the American norm: two to four.

This study concludes that while differences in family planning practices between the three major religious groups in America should not be exaggerated, the variations between them are, nevertheless, consistent and substantial. The fact that these variations exist at all social levels, the authors suggest, "may mean that religious differences will persist long after other traditional differences disappear."

Today's religious climate has importance also at the level of public policy. By inhibiting discussion of population control, it retards public awareness and blocks any kind of concerted public action. It makes of population a politically sensitive issue and constrains public officials to avoid consideration of it. It is such a climate that makes possible an event like the following exchange between Senator J. W. Fulbright, Chairman of the Senate Committee on Foreign Relations, and the Hon. Wymberley DeR. Coerr, Acting Assistant Secretary of State for Inter-American Affairs:

THE CHAIRMAN. Mr. Coerr, in the first part of your statement, you say that the economic growth of these countries is much slower than the population growth. Could I conclude from that that you are concerned about population growth? You think, perhaps, something ought to be done about that?

MR. COERR. I would rather not pronounce on the population growth.

THE CHAIRMAN. You would not?

MR. COERR. I would rather not make any recommendation about the population growth itself.

THE CHAIRMAN. Why not? It is no secret.

MR. COERR. No, it certainly is no secret.

THE CHAIRMAN. Why wouldn't you want to comment on it?

It is a problem in many of these countries. In fact, nearly all of those afflicted countries are in the worst shape economically.

MR. COERR. That is right.

THE CHAIRMAN. A large part of this has been brought about by your program because you are working on health conditions in these countries.

MR. COERR. That is right, improving their health.

THE CHAIRMAN. You talk about health. Why don't you talk about population control? Why is that forbidden to you?

MR. COERR. I think you are right, sir, probably it should not be forbidden to me. I just recognize it as a politically sensitive subject.

THE CHAIRMAN. I know it is. If we are going to continue policies which cause this population increase far out of proportion to the economic growth, it concerns me very much, not only in Latin America. It is a problem in India.

MR. COERR. That is right.

THE CHAIRMAN. The Indians and the Pakistanis have both very frankly said something has to be done about it. Their finance ministers came to me and said something had to be done about this. This is fundamental to the success of the economic program. I do not see why the government should be so reluctant about it.

MR. COERR. Of course, in Latin America we have, as you know, a very different religious attitude from those other countries.

THE CHAIRMAN. I do not know. This is one of the things among others, that causes me a sense of complete helplessness or hopelessness. You are going to spend a lot of money in the health field, which only adds to the problem, are you not?

MR. COERR. Yes, sir. I think as far as the immediate alternatives are concerned, I would have to say, "Yes, sir, we just have to take them."

THE CHAIRMAN. I do not know that we have to or not. Maybe you do. I think this is a matter that at some time we have to consider.

I notice the Japanese and now the Indians and the Pakistanis are all frankly meeting this problem. I do not know why we should be so backward about it.[32]

Despite avoidance of the subject in public, the government is sufficiently concerned about population (at least in the under-developed countries) to have the problem under continual review. The President's Committee to Study the United States Military Assistance Program (The Draper Committee), current research being conducted in the Department of Health, Education, and Welfare, the November, 1960, Report of the President's Commission on National Goals, and the State Department's own July, 1959, Report, "World Population Trends and Problems," give evidence of this interest and concern. But what study there is of the subject is being carried on at echelons below the policy-making level.[33] Fear of disturbing religious sensibilities confines the government's population research to these lower levels and limits its usefulness by the restrictions of extreme caution.

Constraints arising from religion are even more pronounced, however, when it comes to public policy here at home. Americans are far from allowing the government to tell them that they must limit the number of their children. But for ninety years they have allowed government to exercise repressive measures in the opposite direction: on their right to the voluntary limitation of their families. In 1873, Anthony Comstock successfully concluded his virtually one-man campaign against birth control by persuading Congress to enact a statute which in effect branded information on contraception as obscene. Contraceptive appliances and contraceptive literature were excluded from the mails. Read literally, the ban is absolute. But over the years it has been modified by the courts to exclude the traffic in these things between doctors and various other health personnel. Modifications in the statute have been introduced slowly, however, and attempts to alter its provisions through legislation have been unsuccessful. Not until 1931, for instance, in the case of *U.S. vs. One Obscene Book Entitled "Married Love"* did the courts rule that books on contraception were no longer to be considered obscene *per se*.

State practices governing the sale and distribution of contraceptives and contraceptive information have varied considerably. Initially, many followed the precedent set by the Comstock Act, defining contraceptives as obscene and banning their sale and distribution. Today, twenty states and the District of Columbia have no legislation on the subject of contraceptives; seventeen prohibit traffic in them, but exempt professional persons; five ban the sale and advertising of contraceptives. There can be little doubt that as a consequence of these laws there are many couples—particularly in the lower income and less educated groups—who have found it difficult to approach the goal of a completely planned family. This is so despite the fact that these laws have generally been liberally interpreted by the courts and seldom very effectively enforced. One state, Connecticut, which ambitiously prohibits not only the sale, but also the *use* of contraceptives, has no birth control clinics, and officially bars doctors from prescribing birth control appliances for their patients. Repeated attempts have been made to modify this law, but all have failed. As recently as 1961, the Supreme Court refused by a vote of five justices to four to consider an appeal questioning the law's constitutionality, on the grounds that in the absence of cases brought to trial for violation of the statute there was insufficient evidence of a general infringement of constitutional rights. From a legal standpoint, the law may be constitutional—though it should be emphasized that the Court did *not* rule on its constitutionality. But its wisdom is highly questionable. That many couples in Connecticut regularly violate this law can hardly be doubted. Others who may desire to limit their families (particularly those not likely to consult a private physician) are restricted by the inaccessibility of legitimate information and professional advice. That the statute is daily violated by doctors and that contraceptives can be obtained over the counter everywhere in the state does not vitiate the *principle* that the statute constitutes repressive governmental interference in what has now become a generally approved practice.

Today, Connecticut and its neighbor, Massachusetts, are unique in the extent to which their statutes hinder resort to contraception as a means of family limitation. Elsewhere in the United States birth control appliances and information are now fairly readily obtainable. The Planned Parenthood Federation operates 175 centers in 101 cities in 29 states and the District of Columbia. Medical contraceptive information and care is dispensed by 594 maternal health clinics, and the majority of approved medical schools provide some instruction in contraceptive techniques. There may be some truth in the claim of an Indian demographer that, "there is more freedom on the question of family planning in Bombay than in Boston,"[34] but we have come a long way since the days of Anthony Comstock.

Comstock was a Protestant. The statutes which defined contraception as obscene were enacted by a predominantly Protestant Congress at a time when all major religious groups considered contraception to be contrary to God's will. But the perpetuation of restrictive legislation on contraception can be attributed almost entirely to the efforts of the Roman Catholic Church. In fact, future attempts to reverse these laws may well take the position that they violate the separation of Church and State because they enforce the doctrines of a particular denomination at the expense of those with other convictions. This point has already been raised by several Protestant ministers in Connecticut who charge that the law prohibiting dissemination of advice on birth control deprives them of their "liberty, freedom of speech, and right to freely practice their religions."[35]

Nevertheless, the precedent for governmental interference in the private area of family determination has been established in the United States. Like any group in this country, Roman Catholics have the right to attempt to influence public policy and legislation. Their view of "natural law" as binding on all men justifies—in their own eyes—the imposition of their doctrines on contraception on people of other religious convictions. Yet, Catholic influence on policy has resulted in governmental restrictions on the right of parents to determine the number of their children by means now regarded as acceptable by most Americans.

Recognition of this fact has led some Catholic spokesmen to take issue with their church's traditional approach to public policy on birth control. They have added their voices to those of others in questioning whether in a pluralistic society any church should have this much power over the behavior of persons who are not its communicants. Is it advisable, they ask, for the Catholic Church—or, for that matter, any church—to implement its doctrines through legislation, and thereby force its theological beliefs on persons who hold other convictions?[36] And at least one Catholic has taken the position that Catholics themselves "can properly deplore such laws because of their disruptive effect on the community and can even support their repeal."[37]

But these merely indicate the possibility of a rift in the Catholic position. Up to now, the overwhelming weight of Catholic activity has been in support of these restrictive laws. Nor has this Catholic position had to face strong rebuttal from organized Protestantism. One prominent writer on Protestant affairs, Richard M. Fagley, suggests that the traditional Protestant emphasis on the married couples' responsibility for making its own moral decision about family planning has caused the Protestant churches—until very recently—to evade their obligations to provide teaching and leadership in this matter. This laissez-faire approach of the Protestant churches to the question of population and parenthood has extended into the whole realm of public policy, leaving the Catholics, with their much more tightly formulated (and aggressively publicized) position, virtually free of any organized religious opposition to counterbalance the influence they have on public opinion and official policy. By their failure to assert an equally conscientious, if different, position, claims Fagley, Protestants share responsibility for the prevalent official neglect of the population question.[38]

Conflicts between the various religious positions were dramatized when President Dwight Eisenhower, a Protestant, chose to align himself with the stand taken by the Catholic Bishops and against the recommendations of his own Draper committee appointed to study and suggest improvements in United States foreign policy. For a while discussion of population control even made the newspapers. Many Protestant leaders protested that the President had ignored the teachings of the country's other major religions.[39] Yet a few Protestant leaders upheld the President. And no uniform Protestant position emerged to challenge the view expressed by the bishops. The debate soon subsided, and with the July, 1961, publication of Pope John's encyclical, "Mater et Magister," the Catholic view once again filled the publicity vacuum.

In "Mater et Magister" Pope John defined the situation in the underdeveloped countries as the world's most difficult problem, and once again firmly rejected birth control as of any moment to it, while urging, instead, a more equitable distribution of the world's resources. Thus, this latest Encyclical conforms to the "solution" usually proposed by Catholics: not *limitation of* growth, but *adjustment to* growth.

Substantial empirical data can be arrayed to challenge any complacency toward population growth that rests on economic, scientific, or social grounds. But opposition to natality control on religious grounds is completely unassailable by resort to rational considerations. Herein lies the strength of the religious approach and the source of its influence on human behavior in the face of radically changing social conditions. The question of natality control seems still too intimately interwoven with religious convictions and differences for Americans to discuss it calmly and dispassionately. For the sake of preserving harmony, most seem to foreswear consideration of the implications of unprecedented human growth, in the hope, perhaps, that Science or Divine Providence will somehow resolve the difficulty.

5
Attitudes and Values

In today's world of rapidly increasing populations any study of the attitudes people hold toward population growth and its control will have a more than merely descriptive significance, for attitudes are most important determinants of family building patterns. They are specific to a particular cultural setting, however. What motivates a couple in one social system cannot be presumed to operate in another. If we admit, as we must, that a limitation of births is imperative for the welfare of the world's people—in the United States and other economically developed countries as well as in the economically underdeveloped—then an understanding of the determinants of childbearing behavior in a particular culture will be an essential ingredient in any campaign to encourage the spread of birth control. If coercion is to be avoided in this highly private area of life, such a campaign must be based primarily on education and persuasion. Hence, it will be effective only if thoroughly grounded on a knowledge of the complex of attitudes underlying, first, procreative behavior within the individual family, and, second, population limitation at the level of the whole society.

Attitudes toward population growth and control do not exist by themselves. Each has its value premises, whether or not these happen to be either privately recognized or publicly acknowledged. Values will influence the amount and kind of information one acquires, and the interpretation he makes of that

information. Our rate of population growth is amply docu-
mented. Forecasts of the consequences of this growth for our
conditions of life are widely obtainable. But not even a close
familiarity with these materials will guarantee the view that
present growth rates constitute a "problem." In the last
analysis, such a determination will rest upon values.

Not every attitude unfavorable to population control is
prompted by values of a religious nature, although, as we have
seen, these are to be counted among the more influential. The
values that actually influence behavior must always be dis-
tinguished from those expressed in official doctrine. The
practice of birth control is itself a good example of this. For
most couples the ethical principles involved in the choice of
whether or not to practice birth control are hardly as abstract
as those implied in a church's pronouncements concerning the
conditions under which family limitation is morally permissible. Even where religious convictions come most into play,
the determination of family size is likely to depend less on
simple compliance with official doctrine than on a weighing of
these doctrines against concrete personal values—liking for
children and ambitions for them, or style of life to be maintained, for example. These personal values, in turn, will be
affected by the current social and cultural norms surrounding
family life in the groups with which the couple identifies.

When, in the preceding chapter, we considered the bearing
of religious doctrines on family planning and public policy, we
were able to draw upon empirical evidence to show the existence of an association between religious affiliation and patterns
of family limitation in the United States. But when it comes to
the values that underlie attitudes toward population control,
there is no such empirical evidence. Though certain value
preferences are suggested by studies of family planning differentials, any explicit study of the general value orientations
toward population has yet to be undertaken. Hence what we
say here is frankly speculative. It represents an initial attempt

to sort out and identify what appear to be among the more important of these values.

Before taking a closer look at some of these values, we must distinguish between two levels of population limitation. Public debate on this subject has frequently become confused because of a tendency for the participants to shift back and forth between these two levels without making clear which they are talking about. One level refers to control over the number and spacing of births within the *individual family;* the other to the attainment of population stability within a *whole society.*

While most American couples, regardless of religious affiliation, have resorted (or will eventually resort) to some form of birth control, debate over its justification continues to crop up, particularly when laws restricting access to contraception are challenged. Those who uphold these laws on religious grounds argue that because man was created by God, his body belongs to God—not to his parents, not to the state, not even to himself. The prevention of conception (by whatever means) these persons interpret as a violation of a natural human process ordained by God. Those of a less religious, more humanistic persuasion argue, on the other hand, that within legal limits the body belongs to the individual himself. For them the practice of birth control is a human right, justifiable on the sole grounds that a couple should be able to enjoy sexual relations without fear of unwanted conception. As long as we feel, they maintain, that we have to seek justification for birth control on some ground other than that of a human right to sexual relations free of the threat of unwanted pregnancy, we will find ourselves in the predicament noted by Dr. Thomas S. Szasz, Professor of Psychiatry at the State University of New York: "employing methods that are, by our own standards, less than wholesome."[1]

Since every major church in the United States now tolerates *some* form of birth control (at least qualifiedly), most Americans can probably choose to limit their families without feeling morally ambivalent. In fact, for a majority of Americans, the right of individual couples to practice birth control to attain specific personal ends has probably ceased to be a debatable issue. Those remaining laws that limit access to contraception are clearly out of tune with the dominant American values of today.

But when it comes to the wider, less personal question about what to do about population growth at the level of a whole society (whether in the United States or elsewhere), American opinion is much less developed. Probably few in this country consider rapid population growth to be much of a problem; and those who think of it at all seem likely to dimiss it as something confined to economically disadvantaged groups or nations. On the whole, the idea that something may have to be done on a society-wide basis to control population is either only dimly appreciated or else rejected outright as impractical or immoral. Certainly any concern Americans may feel about it is seldom reflected in their private behavior. A recent study has found that in spite of ominous warnings about a population explosion, young married couples from groups which have traditionally had families of smaller than average size now want bigger families and plan to have them.[2]

This tendency to have larger families than in the preceding generation, coming as it does in the face of accumulated warnings about rapid population growth and its consequences, seems supported by two general orientations. One, which we might call positive, is simply the desire of a substantial proportion of American couples to have *at least* three children. The other, which might be termed negative, is a reluctance if not outright unwillingness to countenance control over births as a means of adjusting to population growth.

Obviously, these orientations do not represent fixed, immutable positions on the part of those individuals who hold them. Some who at present would be negatively disposed toward a program of population control for an entire society might well favor such a program under more extreme conditions, or if they were better apprised of the gravity of present conditions. And many who now want an additional child might feel quite otherwise if faced with a different financial, health, or international situation.

Nor are the people holding these orientations necessarily alike in their other views. Those who reject control over natality as a means of stabilizing whole populations may or may not also reject it as a means of limiting the size of individual families. They may or may not be concerned about the consequences of population increase for human welfare generally. But they are all alike in their opposition on principle to control over births as a means of coping with the problems of population growth in the aggregate. How many Americans share this negative orientation we do not know; but we would guess that most would be, at the very least, hesitant about endorsing a society-wide program to encourage birth control as a means to numerical stability—anywhere in the world, but especially in the United States.

The pervasiveness of the positive orientation—the desire for at least three children—is attested to by our high birth rate of the last eighteen years, which has continued in spite of a general diffusion of the knowledge and means of controlling births. Nevertheless, here, too, one cannot assume that all couples who plan families of three or more have the same values and attitudes toward population in the aggregate. Some may be unaware of the implications of our current rate of growth; some may be merely indifferent to them. While others, though aware and concerned, may not interpret this concern as calling for any personal sacrifice on their part—the sacrifice, that is, of having a smaller family than they want.

From the standpoint of behavior, one's values will be indicated by his attitudes toward such cultural items as religious dogmas, ethical principles, political ideas, styles of life. An individual's willingness or unwillingness to restrict population growth is not an isolated attitude. In the United States it appears to be congruent with his attitudes on five basic issues: (1) life and death, (2) the idea of man as an agent of social change, (3) the sexual act in marriage, (4) the role of married women, (5) individual rights and social obligations. The possible attitudes toward these issues range along a continuum, of course. The paradigm on the facing page shows what are generally the more "extreme" positions allowed by the culture. There may be few whose attitudes are at one or another of these positions, as they are presented here. But everyone will *tend* in one direction or the other on each issue; and it is the combination of these tendencies that is, we feel, the determinant of any particular attitude toward population control.* We do not claim that this list is exhaustive, or that all of these attitudes will necessarily underlie a particular orientation toward population control. What we do suggest is that on these five issues Americans who would oppose a program of population limitation for a whole society are likely to hold attitudes which are the converse of those who would favor such a program.

Life and Death

With the possible exception of a few religious fanatics and a small minority for whom life has become completely dispensable, people everywhere will shrink from death and physical

---

* Elsewhere we have noted that in the United States Roman Catholics are the single group which most frequently and consistently holds negative attitudes toward population control. As might therefore be expected, Roman Catholic attitudes in many instances correspond quite closely to those listed as congruent with opposition to population control. We have purposely refrained from labelling these as specifically "religious" or specifically "Catholic" attitudes, however, for it is not necessary to be a Catholic to have these attitudes. Nor can we assume that all who call themselves Catholics will invariably be on the same side of the continuum on any particular issue.

Table 4

Issue	Attitude Congruent with Opposition to Population Control	Attitude Congruent with Support for Population Control
1. Life and Death	Emphasis on life after death.	Emphasis on the condition of mankind here and now.
2. Man as an Agent of Social Change	Emphasis on the necessity of man's complying with absolute moral laws to fulfil supernatural designs or historical necessity.	Emphasis on the freedom and obligation of man to improve his lot through rational action.
3. The Sexual Act In Marriage	Emphasis on: (1) the negative consequences of sexual indulgence and "excess" and (2) the positive results of sexual self-control and self-discipline.	Emphasis on the positive contributions of harmonious sexual relations to marital accord.
4. The Role of Married Women	Emphasis on married women as helpmeets and childrearers, contributing mainly to their families and only indirectly to the society, and having no needs apart from those that can be fulfilled within the family environment.	Emphasis on a varied role for women as individuals—not solely as wives and mothers—with a contribution to make directly to society, and with needs as individuals apart from their status as wives and mothers.
5. Individual Rights and Social Obligations	Emphasis on the primacy of individual rights over the general welfare of the community; stress on individual privileges without corresponding social obligations.	Emphasis on the obligation of the individual to the society; individual rights viewed as justifiably expendable when in conflict with the general welfare.

suffering. Yet there are some so opposed to birth control that they would allow population increase to exact its toll, however great. Such persons may admit the gravity of overcrowded conditions; they may even bend every effort to relieve them by other means. But even if all these other means failed, even then, they maintain, the taboo against birth control would have to remain inviolable. Though not stating it outright, such a view at least implies that adjusting to population pressure through a higher death rate is preferable to adjusting to it through a birth rate lowered by means defined as immoral.

Such a choice suggests that life on this earth has an importance secondary to that of some other existence. Birth is heralded as the creation of a soul destined for eternal bliss. And death, far from being the end of all, represents but the passage from an inferior state of being to one that is more desirable. The loss of spiritual purity—however narrowly this purity may be defined (as not using contraception, for example) —is to be avoided at all costs, even if it means the sacrifice of other, often highly valued, conditions of physical and spiritual well-being. To suffer present afflictions sustained by the promise of a better life to follow is far preferable to the use of means that might risk the sacrifice of these eternal rewards. Suffering, in fact, may even be welcomed as providing a greater assurance of immortal life.*

A belief in immortality by no means precludes concern for the human condition. The recent encyclical of the late Pope John, with its emphasis on alleviating the conditions of poverty in the underdeveloped countries, reflects this concern. Nor is it

* Catholic theology possesses no monopoly of this viewpoint, but the view probably finds its clearest statement there. Cf. William J. Gibbons, S.J., "The Catholic Value System in Relation to Human Fertility" in George F. Mair (ed.) *Studies in Population,* Princeton: Princeton University Press, 1949.

In the Catholic philosophy of life all of man's "various functions and capacities are ordered by nature to a single end—the achievement of beatitude in the life to come. . . ." (p. 108) necessarily true that the obverse—*not* believing in immortality —makes one *more* desirous of improving man's earthly lot. We merely suggest that underlying the negative orientation toward population control there may exist a tendency to give priority to certain other-worldly values as against emphasizing those values that would lead to a maximization of man's welfare in this life. The ultimate choice of adjusting to population growth by raising the death rate instead of lowering the birth rate must surely seem less drastic to the believer in immortality than it does to one who lacks such convictions. As belief in Hell and its eternal punishments steadily ebbs, Death, particularly to one's fellow man, comes to wear its bleakest aspect for those who anticipate nothing beyond.

Man as an Agent of Social Change

Although indications abound that man is forever altering his conditions of life, there are nevertheless those who aver that he *should* not change them—at least not certain of them—because to do so would interfere with "Divine Law," "Historical Necessity," "The Law of Supply and Demand," or some other metaphysical construct. Whether they call themselves "Christians," "Conservatives," "Economic Realists," or "Scientific Marxists," people so disposed have this in common: an unwillingness to endorse man as a legitimate agent of social change. The rationales are different, of course. But whether the chief source

---

Obedience to laws revealed by God through the order of nature (for instance, that the primary purpose of sexual relations is procreation) "may sometimes occasion suffering, even death itself. But sacrifice is integral to man's existence in this world. . . ." (p. 111)

"As a value system, Catholicism endeavours to impress upon men the truth that perfect happiness comes only with the attainment of eternal salvation. Man's temporal life is a testing ground, wherein success is determined on the basis of the individual's readiness to conform to the divine plan. . . ." (p. 113)

"In line with Christian teaching, children are welcomed because they are new souls destined for eternal life." (p. 118)

of change is termed "God," "Nature," "Economic Law," or "The Class Struggle," it is not for man to presume to intervene in the unfolding of its Design.

The notion, for instance, that the earth cannot for long sustain human life at present rates of reproduction is alien to an image of God as Creator. To one who defines Him in this fashion it must be difficult to think that He would not provide for all His Creation, or at least that His Plan for the world would not include some solution to the problem of rapidly increasing numbers. Does not the Bible admonish man to "take no thought for the morrow"? Even if pessimistic forecasts about population growth were realized—if levels of living were to decline and death rates rise—even then, in the logic of this view, it would be man's duty to submit to these conditions as parts of God's Design. It should hardly surprise us that the belief of some Christians in a "Divine Plan" can lead to a denial that population growth is even a problem.

Also affecting one's orientation toward population control will be his attitudes toward social goals and the means allowable for achieving them. In their classic study of "Middletown" (Muncie, Indiana) in the 1930's, the Lynds found widespread opposition to attempts to bring about social change. Detailing what they term "The Middletown Spirit," i.e., what, by and large, the people of Muncie at the time believed, they note the following—among many, many others:[3]

That "progress is the law of life," and therefore: . . .

That "the natural and orderly processes of progress" should be followed.

That change is slow, and abrupt changes or the speeding up of changes through planning or revolution is unnatural. . . .

That economic conditions are the result of a natural order which cannot be changed by man-made laws. "Henry Ford says that wages ought to be higher and goods cheaper. We agree with this, and let us add that we think it ought to be cooler in the summer and warmer in winter."

That depressions are regrettable but nevertheless a normal aspect of business. "Nothing can be done to stop depressions. It's just like a person who feels good one day and rotten the next." ...

> It never is safe to tamper with natural laws—and that of supply and demand is one of them. . . .
> The advancing price of farm products [is] not due to any kind of legislation, but to natural causes which are always responsible for prices whether high or low.*

Similarly, if God is viewed as the ultimate source of social change, the objectives of directed social change or control will be only proximately man's well-being on earth. The ultimate goal of his social efforts will be, instead, to perfect his chances for eternal happiness in union with God. The means used to attain these goals will consequently have to be guided less by expediency than by absolute moral laws—laws which apply across the board without reference to individual circumstances.†

The alternative to this general approach would be the belief that it is possible to guide social change in those directions that

---

* Each of the illustrative quotations (save the second) came from editorials in the Muncie newspaper. Despite this opposition to change in social institutions —an opposition which, though it may now take somewhat different forms from those of the 1930's, is still a common feature of American life—another characteristic trait of American culture is the high evaluation of applied science as a tool for controlling nature, despite the fact that such control, in turn, creates the need for changes in our institutions. See Robin M. Williams, Jr., *American Society*, New York: Knopf, 1951, pp. 426–428, 441.

† See William J. Gibbons (*op. cit.*) for an example of this approach as applied to the limitation of births: "The precise type of contraceptive used makes no difference, neither does the established fact that there are differential rates of effectiveness as between the various types. This moral judgment does not change because conception may occasionally occur or even be 'planned' despite the habitual use of contraceptives. Rather the moral prohibition extends to each individual use of artificial means designed to frustrate the natural purpose of the act."

would maximize for all people the conditions of life most conducive to physical and spiritual well-being in *this* world. We suggest that this latter attitude, or one approximating it, is more likely to underlie an affirmative orientation to the use of society-wide population control. The rationale for this broad objective might well have its origin in religious teachings (for instance, in the value attached to individual worth or on the equality of mankind before God). But the social means to its achievement would not be regarded by its adherents as being so narrowly circumscribed by set moral prescriptions, support for which was derived from divine or historical "law." Instead, the methods used to guide social change would be evaluated in terms of their relative effectiveness and moral worth within a particular social setting. "Effectiveness" implies a standard of evaluation, of course. But those means would be adjudged "best" that, representing the least cost in human welfare (defined in *this*-worldly terms), appeared most directly and most rationally related to the end to be achieved. Their choice would be governed more by observation, and by trial and error in particular social contexts, than by any prior determination of their inherent moral worth apart from the particular social setting in which they were to be applied.

The Sexual Act in Marriage

In the previous chapter we noted that early Christian and mediaeval asceticism exalted the suppression of physical desire as a form of religious sacrifice and spiritual purification. The idea that sexual relations are unclean and spiritually damaging did not originate with the early Christians, however. Purification rites following sexual intercourse, and periods of sexual abstinence preceding important events like hunting or warfare, are common to many ancient and primitive peoples.

What early Christianity did was to elaborate the value placed on sexual restraint into a negative evaluation of sexual relations in general. Sexual abstinence was correspondingly accorded high moral and religous esteem. In the traditional view, sexual intercourse always involved some lapse from moral purity.[4] Fear of impregnation being regarded as the most powerful deterrent to immoral sexual intercourse and "excess," contraception was correspondingly condemned. Only procreation was a purpose sufficiently legitimate to justify such an "impure" kind of activity.

Attempts to lighten or abolish punishment for sexual relations defined as sinful or immoral have always been opposed. In some instances—such as opposition to the use of anaesthetics in childbirth—the opposition has not been confined to "sinful" or "immoral" sexual relations. Prophylactics against venereal disease have encountered vigorous resistance on "moral" grounds, while the cure of venereal disease has been opposed on the grounds that the disease was a just punishment for the sexually impure. This negative view of sexual relations still persists, though in somewhat diluted form. Much of the support for the proposal made a few years ago by Joseph McD. Mitchell, city manager of Newburgh, New York, to deny welfare benefits to mothers of illegitimate children if they have any more illegitimate births seems to spring in part from this same reluctance to allow sexual immorality to escape retribution.

In the United States today, the Roman Catholic clergy is a major group still openly upholding this negative attitude—though the attitude has been considerably softened since the Middle Ages. While they recognize that effective use of the rhythm method depends on a sense of parental responsibility and a high degree of frankness between husband and wife—conditions not often found in those underdeveloped countries where an immediate cessation of population growth is imperative—Catholic spokesmen still shun consideration of any other method. They staunchly maintain that the dangers of unchastity and moral disintegration they see as resulting from the widespread use of contraceptives among these peoples would outweigh the already acute difficulties they face as a consequence of their overwhelming numbers. Certainly a deep distrust of the sexual act, though seldom acknowledged, must underlie much of this negative orientation toward the effective control of births.

Another attitude toward the sex act is reflected in the following statement of the Anglican bishops at their 1958 Lambeth Conference:

> Sexual intercourse is not by any means the only language of earthly love, but it is, in its full and right use, the most revealing; it has the depth of communication signified by the Biblical word so often used for it, "knowledge"; it is a giving and receiving in the unity of two free spirits which is in itself good (within the marriage bond) and mediates good to those who share it. Therefore it is utterly wrong to urge that, unless children are specifically desired, sexual intercourse is of the nature of sin. It is also wrong to say that such intercourse ought not to be engaged in except with the willing intention to procreate children.[5]

What the Anglican bishops chose to emphasize was that sexual relations can greatly enrich a marriage; that sexual intercourse is to be valued not so much as an end in itself, but as a means to strengthening the marital bond. In this view, the use of contraceptives could even come to be regarded as a positive obligation in so far as it contributed to harmonious family relations and better social conditions.

On one side of the continuum, the view taken of the sex act is essentially negative; on the other, positive. In practice, those who take the negative view stress the *means* of birth control; those who take the positive, stress its *ends*.

The Role of Women

Some 95 percent of American women marry.[6] Of these, over 90 percent become mothers.* Hence what is considered suitable behavior for wives and mothers pertains to an overwhelming proportion of all women in the United States. A large body of American opinion has traditionally looked upon any outside activity (but particularly gainful employment) as incompatible with a married woman's roles as wife and mother.[7] A mother's ability to provide the conditions most favorable to the physical and mental development of her children is believed hindered by the demands outside activities place on her time and energy. The growing emphasis parents, encouraged by many child-care professionals, place on the *quality* of the mother-child relationship, rather than on simply the amount of time mother and child spend together, could counter this view somewhat; but it seems more likely it will strengthen it, instead.

Women have always worked. They have always contributed their labor to the economic output of their households (by canning, baking, making clothes, sharing farm chores, etc.). But the Industrial Revolution substantially changed the nature of this work: from unpaid to paid employment; from working in family enterprises to working for unrelated persons; from working in the home to working outside it. Yet, despite this loss of economic functions within the home, and despite increasing educational and occupational opportunities for women (the increase in the number of white collar jobs, for instance), the great majority of married women in the United States are never at any one time employed. Though nearly two-fifths of all those residing with their husbands work at some time during any given year, most of this employment is only part-time. For

---

* This is probably a conservative estimate, since only 9.8 percent of married women age 30–34 in 1959 were still childless at that date. See *Statistical Abstracts of the United States: 1961*, Table 52, p. 54.

but one out of seven is it anything approaching full-time.[8]

Not only are most married women in the United States not employed, but those who are employed have on the average fewer children than do those who are not. Past studies relating differences in family size to the employment of the wife all share a limitation, however—the causal relationship is unspecified. When a married woman works, is it because she is childless or the mother of relatively few children; or does she limit the size of her family more than other married women because she wants to engage in activities outside the home? The answer is probably something of both. One recent study suggests that working wives generally plan to have fewer children. In fact, even the effect of religious differences on family size was found to tend to disappear by the time work experience had reached five years' duration: among wives who had worked this long there was hardly any family size differential between Catholics and Protestants.[9]

In general, the more extreme traditional attitude toward the married woman, in defining her as primarily a helpmeet and mother, emphasizes the needs of her family over any she herself might have for personal development or self-expression as an individual. And it minimizes the possibility of her making a contribution apart from that entailed in the performance of her roles as wife and mother. If she works, it must be justified solely in terms of economic necessity. Any other kind of "outside" activity viewed as competitive with her familial duties is frowned upon as an undesirable personal indulgence. If she has any separate individual needs at all, they must await the prior fulfillment of those of her children and husband.

Compare this with the attitude that is probably more congruent with support for population limitation: married women should be regarded primarily as individuals with needs and social contributions to make apart from, and in addition to, those associated with their familial roles. The assumption here is, first, that family demands can rob a woman of the energy and leisure time with which to nourish her own creative impulses and meet her own individual needs; and, second, that the fulfillment of such needs is important, as much from the standpoint of the welfare of the family as from that of the wife and mother herself. Not surprisingly, women seem to feel this way more often than their husbands. At least one study has found that a strong liking for children among women usually leads them to have *fewer* children, ostensibly in order to give those they have a higher quality of care (one determinant of which would be the physical and emotional state of the mother); whereas a strong liking for children among men leads to a *larger* than average number of offspring.[10]

Individual Rights and Social Obligations

Respect for individual rights and vigorous distrust of government "control" have figured prominently in the American ethos since Colonial times. As we have grown in size and complexity there has also developed an emphasis on the need, and hence obligation, of each individual to share in meeting the requirements of the society. The direction this latter development has taken might at first appear antagonistic to the traditional opposition to government control; for the emphasis on social obligation has been accompanied by a growing acceptance of government as an appropriate mechanism through which to meet social needs and guarantee that the individual's responsibility to society will be discharged. While there is no necessary divergence between these two concepts, we suggest that the individual American will tend to emphasize one or the other: either the primacy of individual rights or the obligations of the individual to the general welfare. And whichever it is, this preference will have its counterpart in his attitude toward the goal of population stability.

For many the phrase "population control" undoubtedly con-
jures up the specter of outside interference, of somebody telling you what to do about what seems a purely personal decision
—the number of your children. If this outside interference is
conceived as government maintaining population stability by
forcibly exercising control over such matters as who can become
parents, when they can, and the number of their offspring, then
objection to such control can hardly be considered an extreme
position. Indeed, it is likely that many of those to whom the
idea of population limitation is repugnant feel this way about
it because they suppose it could only be realized by just such
coercive measures as these.

The extreme position, the one likely to be most congruent
with strong opposition to the limitation of population, would
regard any government regulation of individual behavior as an
unjustifiable invasion of personal rights. Whether it takes the
form of taxation, compulsory social insurance, collective bargaining, or merely persuasion, such interference in individual
action would be opposed as an improper extension of government activities. To persons with such sentiments, individual
rights take primacy over any needs the group may have as a
whole. Any obligation to support community goals at the sacrifice of some freedom of individual action is resented. For such
individuals the ideal form of society would appear to be a collection of atomized individuals, competing freely with one
another within the context of an absolute minimum of both
social obligations and outside constraints.

We should expect the adherents of such views to be found
more often in opposition to a society-wide program of population control than in favor of it—not so much because of a
desire for more people (though that may be there too), but
because of its implication of external, arbitrary controls and,
in particular, of the further spread of government that could
be presumed to accompany them. A person with this attitude

could hardly look with equanimity upon a government program of education in the meaning of population growth and
the desirability and necessity of halting it through a voluntary
limitation of births.

Without going to the other extreme of complete self-abnega-
tion, the alternative to the extreme individualism we have out-
lined here would take a more neutral view. It would recognize
that controls over human behavior are so much a part of us that
we often do not even think of them as controls. Government
would be seen as only one among a great many controlling
agencies that would include the family, neighborhood, corporations, unions, religious bodies. This is not to say, however,
that every particular control would be defined as either necessary or desirable. The question: *who* is controlling *whom* with
what *means* and for what *ends* it always relevant.

Persons holding with this alternative position justify in such
terms as these their willingness to allow government to exercise certain powers over the individual: were everyone able to
act pretty much as he wished, the actual amount of freedom
available to the individual would be trifling. The conventional
view may define freedom in terms of the absence of constraints,
but freedom actually consists of two essential parts, one of
which is, to be sure, a minimum of constraint. But the other—
and no less important one—is a maximum of predictability,
both of the consequences of one's own acts and of the behavior
of others. Few would argue that extreme totalitarianism,
though permitting a maximum of predictability, could ever be
defined as freedom. Yet extreme individualism, as represented
by the near absence of constraints, would bring with it no
greater amount of freedom. Such a condition would be but
Hobbes' "war of all against all," and, as such, constitute an impossible state for any viable social system. As Roger Baldwin
once commented, "My freedom to wave my fist ends where
your nose begins." The American folklore on competition may

intoxicate some; but it is cooperation, not competition, that is the most necessary relationship between men. For this necessary cooperation to exist there must be enough control over behavior to permit a high level of predictability.[11]

Those with a morally neutral attitude toward control will be inclined to accept or reject the agents of control solely on the pragmatic grounds of their capacity to do the job. With its ruling that information on contraception was obscene, the United States government established the precedent for governmental restriction of individual freedom in the determination of family size. Under present conditions it is doubtful whether even the most ardent advocate of population control would favor similarly restrictive legislation in the opposite direction: legislation that would empower the government of the United States to compel people to limit the size of their families. But those who wish to see a halt brought to population growth in this country, and who at the same time are not hostile to government in and of itself, are likely to hope that in a democratic government's capacity for society-wide education and persuasion there lies the possibility of averting both an increase in mortality and the use of coercive measures for the attainment of population stability.

If these are the attitudes congruent with a favorable or unfavorable approach to population limitation, what are the attitudes congruent with the desire of Americans to have at least three children—more, that is, than are necessary for replacement? This question has challenged demographers ever since it began to look as though the post-World War II rise in American birth rates was more than a merely temporary phenomenon. It is especially significant when we realize that many of those who have studied the American family see in this 18-year period of high birth rates a stabilization of the pattern of the 3–4 child family. Whether temporary or permanent, however, it is this pattern of moderate-sized families that accounts for most of our current high rate of growth. What, then, are the attitudes that support it?

Desire for Security and Response

The past few decades have seen a change in the functions performed by the American family. Many of the needs it used to meet (some of the educative, economic, and recreational ones, for instance) have come increasingly to be performed by other groups within the society. Yet the family remains as important as ever. If anything, the value attached to family life has been enhanced by the specialization arising from the loss of these functions. For concurrent with these losses, the family has gained a virtual monopoly over the provision of a stable, rewarding, emotionally satisfying environment for the adult American. Our high divorce rate can, in fact, be viewed as substantiating this. The more the family's functions become limited to the emotional and psychic needs of the individual, the greater the incentives to withdraw from an unsatisfying, unhappy relationship; and the fewer the incentives to remain in it.

Growth in our society has increased the impersonal quality of many of our social contacts. Communities have more residents, doctors more patients, teachers more students, businessmen more customers. In the process, the relative importance of the individual is reduced and the competition for recognition heightened. One has contact with more people, but the contacts themselves are more fleeting, more devoid of meaning.

The past couple of decades have also witnessed the rise of the so-called Organization Man, the employee of a large, bureaucratic-type organization, whose job, though usually affording financial security, may seem to offer little in the way of meaningful personal relationships or in opportunities to make a contribution to the enterprise as a whole.

In this mushrooming of size and anonymity, the family stands out as a haven of intimacy. It often provides the individual with his only retreat from the frustration, indifference, and sense of impotency encountered in a rapidly changing, unpredictable world. Children are seen as providing security, an antidote to the impersonality of one's other relationships, a sense of unique accomplishment. There may even be some Americans who see in additional childbearing a means of increasing the security of the family through multiplying the number of ties made intimate by kinship.

Liking for Children

Americans may also desire more children because they like them. We do not mean to imply by this that children were less well liked a generation ago when the average family size was smaller. What we suggest, instead, is that those economic and social conditions which operated to limit family size twenty to thirty years ago are now no longer as widespread or intense. Under the more favorable economic circumstances of the past fifteen years the value placed on the psychic rewards of the parent-child relationship has been able to result in more couples' deciding to have an additional child.

Essentially, this is an economic argument. It assumes that the effect on family size of a given attitude, such as a liking for children, will vary in response to economic conditions. According to this thesis a liking for children would lead to fewer children in times of economic hardship and to more in periods of prosperity. In developing an economic analysis of the patterns of childbearing, Professor Gary Becker of Columbia University suggests that for analytical purposes family size can be approached in much the same manner as housing, automobiles, machinery. Children thus become "consumer durables." They afford their parents a psychic income and on occasion a monetary one as well. In determining the desired family size, parents will weigh the rewards of this psychic income against the costs entailed in raising a child.[12]

These costs are not all monetary, of course: "Even if one had nothing else to do, the marginal disutility of Cub Scout and PTA meetings rises rapidly."[13] In the more strictly economic line of reasoning, however, such nonmonetary costs of parenthood are given little weight as determinants of family size. Hence, Becker is able to conclude that a rise in income will be used either for increasing the number of children in one's family or for increasing the amount of money spent on the children one already has.

As an explanation for the higher birth rate of today, such an economic analysis may have some merit. Economic conditions are, after all, important determinants of human behavior. Their influence, however, may be less direct than is implied by this kind of analysis. If higher incomes are an explanation of higher fertility, it seems to us that it is because they make the whole process of childbearing and child rearing seem easier and more attractive. In large part this is achieved by changes in living arrangements. There has been, for instance, a marked shift of population to the suburbs over the last two decades. Home ownership, which rose 50 percent between 1940 and 1950, jumped another 7 percentage points between 1950 and 1960, so that now some 62 percent of American families own (or are in the process of buying) their homes.[14] A higher income, a comfortable house in the suburbs with a yard and full complement of "labor-saving" appliances, and a lessening of the physical risks and discomforts of childbearing would all seem to be conducive to having more children.

In the final reckoning, however, there is some doubt about the effect a liking for children actually has on family size. One "likes" children for a variety of reasons. They can provide a source of friendship and response, a fresh outlook on the world, an intellectual challenge, an extension of one's own personality, a touch of immortality. Some may feel that these rewards are multiplied with each additional child, but for others a liking for children may be satisfied more fully by devoting relatively more time and individual attention to a smaller number of them. A study based on data collected in a large survey in Indianapolis some twenty-two years ago highlights the somewhat ambiguous effect liking for children has on the determination of family size.[15] In this study it was found, first, that, whatever their relative social and economic positions, couples with an interest in and liking for children had *not* larger families but *more effectively planned* ones. The greater the liking a couple expressed for children, the greater the care they exercised in achieving the family size they desired. Evidently such couples were motivated to plan the number and spacing of their children in large part because of a desire to realize what they felt to be the best interests of children and parents.

The other major finding of this study we have already alluded to: though there was among husbands in all socio-economic groups a tendency for more interest in children to be accompanied by larger families, a similar tendency was not found among wives. In fact, among those couples who planned the number and spacing of their children the largest families were found among couples where the husband indicated a strong interest in children and the wife only moderate or little interest. But among those couples where it was the wife's interest that was strong, family size tended to be low. Thus the authors conclude: "The wife's liking for children does not appear to be expressed in terms of large family size."

Responsibilities to One's Children

Along with changing attitudes toward the parent-child relationship has come a reinterpretation of what constitute optimum conditions for a child's physical and emotional development. One of the values which helped to establish the small family ideal in the United States was the middle-class emphasis on offering the child as many material advantages as the family could reasonably afford. Fewer children meant more of these advantages for each. Today the emphasis has shifted somewhat from the quantity of the material offering to the quality of the home environment. This may result in part from the general rise in income, the material "advantages" being now more easily obtained.

In the creation of a favorable home environment, brothers and sisters are now thought to be among the most important non-material advantages a parent can give his child. The only child is viewed as encountering numerous psychological hazards from which the child endowed with a houseful of siblings is assumed to be effectively immune. Security, adjustment to life, and the ability "to get along well with others" are all believed fostered by steady contact with brothers and sisters. This contact is thought to be qualitatively different from, and superior to, any the child may have with children outside the family, however close these other relationships may be. Psychologically sound or not, the notion that one owes it to his children to provide at least one sibling and preferably two (or even more) seems to have gained a wider currency in the United States over the past two decades.

Responsibilities to the Society

Some American couples may still believe it their social duty to have a larger family. Contrary to the forecasts made by opponents of birth control that its widespread use would progressively reduce family size and ultimately increase childlessness, the birth rate has been rising in those very groups among which the knowledge and use of birth control is most widespread: the college-educated, urban, professional and managerial groups.

In the past, when population was sparse, a large family could legitimately have been regarded as a form of service and a valuable legacy to the community. This was especially true for those who could provide the material advantages felt to contribute to the making of a good citizen. Before the widespread diffusion of birth control, when differentials in family size between social groups were more pronounced than they are today, it was feared by some that the upper class elements would be outbred. The duty of the wealthy family was thus to try to correct this "unfortunate" imbalance of births.

As wealth accumulates in our society, this concept of social responsibility may have a renascence among those groups that are rich in what the society considers valuable—particularly money and education. To distribute one's affluence among a small number of children may still be regarded as a form of selfishness. The sharing of one's wealth and social advantages with the family of man has, apparently, not yet become an acceptable alternative.

Fad

The importance attached to doing what everybody else is doing must be included in any consideration of the desire for more children. The American emphasis on schools, PTA, Scouts, organized recreation, and similar child-centered activities, particularly strong in the rapidly growing suburbs, may well result in the childless or one-child couple's feeling left out. For most Americans, except the very poor, no matter how large the family, a new baby is still an exciting event, heralded by gifts and visits from relatives and neighbors. A freshly bathed and laundered infant is most appealing and can easily evoke the desire to have one of one's own.

If the three- to four-child family is actually becoming established as the national norm, the parents of but one or two children may begin to feel uncomfortably out of step, that they
have somehow made a mistake in limiting their family to this
size. That the fastest growing areas in the United States are
the new housing developments adds support to the fad theory.
In these areas, where there is hardly an unmarried adult and
only a handful of the middle-aged and elderly, the young couple
is exposed to an unusual degree to people in the process of
forming their families to whatever fashion there may be in
family size. Literally everyone *is* having children. And because
everyone is, parents are likely to find that these housing developments encourage additional childbearing not only by example, but also by providing ready access to playmates for their
youngsters and, for themselves, other young parents with whom
to share child-raising anecdotes and the duties of baby-sitting.

There is too much diversity in family size, even within the
new suburbs, for the fad theory to explain *all* of the post-
World War II changes in the size of American families; but it
may be at least a partial explanation for the increasing concentration of family size within the narrow range of two to four
children.

Since World War II new standards of family size have diffused rapidly throughout American society. Extremes in family
size have been correspondingly diminished. These changes, together with the declines in the birth rate that preceded them,
illustrate the fact that individual values, though highly important determinants of human behavior, are themselves part of a
larger cultural setting. Changes in this cultural setting will
bring with them changes in the proportions of the population
holding various attitudes relevant to natality. With the means
of family limitation almost universally available in this country, and with all groups coming under the potential influence
of a single system of mass communication, one of the most

crucial factors in any couple's decision about the number of its children may well come to be the desire to conform to prevailing cultural values about family building. It is this susceptibility of individual values to the cultural milieu as a whole that affords us a kind of cautious optimism concerning the practicability of voluntary limitation sufficient to stabilize the size of our population.

Part III

The Arguments
Against a Stable Population —
and Why They Are Invalid

6

The Economic Argument

GIVEN THE ATTITUDES and values of Americans concerning population limitation in the United States, it is not surprising that,
to date, the case for population stability has failed to receive the
hearing accorded its opposite: the case for population growth.
In fact, arguments in favor of continued population increase
predominate to such an extent that they suggest the existence
of an "American Fertility Cult." Enthusiastically endorsing
our abundant growth, the apologists for further population increase in the United States ignore all evidence of its detrimental consequences, and in some instances even go so far as to
claim that our prosperity and very survival depend upon maintaining growth at its present high level.

Most arguments for population increase were formulated
during the 1930's as antidotes to the sharp declines in birth
rates that the western industrialized countries were then experiencing. Yet, their influence, despite the substantially different circumstances, seems at its height today. The average,
well-informed American probably has a clearer idea of these
arguments in favor of maintaining growth than he has of the
reasons why a rich country like ours should be concerned about
additions to its population. However anachronistic, the arguments in favor of growth would seem to carry sufficient weight
with contemporary American opinion to warrant a separate
examination here. They are of four general types: (1) Economic;
(2) Scientific; (3) Military; and (4) Eugenic.

The "economic" argument holds that population growth is

necessary for the maintenance of our current level of economic prosperity, and a requisite for any long-range prosperity, as well. With a spirit reminiscent of the Couéism of 1923—whose followers went about proclaiming, "Day by day in every way I am getting better and better"[1]—a self-styled "public service" advertisement in the New York subways informs us: "Your future is great in a growing America. Every day 11,000 babies are born in America. This means new business, new jobs, new opportunities." In the same vein, a 1958 issue of *Life* greeted its one million subscribers with a cover picture of three dozen children and the title: "Kids: Built-in Recession Cure— How 4,000,000 a Year Make Millions in Business." Inside, it was "Rocketing Births: Business Bonanza."

Oversimplification of this sort is not confined to businessmen. It has even been indulged in by some economists. If many are cautious in their pronouncements, there are others unembarrassed by doubt, although, as we have already noted, the exact relationship between population and economic conditions is an uncertain one at best. Either the necessary data do not exist, or they are beset by inaccuracies, changing definitions, incompleteness.

Only with the greatest difficulty, it seems, does man withstand the siren song of *post hoc* thought. Does B follow A? Then A is the cause of B. *Post hoc, ergo propter hoc.* What could be simpler? What could more readily support a chosen position? The great population expansions in Europe and the United States coincided with increases in both production and per capita income. In terms of *post hoc* logic two conclusions can be drawn from this association of events: either population growth is necessary to bring such increases or it is, at the very least, no hindrance to their realization. Here, for instance, are the words of Colin Clark, an internationally known Roman Catholic economist and leading advocate of unchecked population growth:

The first people in Europe to feel the pressure of population upon a limited area of land were the Dutch, in the sixteenth century. This spurred them on to the astonishing achievements of fighting a successful war against Spain, the greatest power of that time, becoming the world's greatest maritime, commercial, and colonizing power, ranging the world to found New York, Cape Town, and Djakarta, importing most of their food supplies, from the proceeds of their shipping and commerce. At the same period they also produced some of the world's greatest art.

He contrasts this with France where

the Black Death . . . of 1348 . . . was . . . followed by a whole series of devastating epidemics compounded by the Hundred Years' War . . . and . . . civil war . . . The result was a loss of population from which France took centuries to recover . . . Before the Black Death the population of France had reached an unexpectedly high figure of more than 30 million; and with this population growth had developed an economy more productive, with considerable interregional and international commerce, lower taxes, wealthier, and certainly freer than the highly regulated economy of France in the seventeenth and eighteenth centuries. French history, in short, suggests a connection between economic vigor and rising population.[2]

These data cited by Clark in support of his view that population increase is a requisite for economic growth are all for periods when the countries in his examples were relatively sparsely settled. It would be equally logical to claim that the prosperity of these countries was due not to population growth but to relative emptiness, instead.[3] But quite apart from this, assuming his description to be an accurate one of a period for which economic data are in notoriously short supply, it is curious that Clark makes no comparison with conditions in more recent years for which the data are more numerous and demonstrably superior. For instance, he omits all mention of

Japan and the European Economic Community. Neither of these is experiencing more than minimal population growth, yet each is currently undergoing a truly phenomenal economic expansion.

Concerning contemporary India, Clark asserts, "There is no need for pessimism; . . . Population pressure is probably the only force strong enough to overcome the intense conservatism of the Indian peasant. In the unlikely event of that pressure's being removed by the wholesale adoption of family limitation, most of the stimulus to economic development would be removed with it." In other words, for Indians to live more decently there must be even more of them suffering from malnutrition, even more dying prematurely from diseases of poverty, even more sleeping in the streets of Calcutta and Bombay to which they have migrated in search of jobs that do not exist. For without these pressures there would be insufficient incentive; insufficient willingness to make the changes necessary to bring economic progress; and—horrible thought!—stagnation. What this particular approach may lack in reasonableness is at least partially offset by its dogged certainty and, in contrast to others like it, its immaculate logic. When world population reaches that figure of 28 billion which Professor Clark claims (in shining isolation from serious students of the matter) to be the maximum the world could feed at the present levels of the most prosperous countries, people will have become "a thousand times as economically productive as Americans are today. The construction of *artificial space satellites on which to live* should present to them no difficulty. . . ."[4] (italics ours)

Here we have a quixotic example of the logical extreme to which the economic argument for population growth can be carried. Based as it is on the "post-hocian" application to present conditions of a combination of mediaeval dogma and data of uncertain reliability from pre-industrial and pre-demographic transition societies, it could be good-naturedly shrugged off were it not for the widespread publicity it receives and the support derived from it for certain economic fixations in the United States.

The belief that an increasing population is beneficial for business and even essential for business growth seems to rest on the assumption that population increase raises total buying power. In other words, whatever increases population growth may bring in operating costs (for materials, transportation, taxes, distribution), will be more than offset for any individual firm by the addition population growth brings to total demand. Underlying this assumption seems to be the belief that population growth is a surer, and certainly preferable, means to increase demand than would be any reduction of prices or any equalization of income.

Actually, a population's rate of growth generally has only slight short-run economic consequences, save in those countries classed either as "overpopulated" or as grossly "underpopulated" (Colonial America, for instance). And in the long run, as we pointed out in Chapter 3, continued growth will be at the expense of both economic welfare and the quality of life.

In what way, then, do demographic conditions affect economic? There is, of course, feedback—or "mutual causation" —always going on between the two. Population conditions affect economic; and economic conditions, in turn, affect population. Moreover, neither operates within a social vacuum. Each is only one set of variables within a multiplicity of variables that together determine a country's economic situation. In none but the most extreme circumstances could either be considered of prime importance in determining the characteristics of the other.

With these general considerations in mind, the economic consequences of demographic conditions may be considered under five heads:

1. Absolute size

2. Rate of numerical growth or decline

3. Composition (age, sex, intelligence, genetic endowment, physique and health, marital status, and family status)

4. Degree of residential and commercial concentration (i.e., spatial concentration)

5. Degree and direction of geographical mobility

In terms of economic roles people are both producers and consumers. The five demographic factors listed above may affect each of these roles in various ways. The most direct relationship is that between the size of the population and the *potential* numbers of workers. Obviously, there can be no more workers than there are people, nor can the number of different specialties in operation at any one time exceed the number of people available to undertake such specialization. The number of these specialties will be further limited by the fact that for every one person in certain specialties there must be several persons in various others. To keep one textile designer busy, for example, requires the activities of more than a score of mill workers.

Economic production is also affected, though less directly, by marriage and childbearing. In some societies nearly everyone may be defined as a worker,[5] but as economic development proceeds, the general tendency is for certain sections of the population to withdraw from active participation in the work force. Married women remaining at home still work, of course, but their labor does not ordinarily count as "economic" activity, or its results as "economic" production. In the United States, 77 percent of all single women 25–44 years of age work full-time. But among their married sisters this proportion is only 29 percent.[6] Among married women the proportion in the labor force either full or part-time is over three times as high for those with no children under the age of 5 as it is for those who have children in this age group.[7] To the extent, then, that marriage or childbearing affects the degree to which certain sections of the population are likely to participate in the labor force, the marital and family status of that population will have a direct bearing on the number of potential workers.

Family status also has a bearing on the mobility of the work force. Americans are traditionally a footloose people. Each year, one out of five changes his residence, one out of 15 moving to a different county.[8] Not all of these moves are economically inspired, but a large proportion of them certainly are. At the younger ages, married persons are more mobile than unmarried, while at ages 35 and over this relationship is reversed.[9] Hence one's marital and family status may well be among the factors determining not only the likelihood of his being in the labor force, but his willingness to seek employment outside the local community.

When it comes to consumption, the relationship between demographic and economic conditions is even less direct than it is with production. Only if a people lived at the barest subsistence level would the ultimate limit to how much was consumed be determined directly by the size of the population. There would be a minimum of some sort, of course. But it would be so low under such conditions—being the amount just adequate to enable a people to reproduce themselves—that it would have no practical relevance to any but the most sterilely theoretical discussion. Apart from setting a theoretical minimum for the amount consumed, purely demographic factors are probably as little determinant of consumption as they are of production. The number of people sets a limit on the *ultimate* minimum that can be consumed without a society's atrophying. But within these very broad limits what is actually consumed will be determined almost completely by the cultural attributes of the people: by their knowledge, beliefs, values, and attitudes; by their system of social stratification and the character of their institutions.

On the basis of the available data it seems fairly certain that the purely demographic characteristics of a people—their number, age and sex composition, and rate of growth or decline—are of progressively less economic importance as an economy becomes more productive. The reasons for this are two: First, high productivity must necessarily rest on a high capitalization per worker, that is, on a substantial investment in machinery, scientific and technological knowledge, greater and more efficient amounts of energy. Second, high productivity requires also a high rate of consumption—a rate far higher than can be brought about by the addition of mere numbers. High capitalization and a high rate of consumption are both essential to high productivity. Neither can exist by itself.*

Still, within a high-production high-consumption system like ours the effect of demographic factors on the economy cannot be entirely discounted. What has probably received the most attention from demographers and economists is the relation of demographic characteristics to the size of the labor force and to the ratio of workers to total population. Considerable effort has been made to determine changes over time in the number of persons supported by each worker: to show, that is, the number of infants, school children, wives, incompetents, retired and institutionalized persons per worker. Since most of these people are outside the work force, their support must, by definition, come from the work of others. This is a sign of our higher productivity and our greater industrialization. No more are children sent to work in the mills and mines at ages of six or seven. As a people we can afford to keep them not only in school, but in economic idleness, as well. We can also afford to force retirement upon older workers, and to discourage wives and mothers from seeking employment. In terms only of economic

---

* The requisite high rate of consumption need not entail a generally high level of living, however. Consumption may be in a large measure a function of government (as during wartime), businesses (as under programs of rapid or extensive capitalization), or a privileged class with wealth far greater than that of the rest of society.

function, married women without children under the age of twelve (some 25 million in all)[10] may be said to comprise the largest leisure class in the United States.

What does all this mean so far as the relation between population and the production function is concerned? It means, simply, that within the very broad limits already discussed, it is the cultural, and not the demographic, characteristics that will determine how many producers there are and how productive they will be. What makes the aged a problem, for instance, has little to do with the fact of their age, or even with the proportion they are of the total population. They will be a social problem to the extent they occupy a disadvantaged position in the society.[11] They will be a drain on the economy to the extent they have an inferior financial position and are unable to obtain employment by which to improve it. The same goes for every other such group. The explanation is to be sought in the *cultural* characteristics, not the demographic.

On three nights late in July and at the beginning of August 1943 [Professor Galbraith writes], the heavy planes of the R.A.F. Bomber Command droned in from the North Sea and subjected the city of Hamburg to an ordeal such as Germans had not experienced since the Thirty Years War. A third of the city was reduced to a wasteland. At least 60,000 and perhaps as many as 100,000 people were killed—about as many as at Hiroshima. . . . Adolf Hitler heard the details of the attack and for the only known time during the war said it might be necessary to sue for peace. . . .

Yet this terrible event taught a lesson about the economics of war which very few have learned and some, indeed, may have found it convenient to ignore. The industrial plants of Hamburg were around the edge of the city . . . or on the harbor. They were not greatly damaged by the raids; these struck the center of the city and the working-class residential areas and suburbs. In the days immediately following the raids production faltered; in the first weeks it was down by as much as 20 or 25 per cent. But thereafter it returned to normal. By then the workers had scanned the ruins of their former homes, satisfied themselves that their possessions and sometimes their families were irretrievable, had found some rude clothes and the shelter of a room or part of a room in a still habitable house, and had returned to work. . . . [T]he efficiency of the worker as a worker was unimpaired by this loss. After a slight period of readjustment, he labored as diligently and as skillfully as before.

There is a further chapter to the story. Before the attacks, there had been a labor shortage in Hamburg. Afterwards, despite the number killed and the number now engaged on indispensable repairs, there was no shortage. For, as a result of the attacks, thousands who were waiters in restaurants and cafes, attendants in garages, clerks in banks, salesmen in stores, shopkeepers, janitors, ticket takers, and employees in handicraft industries (which, being small and traditional, were more likely to be in the center of town) lost their places of employment. They had previously contributed nothing to war production. Their contribution to the standard of living proved dispensable. Now they turned to the war industries as the most plausible places to find employment.

Even in the presumptively austere and dedicated world of the Third Reich, in the third year of a disastrous war, the average citizen had access to a wide range of comforts and amenities which habit had made to seem essential. And because they were believed to be essential they were essential. . . . The R.A.F. broke through the psychological encrustation and brought living standards down somewhere nearer to the physical minimum. In doing so it forced a wholesale conversion of Germany's scarcest resource, that of manpower, to war production.

In reducing, as nothing else could, the consumption of nonessentials and the employment of men in their supply, there is a distinct possibility that the attacks on Hamburg increased Germany's output of war material and thus her military effectiveness.[12]

If a labor shortage threatens in the United States (and none seems even remotely in the offing), population increase will hardly serve to mitigate it. If we seek more workers, they can be obtained in greater numbers, far more rapidly, and at much less social cost if resort is had, instead, to various groups already in the population. Nonwhites, women, the aged, and disabled are all victims to some extent of discriminatory hiring practices. As the experience of World War II well shows, such discrimination diminishes greatly in the face of a genuine labor shortage. We could also make greater use of part-time workers from among, particularly, the aged, housewives, school children, and the disabled. And, of course, we could lengthen the work week. Adjustments like these would necessitate some changes in our thinking, but the costs—monetary and otherwise —would be negligible beside those which population increase would entail, and the results would surely be more certain.

But what of the division of labor and the economies of large-scale operation? These are, after all, of real concern to some economic systems. Writing in 1947, the Australian demographer, W. D. Borrie, concluded that "Even allowing for the improved efficiency of industrial techniques as a result of the war-time experience there is little doubt that Australia has not the human resources necessary to take full advantage in the immediate post-war period of its potential industrial capacity."[13] Borrie saw no shortage of demand. What he did see was that *within the social and cultural context* of the post-World War II period, *full* development of Australia's industrial potential would require more than the 7.7 million persons inhabiting the country at that time. He had little doubt that this number was sufficient to provide a high level of living, and subsequent per capita income figures have borne him out, but he felt that a larger labor force would make possible a still higher per capita level of living—*other things being equal,* of course.

Australia is in an unusual position. It has an industrialized economy and a small population inhabiting a vast territory so far removed from potential markets and sources of supply that transportation costs are at a maximum. Yet it has one of the highest levels of living in the world, a level only somewhat lower than the United States'. A labor force too small to permit adequate specialization of labor or the economies of scale is quite believable for such an economy serving so few people. But it most assuredly is not for an economy, like ours, which supports a population currently eighteen times as large.

So far we have dealt with only one factor of production, the labor force, a factor whose characteristics in highly industrialized economies are seldom of transcending economic importance. We have described various ways of recruiting a larger work force, but said nothing of increasing the level of productivity of the workers we already have. Since gains from the latter have throughout the history of industrial economies exceeded in importance those from numerical additions to the work force, let us turn to a discussion of this alternative approach to raising the quantity of a people's goods and services.

Capitalization per worker once comprised little more than a few tools, a crude workshop, and the energy supplied by animal, wind, and water power. This is still true of much of the world. In the industrialized countries, however, a worker may operate equipment costing tens of thousands of dollars; his knowledge and skill will have been acquired at a cost of several thousands more. He is already highly capitalized and becoming more so every year. There seems to be no real limit to this process.

More production can be far better achieved by further capitalization than by any increase in the number of workers. More efficient machinery, further scientific and technological development, better schooling, better on-the-job training, improvement in the sources of energy are among the many productive avenues open to additional capital expenditure. So also are such economically relevant social expenditures as those for better health facilities, air and water purification, conservation, recreation, and rehabilitation.

There are other ways, too. More efficient management is one. Another is the further development and improvement of built-in economic stabilizers by which to flatten out the peaks and troughs of business fluctuations. Such improvements as these latter would, incidentally, help management to be more efficient by increasing its chances of making accurate forecasts of business conditions. Finally, increased production could come, as it did in the Hamburg described by Galbraith, from a re-allocation of talent and energy into more productive activities. Would society fall apart with fewer taxi drivers and more doctors; fewer race track touts and more teachers; fewer chorus girls and more social workers; fewer stock brokers and more probation officers?

So much for the production function. What now of the relation of demographic factors to the consumption function? Were numbers alone sufficient to create demand, the greatest market in the world would be China. Yet it was her very lack of demand for the goods of industrializing Europe that helped so much to keep China from becoming a part of the European trade empire when this was being created in the 18th and 19th centuries.[14] We have already noted that the number and composition of a people establish only the theoretical minimum of consumption. They do not determine the maximum except in the case of a people living at the barest possible subsistence level, a situation in which, by definition, maximum and minimum would be the same. Any increase in numbers, no matter how small, would bring starvation to a people in such extreme circumstances. Perhaps the closest approach to this is found among the Bushmen of the Kalahari Desert. Yet even here, there is enough of a surplus of time, energy, food to permit of music (both instrumental and voice), decorative clothing, dancing, story-telling, carving, games.[15]

In short, no people lives at a level adequate only for biologic maintenance. They may be continually hungry; but enough live long enough for them to reproduce themselves. Nor do they spend every waking moment in a continual pursuit of food, whatever their degree of hunger. There is always something—both time and substance—left over for art, play, invidious distinction, religion, magic, and the free play of curiosity.

Just as their culture determines a people's *productive* behavior, so also does culture determine their patterns of *consumption:* what they will consume, when and how they will consume it, how much they will consume, and who among them will consume what. Culture is subject to enormous variations among peoples and over time. To the extent that demographic conditions affect the rate and nature of consumption they do so only through this mediary of cultural prescriptions.

Still, probably the single most important factor accounting for the positive enthusiasm with which so many American businessmen regard the high birth rate in this country is the belief that population growth is necessary for the maintenance of consumption levels. But whatever they may say about a larger market's resulting from an increasing population, few businessmen act as though they have much faith in it. Their bets do not go uncovered. Perhaps nowhere is this better evidenced than in the development of advertising.

Whether or not we accept Professor Potter's judgment that it "now compares with such long-standing institutions as the school and the church in the magnitude of its social influence," there is no doubt that advertising occupies a position of great importance in today's America. The industry has grown a lot since its inception a century ago. From an activity "involving relatively small sums of money" and "practiced principally by retail distributors who offered items without the mention of brands," advertising today "dominates the media, . . . has vast power in the shaping of popular standards, and . . . is really one of the very limited group of institutions which exercise social control." And what is the purpose of this control?—the stimulation of man "to consume or to desire to consume."[16] Were population growth sufficient in itself to create this demand, there would be no need for advertising beyond the merely informative type still featured by grocery stores. Whether there would be as much material abundance without advertising is doubtful; for whatever else it may do, advertising increases the likelihood that demand for a product will be sufficient to guarantee its producer enough return on his investment to keep him in production.

The businessman's fear of depression is another sign of his incomplete faith in the assumption that population growth in and of itself leads to economic prosperity. It is not because unemployment reduces the quantity of goods and services that depression is so feared, but because it reduces the amount of money people have to spend.

No matter how many people there are, demand by itself will not bring sales. In a society like ours where so much is distributed by means of the market mechanism (i.e., through sales to private individuals) demand alone is never enough. To be effective, it must be supported by various social conditions, among them, as in this case, the possession of money.

Despite this evidence of incomplete conviction within the business community itself, the belief persists—and not just among businessmen—that population growth is good for business, and stability or decrease bad. Why? Is there fear that we will find ourselves short of workers? If so, it must surely be put down to irrationality, what with automation looming on the horizon and an unemployment figure that has averaged more than 5 percent of the work force since 1953.[17]

Then is it fear that there will be too few customers? This fear does, indeed, seem to be widespread. It is ordinarily expressed in positive terms, however: more people equalling more consumption, not fewer equalling less. Negative thinking, it seems, is taboo even for negative ideas.

What kinds of evidence can be adduced to substantiate these persistent fears? Ironically, one origin of these fears is certain beliefs of businessmen themselves. If potential investors believe that declining numbers (or at least a cessation of population growth) necessarily brings less consumption, there will be a lesser willingness on their part to invest, either in new enterprises or in the further expansion of old. The situation will have been defined like this: a lower rate of population increase = less potential demand = less potential profit. The result? A lower rate of investment, and one more example of what Professor Robert K. Merton has termed "the self-fulfilling prophecy."[18]

We have no assurance that population growth necessarily leads to greater consumption unless other conditions are favorable to it also. Nor have we any assurance that a cessation of growth will necessarily entail less consumption. To accept either contention is to reject not only the evidence to the contrary, but also the numerous findings on the socio-psychological origins of wants.[19]

A cessation of population growth may well lead to reductions in *certain kinds* of consumption, however, quite apart from any changes in *total* consumption. Fewer babies would obviously mean a lower consumption of baby food; fewer families, a reduction in the need for certain types of housing.

But it is probably the local merchant who is most likely to experience whatever decline in consumption might follow upon a decline in numbers. He can almost always accommodate more customers without increasing his overhead; but any loss of customers (for *any* reason) will increase his costs per unit sold, and hence reduce his margin of profit. There is always the possibility, of course, that increases in per capita consumption will more than make up for these losses, but the extent to which this can occur at the local level must surely be limited in the short run. As he lacks any real control over his market, and is usually a resident of the same community as his competitors, it is hardly surprising that the neighborhood merchant stakes his business' success on local population growth. Such growth has the *appearance* of being a sure source of increased sales; a substantial body of business opinion confirms it as such; and it occasions no hard feelings on the part of his neighbor-competitors.

Support for the belief that a growing population raises consumption and lowers costs can also be derived from the patterns of settlement in certain parts of the country. Space itself can be a cost, as is probably nowhere better illustrated than in the Great Plains states and Canada's Prairie Provinces. There are many compensations to living in these areas—they have the highest life expectancies, for example—but there is no denying that the sparseness of settlement works to increase the per capita costs of schooling, electrification, medical care, and the like.[20]

Financial failures in abundance attended the development of these states. Greater population growth would surely have forestalled many of these. But can the lack of population increase be held accountable for the failures of speculators who banked on large population increase in a region manifestly unsuited to it? These Great Plains states are still losing population as their numbers come more into line with the supporting capabilities of the region. There have been business failures. But their source was over-speculation based on an over-optimism rooted in ignorance of the true nature of the region to be developed. The result, apart from the personal hardship, has been the ruination of one of the world's most extensive grasslands and "cities" of fewer than 1000 inhabitants whose names (Dakota City, Rising City, Republican City, Big Stone City, Kaw City, etc.) embody the speculative boosterism of their founders.

Additional historical support might be obtained from the fact that numbers can impose limits upon the specialization of labor, an argument which goes something like this: had there been more people, there would have been more rapid economic development because of the greater possibilities for specialization. But the opposite argument can also be offered, and with seemingly greater cogency. Fewer workers can limit specialization, but they can also lead to a greater emphasis on labor-saving machinery and techniques, thereby actually raising per capita productivity.

Finally, with reference to the converse assumption—that a stable or decreasing population is a very bad thing for business (that, for example, if a couple with three children fails to have a fourth their expenditures will *not* increase)—we can note that there have indeed been instances in the past when slackening population growth has seemed to result in subsequent economic difficulties. But population was in every instance only one of many factors involved. As Professor Borrie has pointed out, ". . . the fact that Sweden and France—both countries in which population was comparatively stable in the 'thirties, and in which the decline in fertility was of long duration—suffered less severely than many other Western countries in which the rate of expansion of population was higher, may justify the opposite conclusion that with an economic readjustment the level of economic activity can be stabilized more readily in a stationary population than in an expanding one . . . [T]he effect of the depression in the 'thirties on various countries must be considered in relation to the whole framework of the economic organization and of the resources of each, and not merely to the level of population growth."[21]

Resting as it does on "evidence" which is at least ambiguous and in some instances demonstrably false, why should the "economic" argument for further population increase continue to

attract so many adherents? That an economic dogma should be
supported by "economic" argument should hardly surprise us.
To use any other would be a departure from the position of
"hard-headed realism" so beloved of American businessmen.
Yet the quality of this "evidence" suggests these "economic"
arguments are resorted to less for themselves than for the seemingly rational support they give to positions taken for quite
irrational reasons.

Accordingly, we should like to suggest certain other elements
which seem to us to underlie the widespread American belief
that economic well-being somehow depends on continued population growth. These, we feel, are more often the *fundamental*
elements, whatever form the verbal argument may assume.

The first of these is the ordinarily unquestioned assumption
that growth, bigness in any form, is a desirable characteristic in
almost anything. We have the "deepest" canyon, the "tallest"
building, the "largest" stadium. The folder of souvenir snap-
shots tells us that the statue of the Iwo Jima flag-raising cere-
mony is "the biggest ever cast in bronze." After every census
dozens of mayors and Chambers of Commerce take vehement
issue with census takers over the number of people enumerated
in their home towns. The mastheads of newspapers and signs
on the outskirts of small towns urge all and sundry to "watch
us grow!"

"Bigger and better" is not just a handy alliteration. It is part
of the very fabric of our society. Growth stands for youth; the
cessation of growth for old age. A population that has ceased
to grow is considered weak, unprogressive, lacking in vigor;
even, somehow, impotent or sterile. The "cult of youth" is an
important part of American culture.[22] Not only are Americans
as individuals reluctant to grow old, they seem reluctant also to
think of their country as growing old. It may never be expressed in these terms, but we suggest that the feeling that they
will retain their youth as a nation so long as they manage to

keep growing is important to much of the support Americans give to continued population increase.

Another source of support comes from the vested interest. Among the most active propagators of the "benefits" of population growth is a magazine with one of the nation's largest circulations. Since in this country any profits to be had from operation of the various media of mass communication will come from advertising revenues and not subscriptions, these media have a vested interest in fostering a general attitude of optimistic boosterism. In the case of population growth, it takes a form such as this: More people means more consumption; more consumption means the advertisers had better get into gear and put their messages across to the consuming public; the more "messages," the more revenue for the media.

Publishing is not the only business that stands to realize a short-run gain from population growth; housing construction and real estate are two other examples. House-buying is widespread in our society; so is changing houses, whether because of a change in jobs or a desire for something "better."[23] For the average person, buying a house is the only financial speculation he makes in a lifetime. He wants not only to preserve his equity, but also to make a profit. With such an attitude, he is already primed for an argument in favor of population growth as a means to keeping up the demand for housing. It sounds reasonable—and the cost is never mentioned. Many of the great American fortunes were acquired in precisely this something-for-nothing way. Why should not the little fellow share in the bounty of capitalism?

The construction business can also anticipate gains from the greater demand for schools, roads, dams, etc. that population growth makes necessary. The textile and food processing industries have similar vested interests.

And finally, there may be another reason for claiming that economic well-being depends on population growth. Suppose you object to family limitation on, say, religious grounds. A purely religious argument will ordinarily win few but coreligionists to your position. But economic arguments have much broader appeal. Besides, to the extent you accept them yourself, they can serve to strengthen your own conviction. The same can be said of any other argument based on evidence that is ostensibly empirical rather than philosophical or theological.

Cessation of population growth may be accompanied by economic problems: less labor mobility, further shifts in demand from the more basic commodities to those goods and services (recreation, for example) for which the demand is more variable, more unemployment because of seemingly fewer opportunities for investment, and greater public and private indebtedness, for example.[24] But in no instance are demographic changes the sole or even the most important forces leading to these conditions. To the extent these conditions do accompany the cessation of population growth, it is not (except within the broadest of limits) the number of people or their demographic composition that is the cause, but rather, the factor of change itself—in numbers, in composition, or in rate of growth. If population size were stabilized, there would be no demographic reason for a community or business to overcapitalize itself; no demographic reason for businessmen to invest unwisely on the assumption that population growth would somehow compensate for errors in judgment. Admittedly, this would reduce the chances for a quick speculative profit in real estate. And, undoubtedly, over the short run, the sum of these changes might mean less employment, or a lower income per capita. Change is always disruptive to some extent. It requires new patterns of thought, and new patterns of behavior, none of which is likely to be enthusiastically undertaken. Those new patterns of thought and behavior occasioned by a transition from a condition of rapid population growth to one of relative stability should become more palatable, however, when we recognize first, that the end product of this transition will be a more stable, predictable economy; second, that it will enable the preservation of qualitative aspects of life that would otherwise be progressively eroded; and finally, that, in the long run, whether we like it or not, population growth is going to be limited anyhow—if not by lowered natality, then by increased mortality.

7

The "Scientific" Argument

THE ECONOMIC CASE for complacency about population growth
may have wider appeal than the religious, but in today's
America faith in science is doubtless the most potent tranquilizer
of all. The resort to "science" (for which read: science-and-
technology) in defense of our present increase rests on the
assumption that scientific and technological development will
somehow keep up with any population growth we may experience (or perpetrate). Quite often the "scientific" argument is
adopted by those who oppose the use of population control on
moral grounds. The need and desire of persons with such
values to find alternative measures for adjusting to population
increase prompts them to rely heavily on solutions of a "scientific" nature. Thus the Catholic bishops assure us:

> . . . The thus far hidden reservoirs of science and of the
> earth unquestionably will be uncovered in this era of marvels
> and offered to humanity by dedicated persons with faith in
> mankind, and not by those seeking short cuts to comfort at the
> expense of the heritage of their own or other peoples.
> . . . The "population explosion" alarmists do not place in
> proper focus the idea of increasing the acreage or the acreage
> yield to meet the food demands of an increasing popula-
> tion . . .[1]

A lay writer displays similar optimism:

> . . . If we can but learn to farm and harvest the seas, we need
> not fear starvation, even though the world's population should
> increase sevenfold.[2]

But there seems yet another reason for this frequent resort to "science." One of the distinct advantages of basing support for population growth on assumptions about the inevitability of scientific progress is the appeal of such an argument to the self-styled "realist." Though the observation is no longer new, science in mid-twentieth century America has become almost sacrosanct. It receives the financial support, the dedicated services of its practitioners, and the obeisance and unquestioning faith of the multitude in a measure hitherto reserved to the Deity. What is probably the most rewarding feature about trusting in man's scientific acumen is that by so doing one can enjoy the confidence of the True Believer while maintaining the facade of the Rational Empiricist.

Like any other form of utopianism, belief in the omnipotence of science rests ultimately on faith, not reason. In the truly long run, nothing that fails to halt population growth can save us. Remember Professor Coale's *reductio ad absurdum:* if current growth continues, in about 6,500 years, "the descendants of the present world population would form a solid sphere of live bodies expanding with a radial velocity that, neglecting relativity, would equal the velocity of light." And since population increases geometrically, doubling itself every 40 years at present rates of growth, there would have to be *two* such spheres 40 years later, *four* such spheres 80 years later, *eight* such spheres 120 years later . . .

Obviously, to be at all meaningful, the question of science's ability to provide must be asked relative to some specific period of time and to some specific level of living. Can science provide adequately for us in the very short run of the next decade or two? Probably it can—but it depends on what is meant by "provision." The chances will be better if we limit ourselves to Americans than if we include people in other countries, especially in the underdeveloped and overpopulated areas; better if we demand no improvement in the material levels of living; better still if there are actual reductions in these levels.

If we are going to reject population control and rely, instead, on science to meet the ensuing population increase, we should recognize the consequences of our choice, even for the short run. There is no question that extensive development in science and technology is both possible and probable. The production of food can be increased and undoubtedly will be. Nor would anyone deny that science is capable also of substantially increasing yields in the areas of energy, or minerals, renewable resources, or water. In the years to come we will have to depend very heavily on these scientific and technological developments merely to make adequate provision for the three billion people who already inhabit the world, and the children who will follow them.

But though the importance of scientific development to human survival is incalculable, we feel that any discussion of the contributions science may make to the alleviation of population pressure is essentially irrelevant to the problems facing the United States. Our concern here is with the quality of life, whereas claims about the ability of science to maintain ever larger populations imply that all we need worry about are man's physical needs.

Parks, wildlife, open spaces, recreational facilities are not essential to man's physical survival. The two million Americans in our nursing homes, mental institutions, convalescent hospitals, and prisons bear daily witness to the fact that man can survive without them. For that matter, men have learned to adjust for a time to conditions in which the available nutriment and shelter were barely enough for survival. Man can indeed exist on bread alone. But is this to be our criterion by which to judge the course of events? Man can *exist* on bread alone; can he live on it? Apologists for continued population growth who put their faith in science reduce man to a mere bread-and-potatoes phenomenon: let him increase as long as he can be fed.

Unquestioning faith in science and a ready enthusiasm for new gains in providing for the world's people are inherently dangerous, for they may well lead us to overlook the fact that these gains are not without their price—in both quantitative and qualitative terms. Much can be done with planning and further scientific development to postpone eventual reckoning with the consequences of population increase. But continued additions to our population will make the expansion of these activities (requiring, as they do, greater outlays for research and development, schooling, libraries, laboratories, etc.) more difficult and more costly at the very time it makes them more necessary.

Science may well provide us with new supplies of raw materials, with substitutes for them, or with more efficient procedures for their utilization. But it has not yet done this at a pace rapid enough to maintain real costs at their earlier levels. Improved management, coupled with further development in science and technology, may, of course, eventually enable us to meet these higher real costs without any reduction in our material levels of living; but we should at least recognize that, so far, the real costs of producing these materials have been rising and that they give every indication of continuing to rise as present supplies are diminished and resort is had to sources that are ever more difficult to utilize. If the present and the immediate past are any indication of the future, it seems far more likely that real costs will continue to rise than that they will be brought down by any advances in science and technology. Should they continue upward, the result will eventually be such a drastic reduction in consumption as to effect substantial reduction also in levels of living, both here and abroad.

Food

Economic costs are only part of the story, however—and by no means the most important part. To increase our food production, for example, will require not only additional expenditures, but also extensive changes in our conditions of life and work, in our diet and our recreation. The larger the number of people to be fed, the greater will be the changes required. This may sound unduly pessimistic at a time when the well-publicized cost of storing "surplus" food in this country runs to some $1 billion each year.[3] But the whole of this surplus, which has taken years to accumulate, would supply only the following proportions of a single year's consumption by Americans at their present dietary levels:

Commodity	Inventories in 1960 as a percentage of U.S. consumption in 1960
Wheat	155%
Corn	27
Barley	17
Soybeans	4
Oats	1

Source: Calculated from data in *Statistical Abstract of the United States: 1960,* Table 870, p. 633, and *Statistical Abstract of the United States: 1961,* Table 894, p. 647. Consumption is conservatively estimated as equal to total production, less total exports.

Only of wheat have we as much as a year's supply in storage. For none of the other commodities is the amount stored as much as a third of the amount consumed in one year. With half the world's people hungry, these foods are "surpluses" solely because a profit-making economic system defines them that way. When, in the spring of 1961, their distribution to Americans was taken out of the market system by the emergency food program for unemployed workers, the effective demand for these "surpluses" rose considerably. It would rise even more if, in addition, their international distribution were also carried on outside the market system.

What can science contribute to the production of food in

sufficient quantity for a continually growing population? Extension of currently cultivatable land area is one possibility, although even the most optimistic see a possible increase of no more than 50 percent—and that in the essentially marginal tropics and far north.[4] Moreover, the migration necessary to utilize these areas would raise numerous political problems, while getting them into production would require huge outlays of capital for the removal of undesirable plant growth, the development of irrigation and drainage systems, the reduction of disease, and the development of suitable crops, livestock, and agricultural techniques.[5]

Another possibility would be to farm more intensively. Assuming that cropland could actually be increased some 50 percent and that, in addition, cropland over the whole world could by dint of very hard work and extensive capitalization be made as productive as that in Europe, Professors Brown, Bonner, and Weir of the California Institute of Technology conclude that the world's level of productivity would be only about twice what it is today—a level it would have taken some 500 billion dollars (two-thirds of the annual income of the entire world) to achieve. And for what?—for meeting merely the nutritive needs of the population we can expect in another 40 years (in the lifetime of one-half of the Americans living today) if present rates of growth continue. Is it any wonder that after two decades of extensive population increase, the average Indian eats less well today than he did in 1939, despite "vigorous governmental efforts" to improve the food supply?[6] Even with the most optimistic assumption, the enlargement of the area suited to agriculture, or the intensification of its use, can offer but limited hope for meeting our future food requirements. Those commodity "surpluses" may be something of a burden today, yet we may be very glad to have them in another decade or so—and sooner than that, in the event of a couple of bad crop years.

But there are still other possibilities for increasing the world's food supply. Insects, fungi, and animal pests consume about a third of the food which might otherwise go toward the maintenance of man. Further destruction of these pests could, therefore, conceivably increase the amount left us. But the tremendous financial cost of such an assault, and its numerous deleterious side effects, make it questionable whether there is actually much to be gained from embarking upon such a program.*

Drastically upsetting the balance of nature, such wholesale destruction of life—any form of life—is too fraught with harmful consequences to be taken seriously as a means to augmenting very greatly the world's supply of food. Pesticides all too often wipe out many useful forms of life as well: small animals, birds, fish, plants, even organic matter within the soil itself.[7] The destruction of bird and animal species—creatures whose evolutionary development took millions of years—would, of course,

---

* There is, however, no shortage of self-interested optimism from some of the commercial interests:

"Thursday, November 13, 2026. Remember this date. . . . It's *Doomsday*. This Doomsday is nothing to scoff at. . . . It is a carefully considered estimate . . . by three serious scientists [who have] calculated ahead and concluded that on November 13, 2026 the planet earth will contain 50 billion people. . . . That's the population explosion you've heard about.

"Cyanamid has heard about it, too. That's one reason why several hundred Cyanamid scientists and technicians are at work in a new Agricultural Research Center . . . near Princeton, New Jersey.

"There . . . they consider . . . that in 2026 [New Jersey] will have *10,000* per square mile . . . which makes them search a little harder for ways to match that population explosion with a food explosion. . . .

"The people of Princeton are confident that they can do it. Already they are discovering which nutrients produce the biggest, healthiest livestock. . . .

"They're discovering better ways to cope with insects, too. . . . Cyanamid's . . . chlortetracycline has enabled a farmer to bring a plump, tender broiler to market in 6 weeks instead of 12.

". . . A new insecticide called CYGON dimethoate is stopping our old friend *musca domestica,* the common house fly, in his tracks. Fly-free cows, science knows, will grow fatter and give more milk.

"Cynamid subscribes to the often-ignored axiom: Look after the future in the present. . . ." (Advertisement of American Cyanamid Company in *Scientific American.* May, 1962, p. 37. Italics in original.)

be for all time. During the past two centuries Americans have destroyed 20 species of wild mammals and birds and dangerously depleted another 57, along with 5 species of fish.[8] So there can be little doubt of either our capacity or readiness to destroy others. The destruction of insects, however, would have to be continuous, for their breeding rate is so rapid that mutations resistant to the insecticides in use at any one time would necessitate a steady expenditure of money and effort for the development of new ones. Some of these chemicals kill outright; others produce sickness or sterility in the creatures that come into contact with them. When such contaminated creatures or their products (eggs, milk, etc.) are eaten by man the poison is, of course, transferred to his own system. And what is the end of all this? The effectiveness of sprays and insecticides is frequently short-lived. Treatment must usually be repeated year after year—at additional financial cost and at the sacrifice of ever more growing things. And as a final irony, chemical blanketing at times has an adverse effect even on the very crop it is used to improve.

Still another possibility would be to consume a greater proportion of the food currently produced, beginning, for example, with feeding our garbage to pigs—a practice which used to be widespread in this country. Then, as the need for food increased further, we could try eating more of what is already produced. As it is now, man consumes an average of only about 20 percent of the plants he grows for food, ordinarily limiting himself to the seeds and rejecting the stem, leaves, and roots.[9]

Then, as our growing numbers made necessary the production of even more food, we could abandon meat and the other animal products, such as eggs, butter, milk, and cheese. Animals are a notoriously inefficient source of nutriment. They return only about 10 percent of the calories they consume while using the remaining 90 percent for moving and keeping warm.[10] The only excuse for retaining them for food is the pleasure we derive from eating their flesh and products and from viewing the open countryside where they are raised. But in a brave new world of adequate diets and ever-increasing numbers, what is produced and consumed will have to be determined by the need to supply basic nutritional requirements with the least expenditure of space. There will be no room to cater to gustatory or aesthetic tastes; no room for such inefficient luxuries as the charcoal-broiled steak or Thanksgiving turkey.*

Greater dependence on fisheries—ocean and fresh water—is another possibility, and certainly more acceptable to most than vegetarianism. But fish are an even less efficient source of nutriment than animals—it takes a thousand pounds of diatom to produce but one pound of commercial fish, for example.[11] Moreover, much extension of the yearly harvest of fish would soon exhaust the source.[12] From a nutritive standpoint, far more could be gained if we were to ingest the algae directly, rather than going through the nutritionally wasteful stages by which it is converted into fish. This, in turn, suggests another alternative, namely, the development of new sources of food.

To the aborigines of Arnhemland, Australia, the witchetty grub they find in the trunk of the eucalyptus tree is a succulent delicacy. Some of the Plains Indians of the United States were known to eat grasshoppers. In certain New York delicatessens the gourmet can purchase chocolate-covered ants. It's all in getting used to it. If our program of pest control leaves any survivors among these creatures, we might profitably explore their nutritive potential. So also for snakes, lizards, mice. Unfortunately, though, these species are seldom found in any abundance, and they would be even less numerous to the extent they had to contend with more and more people, pollutants and insect sprays.

Greater use of sugar or sea algae, yeast or chlorella[13] would

* Or American Cyanamid's "fly-free cows."

add considerably to the number of people who could be fed; but the economic problems attending their use would be enormous—to say nothing of the political and social—while their most readily acceptable use (as livestock feeds) could only postpone, not prevent, the eventual rejection of meat as an altogether too inefficient source of nutriment.

Water

Back in 1950, public-spirited New Yorkers forswore shaving and bathing on Fridays as part of a program to alleviate the shortage of water. Fortunately, the need for such sacrifice was temporary, else the good humor with which it was faced might have soon worn thin. Since that date, the city has had to go ever farther afield in search of water. So far, its efforts have been reasonably successful. But the same cannot be said for certain other localities. A 1957 study by the United States Geological Survey found some 1000 communities, comprising 15 percent of our population in 47 states, that were forced to restrict the use of water.[14] For a time, people in Dallas were lining up to buy water at 50 cents a gallon.[15] Water shortages, ever-present in much of the Southwest and Great Plains, are now a common feature throughout the country. "The problem is not just in the low-rainfall states. For ten years, New Jersey, which has far greater than average rainfall, has lived with a critical water shortage that approached catastrophe in 1957 when rainfall was below normal. Even with adequate rainfall its water supply barely equals consumption, and lack of rain, even for a short time, creates a crisis."[16]

Yesterday it was 1000 communities; tomorrow we can expect it to be many more. All trends point to more severe and more widespread restrictions in the future. Between 1900 and 1960, the per capita daily use of water in this country rose from 526 to 1732 gallons, for an increase of nearly 230 percent. The median prediction for 1975 is 1968 gallons, which would mean an increase of 314 percent over that 1900 figure.[17] In 1955, Americans used slightly less than 250 billion gallons per day. But the median estimates for 1980 put this figure at 600 billion gallons, for an increase of 240 percent in only 25 years.[18]

About 43 percent of the water used in 1960 went for irrigation; about 25 percent for industrial uses, and another 25 percent for the generation of steam electric power.* Domestic and public categories of use took the remaining 7 percent.[19] Allocation will probably undergo some changes over the next few years, but no major use is expected to take less in 1980 than it does now.[20] Nor is any expected to take less in the year 2000 than in 1980.

How long this can go on depends on the interaction of (1) population size, (2) the growth of industrial and agricultural processes that make heavy demands on water, (3) the extent to which we will be able to increase our control of run-off and our re-use of what water we have, and (4) the development of economically feasible means for the de-salinization of sea or brackish inland water. The technological developments for meeting these future needs have already been launched. Probably more than any other resource, the supply of usable water is susceptible of increase through expenditure of greater money and effort. The expenditure has to be considerable, though, and it has to come soon: $54 to $74 billion over the next 20 years for dams, reservoirs, and pollution abatement, for example.[21] And that will be just a starter.

De-salinization has been more prominently proposed of late, particularly as various methods have proved to be technologically (if not yet economically) feasible. President Kennedy,

---

* Though the direct users of 93 percent of the water were industries, farms, electric companies, etc., the ultimate consumers were, of course, the people supplied by these producers. Once again, what is consumed is a function of both numbers of people and levels of living.

echoing a report of the United States House of Representatives Committee on Science and Astronautics, has called for increased effort in this direction. Surely the sea is the most obvious source of water. But de-salinization is still very expensive (though far less so than the 50 cents a gallon paid by those residents of Dallas); and the costs quoted never include the possibly greater costs arising from the need to transport water so obtained to the farms and industries that need it.

With most of the earth covered by water in some form, there is no likelihood of our eventually running out of it. Rather, the question is whether there will be enough of the right kind of water, in the right place, at the right time—and whether that water will be at an economic *and social* cost that we will be able and willing to bear.

Space

Suppose man receives enough nutriment and water and has access to sufficient quantities of raw materials (natural or synthetic). What then? If his numbers keep on growing, can he avoid the prospect of ever more crowding, of a "beehive world"? The "scientific" faithful are notoriously reticent on this score. Most, in fact, ignore the question. Yet this is the most important reason for rejecting the argument that developments in science can continue to keep pace with population growth.

Where is this ever-increasing population going to live? Where will it be housed—and how? Improvements in transportation could, of course, make possible the further diffusion of settlement within our metropolitan areas. Such a process has gone on for generations, though only over the past couple of decades, with industrial relocation and extensive development of suburban and exurban areas, has it begun to accelerate rapidly. A considerable portion of the shorter work day has already been transferred to commuting time—and we might

note, somewhat parenthetically, that for many the *energy* saved
by the shorter work day has received a similar transferal. Perhaps another shortening of the work day will make available
even more time and energy for commuting.

But such diffusion would take land from other uses: agriculture, recreation, and watershed, for example. It would also
mean further—and, because of the diffusion, far higher per
capita—capital expenditures for transportation facilities, sewage
disposal, water, electricity, and roads, as most residents of new
suburbs can readily testify. Water will be a particular problem
if any real effort is made to extend settlement to the more open
land areas in this country (and such settlement would have to
take place if further diffusion were to be a "solution" of more
than a generation or two's duration to our need for living space).
Apart from mountains, swamplands, and polar areas, those
regions which are today relatively sparsely settled have remained
so primarily because of their lack of water. If they are now to
become more densely settled, the provision of water for this
increase in numbers—quite apart from that for the industries
that would ostensibly employ them—would be an extremely
costly, if not technologically insurmountable, task. There are
other possibilities, however. We could continue the drainage of
swamplands for replacement by housing developments, though
this process often destroys wildlife breeding grounds and lowers
the water table. We could also build dikes against the sea. The
energetic Dutch have obtained additional land in this way for
centuries—but only at great cost and by no means fast enough
to keep up with their growing population. Conditions in the
Netherlands are so bad, in fact, that ever since 1914, the Dutch
government has lent official encouragement to efforts to expand
emigration from that crowded country. In 1952 it established a
special bureau to serve that purpose. And there are several
dozen other official, quasi-official, and private organizations
devoted to the same end.[22] The Netherlands government hopes

soon to achieve a net emigration of at least 50,000 a year,[23] two-fifths of its annual increase. With a population as small as the Netherlands', such a high rate of emigration can be carried on for generations without influencing very much the population picture elsewhere in the world. But for the United States— where the same annual rate of emigration would involve 24 times as many people—migration on such a scale would be clearly impractical.

Deus ex Machina

To a generation reared on "Buck Rogers" and others of that genre, the recent exploits a few miles above the earth's surface offer ample proof that science has not failed us, that it is this very moment in the process of providing an escape from the realities of a finite universe. Are we depleting our resources? There will be plenty more on the moon. Are we running out of space? We'll simply migrate to other planets.

But astronomers are remarkably less sanguine. After a detailed analysis of the problem, Sebastian von Hoerner of the Astronomisches Rechen-Institut, Heidelberg, Germany, reaches this conclusion:

> . . . The requirements . . . have turned out to be such extreme ones that I, personally, draw this conclusion: space travel, even in the most distant future, *will be confined completely to our own planetary system,* and a similar conclusion will hold for *any other civilization, no matter how advanced it may be.*[24] (italics added)

Though admitting the possibility that quarters of a temporary nature might be established on Venus or Mars, Professor Garrett Hardin of the University of California (Santa Barbara) concurs with the general run of astronomers in rejecting the notion that these, or any other planets of our sun (save Earth, of course), could become the abode of man.* But what of the possibilities outside our solar system? Might not von Hoerner and his colleagues be unduly pessimistic?

The nearest star, Alpha Centauri, is 4.3 light-years away. Were we to travel there at the maximum velocity of the rockets currently being readied to send to the moon (19,000 miles per hour), the journey, writes Hardin, would require some 129,000 years. The question, then, is how likely are improvements in space travel that will "significantly cut down the time required to make such an interstellar journey?"[25]

Relying on the calculations of L. R. Shepherd[26] who "presumes a technology in the release and utilization of nuclear energy that may take several centuries to achieve," Hardin gives "the worshippers of Progress the maximum advantage" by assuming for sake of argument that "such advanced technology is available *now*." (his italics)

Under these "fantastically optimistic assumptions," how long would it take to travel to Alpha Centauri?—a mere 350 years (or 350–4.3 = 345.7 years, if relativity is taken into consideration), during which the average speed of the space craft would be 7,000,000 miles an hour.

To solve our population problem by shipping only the current annual population increase of the United States would require spending on this purpose alone—allowing nothing for any other use, not even food—an amount equal to some 20 times our current national income. And all this assumes that

---

* As recent explorations have found, Venus is far too hot and Mars far too dry. All the other planets are either too hot (Mercury) or too cold (Jupiter and beyond). Even a student of the moon so optimistic as to suggest that certain amounts of water *might* be derived from the moon's rocks limits himself to discussion of the ways by which personnel involved in temporary exploration of the moon might be able to meet but a fraction of their needs from materials available on site. (See Jack Green, *The Geology of the Lunar Base*, North American Aviation, Inc., Space Sciences Laboratory, May, 1962)

our nearest star has planets; that at least one of these planets is suitable for human habitation; that this suitable planet is uninhabited—or, if inhabited, that the humanoids thereon will gracefully commit suicide when they find we need their planet for our *Lebensraum*. . . .

And what would life en route be like for these interstellar migrants?

For 350 years the population would have to live under conditions of complete sociological stasis, the like of which has never been known before. No births would be permitted, except to replace the dead. . . . Marriages would certainly have to be controlled, as would all other social interactions, and with an iron hand. In the spaceship, Progress would be unendurable. The social organization would have to persist unchanged for 10 generations' time, otherwise there would be the risk that some of the descendants of the original crew might wish to change the plans.[27]

Without any change in the ratio of births to deaths, this "adjustment" to population increase would confine to the "closed universe of space-ships" a population six times as great as that of the earth—all because we were unwilling to admit living in a closed universe. Even if we could one day develop the technology to achieve this kind of interstellar migration, its perfection would necessarily be so far in the future that in the meantime we could not have avoided coming to terms, anyhow, with the problem of population growth.

No discussion of "scientific" escape valves would be complete without reference to predictions of human behavior that are based on observation of nonhumans. The late science editor of the *New York Times* summarizes the observations of the cosmologist, Fred Hoyle, as follows:

[C]ertain species of song birds automatically limit their number without starvation by a division of good and poor territory from the standpoint of food supply. Territory is divided not into a number of units equal to the number of contending birds but into the number that can provide enough food for a brood of chicks. If the number of contenders exceeds the number of good territorial units, there is fighting. Fighting means not death but the separation of the contending birds into two groups. One group appropriates the available rich territory and breeds; the other group contents itself with poor territory and does not breed. Thus the birth rate is determined automatically by the amount of food that is available. The unsuccessful birds do not starve to death. They find just enough food for subsistence. . . .

What happens if the [human] population gets too large? Is death by starvation inevitable? In the case of the songbirds . . . no deaths are caused by starvation, there is simply no more breeding among the poorly fed. This is likely to happen in a human population. The excess will not necessarily die of starvation; it will cease to be born.[28]

This may be the way songbirds behave. (Fruit flies behave the same way, and so also do some mammalian species.[29]) But it is not the way humans behave. Any claim that it is has to flout the evidence from every study ever made of human reproductive capacities and behavior. We can find both high birth rates and low birth rates among both impoverished peoples and affluent peoples. If crowding itself were eventually to prevent population increase (and we have no doubt of its ultimate ability to do this), it would do so through increasing mortality, not through any lessening of human reproductiveness. As a solution to population increase among humans this songbird analogy must be relegated to the same category as Colin Clark's space satellites.

In the past, restrictions on human activity came largely from physical and biological limitations in combination with man's lack of economic means and society's ideas of right and wrong. Science and technology have lessened many of the restrictions originating in physical, biological, and economic conditions;

but they have claimed a price. By reducing mortality, they have in recent years brought into being a new limitation on man's activity: the weight of human numbers itself, a limitation which would appear far less tractable than either custom or poverty.

Any future contribution science might make to man's welfare is also likely to exact its price in economic and social terms. Even if we accept the value assumption that man should increase because science can provide, there can be little doubt that social and economic conditions would severely restrict the ability of science to expand indefinitely the ingredients necessary to man's physical survival. The "scientific" case for continued population growth thus merits scepticism on two counts: first, because of the values that underlie it, and, second, because of the claims it makes for science itself.

8

The Military Argument

TWO ASSUMPTIONS underlie the support for continued population growth that originates in a concern for the military position
of the United States: (1) a large population is a necessary basis for
military strength; and (2) the larger the population, the greater
will be that strength. Neither of these assumptions is more than
partially valid.

650 million Chinese; 220 million Russians; 190 millon Amer-
cans. 1.05 billion in the Communist bloc; .85 billion in the
"Free World." To the American who sums up world power in
terms of human numbers, the international situation must look
bleak, indeed. But the future must look even bleaker. Today,
the difference is 200 million. A decade from now it may well be
280 million; and a generation from now 435 million. No matter
how rapidly our population grew, these others would be ahead
for many generations. Those who propose that we maintain
population growth to preserve a military advantage are actually
suggesting that we compete with "the enemy" on a ground on
which he is already pre-eminent and likely to remain so for the
foreseeable future.

But in today's world, national military strength is by no
means a reflection of sheer size alone.* Under some circumstances a large population may actually lead to military

* Nor has military victory always gone to the largest population in the past.
Witness the Greek victory over the Persians, the Mongol conquests of China,
the Spanish conquests in Mexico and South America, the World War I German
defeat of Russia.

weakness. As with economic conditions, a country's potential military strength results from the interaction of many different constituents. With military strength these can be separated into three broad categories:[1] (1) *Economic capacity,* which would include population, resources, scientific and technological development, productive facilities, skills; (2) *Administrative competence,* comprising military and governmental (including diplomatic) skills and organization; and (3) *Motivation for war* —particularly, in this age of modern military technology, on the part of those who control the machinery of government. All three must be weighed in any assessment of a country's relative military position.

Population size is only one factor among several that influence the level of military power, and it, like the others, has no independent relationship to it. The *ultimate* number of persons available for military or para-military activities does, of course, depend on the size and composition of the population. Just as there can be no more workers than people, so also can there be no more soldiers or war production workers than people. But within the very broad limits thus established there are many possibilities for either reducing or expanding the number of persons available for military activities. As Germany and Russia demonstrated during World War II, there is no *military* necessity for limiting conscription to men between the ages of 18 and 35. Boys of 15 and 16, and men in their forties and fifties, were eventually called up with the others. As both Russia and Israel have shown, there is, in fact, no *military* reason for exempting women. In both countries, women have been found to be effective front line fighters. By the beginning of the Korean War, the United States had concluded that there was no *military* reason either, for exempting homosexuals or those afflicted with any of a number of physical and psychological disabilities that had formerly served as grounds for rejection. If conditions appear to warrant it, existing military manpower can always be augmented by conscription of those ordinarily defined as "unsuitable": the young, the old; women, homosexuals, the physically and mentally "unfit"; those in "essential" occupations. In fact, as war becomes increasingly total, the distinction between "military" and "nonmilitary" personnel becomes correspondingly obscure, if only because the weapons of destruction do not discriminate.

Obviously, however rigorous the controls, a people cannot be wholly engaged in either productive or military activities. Even in wartime, a population continues to consume. The military establishment itself, and the maintenance of international diplomacy based on its apparent strength, requires the consumption of a mobilized surplus of capital, energy, time. Though some of today's most destructive weapons can be produced relatively cheaply,[2] the requisites of an effective military force still make heavy economic demands, especially if the purposes for which that force is to be made ready encompass all kinds of international violence, ranging from full-fledged nuclear exchange to a number of limited local wars. And all the while, the economic demands of the military are in constant competition with the population's needs and preferences for non-military goods. Mobilization of the surplus necessary to support large scale military efforts requires expenditures for a central government strong enough to force the populace to save (usually effected through taxation) and to allocate these savings to their most efficient military use. Thus, a minimum population size is established not only by the need to supply manpower for the armed forces but also by the need to guarantee a level of economic productivity sufficient to meet the various ancillary demands of a modern military establishment.[3]

But just as a country may have too *few* people available to implement its military objectives (and the political, scientific, and economic activities on which they depend), so also may it have too *many* people to meet the requirements of an effective military establishment. If population were the sole, or even the most important, ingredient in military power, China and India would today be far more powerful than either the United States or the Soviet Union; Indonesia, Pakistan, and Brazil—each more populous than any European nation (save Russia)—would be only somewhat less so. The fact that they are not arises mainly from the generally underdevolped state of their respective economies. They are less strong because of their poverty, and they are poor, in part, because of the pressure of population on their resources. Such a high proportion of total output goes merely to maintain these large populations that the amount left over for investment in economic expansion or for allocation to military pursuits must, necessarily, remain limited. Also limited must be such nonmilitary avenues to international influence as economic and military missions abroad, cultural exchange programs, and short-wave propaganda broadcasts. The overpopulated country is customarily forced into a defensive position in international affairs: it is the object, and not the disseminator, of propaganda; the recipient, and not the donor, of economic aid. Professor Kingsley Davis of the University of California (Berkeley) concluded some years ago that India "would have a much better chance to become one of the great powers if it had 100 million fewer citizens than it has." At that time (1954), this would have meant a reduction of over one-fourth in the population of India. The greater military advantage of this inverse relationship—an increase in power with a reduction in numbers—Davis claims, would also obtain in the case of Egypt, Japan, Italy, China, Pakistan, Mexico, Haiti, Ceylon, and Israel,[4] to which we would add Indonesia.

Nor are the military disadvantages of overpopulation based entirely on the economic burdens resulting from too many people. The low levels of living that are a concomitant of underdevelopment take their toll also of human vitality, partly through higher mortality (only 58 percent of those born in

India in 1941–1950 period could expect to live to age 20, compared with 95 percent in the United States[5]) and partly through the greater incidence of disease. Malaria, and also intestinal worms, dysentery, and cholera—the diseases of filth and of undernourishment and malnourishment—are the common lot of the ordinary individual in most of the underdeveloped countries.

But what of a highly industrialized country like the United States? Since it is hardly likely in the near future to revert to a condition of economic underdevelopment, can population growth be said to have any detrimental effect at all on its military strength? Certainly not by itself. But in combination with a high level of demand for resources and for nonmilitary services the production of which involves skills and procedures not readily convertible to military use (as is the case in the United States today) a large population would doubtless be something of a handicap in any situation demanding rapid mobilization. The source of the difficulty, however, would lie less in the number of people *per se,* than in the combination of numbers with habits of consumption. As with World War II Hamburg in our earlier example, a sizable population at a high level of living could result in an uneven competition between military and nonmilitary needs for goods, resources, and manpower that would eventually work to the detriment of the military.

Another possible handicap to the military effectiveness of a growing population arises from the character of its age structure. Such a population is always younger than a stable population with the same mortality rates. This means a somewhat higher ratio of dependent children to supporters (the size of the discrepancy varying directly with the rate of growth) and, so far as the United States is concerned, a somewhat higher percentage of women likely to remain out of the labor force in order to care for them.

But with no population increase, is it not possible that a

dependency of age would be substituted for a dependency of youth? To be sure, a stable population with the same mortality rates would have a higher proportion in the older age groups and, thus, a conceivably higher proportion of dependents. But though many of the aged would be dependent because of impaired health and vigor, many others of them would retain their productive capabilities virtually intact. The tendency has been to underestimate this as we retire older workers in order to make jobs available for younger ones. But whether or not one is "dependent" is at least partially a matter of cultural prescription. In a country like the United States, characterized by urbanization and high levels of living, the *necessary* dependency of the young will be substantially greater than that of the old. It will cost more to feed and clothe them; far more to educate and train them.

However, those who equate population with national strength are not concerned about the military hazards of too *many* people; the situation they fear is too *few*. In the context of a population of 190 million this apprehension is surely misplaced. That world in which military might essentially depended on the number of men who could be readied for combat, rather than on military technology, organization, or production, no longer exists—at least not in that international setting of which the United States is a part. For New Guinea tribes it may be different.

The Industrial Revolution changed military conditions no less than it did economic. The human being, represented in the form of tactical skill, individual bravery, physical stamina, or sheer numbers, has steadily given way in importance to the machine, to economic productivity, to the technician. We have reached a point where "a decisive superiority in weapons and in their tactical employment may well offset, and perhaps more than offset, any inferiority in the size of the armed forces . . ."[6] Though generals and statesmen have not been without some importance in determining the course of history, it is probable that only with the advent of nuclear weapons have they actually come to occupy a position of importance in any way approximating that customarily accorded them in the history books.* For their activities are ever circumscribed by the force of events and the fundamental attributes of the society. "In politics, as on the stage, brilliant acting alone cannot bring success. A good setting and a good drama are also required. It is not so much what Wilson or Hitler *did* which affects history, but rather what they *could* do."[7] And with the variety and destructiveness of today's weapons, what the military and their civilian cohorts can now do far exceeds anything ever before possible in human history.

What, then, is the minimum size population a country must have to achieve and maintain top rank under conditions prevailing today? Davis estimates 60 million[8] (less than one-third the population of the United States)—a figure that happens to be larger than the population of every country save China, India, the Soviet Union, the United States, Japan, Indonesia, Pakistan, and Brazil (in order of population size). Any such estimate depends, of course, on the use to be made of that population, quite apart from its industrial production. Foreign occupation would require much more manpower than the operations of a Peace Corps, for example. As other nations join

---

* The myopia of all but recent historians on this matter is understandable if we recognize their dependence on written documents. Not until the last century did literacy spread much beyond the upper classes and those serving their interests. The result is a plethora of materials on diplomacy, warfare, fashion, court intrigue and gossip—that is, on upper class interests and activities—and a comparable paucity of data on economics, science and technology, public opinion, morals, and the living conditions of "that other" 98 percent of the population. In fact, the historian was in the past confined largely to upper class subjects not only because of the nature of the data available to him, but also because of his own class origins and the narrow spread of literacy. Thanks to the more comprehensive studies of ethnologists, we may know more about the lives of South Sea islanders and Indian villagers than we know about the lives of our own European ancestors.

the Nuclear Club (or the Poison Gas Club, or the Biological Warfare Club, as the case may be), the minimum number necessary for world power could conceivably drop to a figure far below this—if it has not already done so by virtue of the stockpiles in the United Kingdom and France (populations: 52 and 45 million respectively).

So far, we have implied that a nation's relative strength is to be measured in terms of its nuclear striking power. Is this view realistic? Not if we listen to the proponents of nuclear deterrence. For it is their assumption that the capacity to destroy one another's cities and industrial potential, and to kill all or a major share of one another's people, will be enough to dissuade the world's leaders from ever launching an all-out nuclear attack. If this is true, then the ability to launch such an attack will fade in importance alongside the capacity for waging wars of a more "conventional" nature. It will, however, remain in the background as a tactic of last resort. It is these "conventional" wars that make the greatest demands on manpower, for the largest of them (i.e., those on a scale equivalent to that of World War II) would require not only large armies, but large productive forces, as well.

In the years since World War II, the United States has been involved to some extent in several of these "conventional" engagements. One (Korea) was comparatively large; three (Iran, Guatemala, and Cuba) were very small, and made even smaller for Americans, perhaps, by the fact that others did the fighting. The United States has come close—how close depending on your informant and your credulity—to military action (which would probably have been "conventional") in four other areas (Indo-China, Quemoy and Matsu, Laos, Berlin) and has sent conventional armed forces into two other areas: Lebanon and Southeast Asia.

This type of military activity may continue for some time. Whether any "conventional" warfare involving a Great Power (i.e., one possessing nuclear, biological, or gas weapons capable of mass annihilation) will ever again attain the magnitude of the Korean conflict without evolving into a "nonconventional" war—one in which resort is had to weapons of mass annihilation —is a matter for speculation. It seems doubtful that the Korean War could have lasted as long as it did and on the scale that it did if the United States had not at that time possessed a nuclear monopoly. In a comparable war today, the threat of the losing government's turning in desperation to "nonconventional" weapons, especially if its homeland were invaded, would hang over both sides and affect the entire conduct of hostilities.

Still, "conventional" wars of lesser magnitude than the Korean War should not be ruled out as a possibility—nor, for that matter, should ones of the same or even greater magnitude. Wars of this kind must figure in any calculation of military needs for a country whose leaders are committed to a policy of retaining for it a position of prime military power. There is no denying that a large population is one of the enabling conditions for waging (or threatening to wage) limited wars. But does it follow that we in the United States must have a still larger population to strengthen our hand? We would judge not, and for these reasons: first, the heightened destructiveness of "conventional" weapons; second, the much greater relative military importance of the economic, as opposed to the purely demographic, variables; third, the fact that further population growth in the United States would bring with it problems of an economic and social nature the solutions to which, insofar as they were possible, would reduce the amount of the nation's energy, resources, and time available for allocation to military pursuits.

The diffusion of weapons of mass destruction may well lead to a revolution in the conduct of war. It seems likely that wars using "conventional" weapons will tend either to last but a short period of time (measured more in weeks or, at most, months, rather than in years) and be waged not for "total victory" but for limited ends, or that they will lead eventually to the use of weapons capable of annihilation on a mass scale. Never again is a Great Power likely to wage war with massed armies on a battlefield. The military unit which is now more suited to the exigencies of the limited-war-backed-by-threat-of-annihilation era is not millions of conscripts massed on predetermined borders, but, rather, a much smaller, exceptionally well-trained and disciplined force, armed with the most deadly of light weapons and organized into highly mobile units capable of being transported at a moment's notice to any "trouble spot" in the world. And how many people would this specialized fighting force require for both its personnel and their provision?—surely no more than could be made available in any industrialized country or alliance of industrialized countries with Davis' minimum population of 60 million.

Science and technology, while they have enhanced the potential power of statesmen and generals, have steadily reduced the direct military importance of the individual soldier. This they have done by increasing his "firepower" (that is, his ability to kill human beings, for let us not delude ourselves with such euphemisms as "bombing cities," "sinking ships," "knocking out tanks," "downing planes," "wiping out machine gun nests"). Vast differences in killing power separate the automatic rifle equipped with telescopic lens from its crossbow ancestor; the intercontinental missile from the cannonball; and the thermonuclear warhead containing three times the total of all the explosives used in World War II from the "little" bombs that killed 170,000 and seriously injured another 170,000 people in Hiroshima and Nagasaki.[9]

Coincident with the declining military importance of the individual as a wielder of arms has been a heightening of his military importance as a producer of arms. Rockets, missiles, nuclear-powered submarines, and all the other paraphernalia of modern warfare require far more precision and complexity in their manufacture than did the rifles and cannon of that less destructive era of two decades ago—just as these in their turn required far more precision in manufacture than the crossbows, battle axes, and staves with which men of still earlier ages did in one another. Even so—in terms of today's population size— the manpower requirements for the production of these weapons are quite modest. Though it was customary during World War II to define "war work" in the broadest of terms,* the actual number engaged in military pursuits—the fighters, those who supplied them, and those who took care of them—pared down to the essentials, could hardly have exceeded 5 to 10 percent of the adult population.[10] In today's nuclear age this proportion would be even lower—though in the event of a nuclear "exchange," nearly everyone would be victimized, either directly (through death or permanent disablement) or indirectly (through the death of loved ones and genetic damage from exposure to radiation).

But it is not just the introduction of nuclear weapons that has diminished the military effectiveness of sheer numbers. The whole of modern military technology—the airplane, the missile, the flame thrower, the napalm bomb, the automatic rifle—has had this effect to some extent. No longer does a substantial population differential between countries at comparable levels of technological development indicate a considerable difference, also, in military might. These weapons, like the six-shooter in the Western movie, have become "equalizers." The ultimate "equalizers" are, of course, the nuclear, gas, and biological weapons. If controls are not soon devised, the fact that they cost relatively little to produce, require little manpower to manu-

---

* This was apparently done on the assumption it would raise morale. Newspaper correspondents, professional athletes, movie and radio entertainers were only among the better-publicized members of a category broad enough almost always to include local politicians and in some instances even dance hall proprietors, street cleaners, and real estate brokers.

facture, and can be technologically diffused with relative ease will spread this lethal "equality" to every continent and every major country in the world—and undoubtedly to some minor ones as well. Solely from the standpoint of the capacity to kill and destroy, the United States, the Soviet Union, and the United Kingdom, with their respective nuclear stockpiles and means for delivering nuclear weapons, are in no need of any further strength of the kind that in another age might have been presumed to come from population increase.

What, then, about the defensive capacity of the United States? If this country needs no more people to improve its offensive military position, might not additional numbers be needed to improve its capacity for survival in the event of a nuclear (or biological or gas) attack upon it? Such a question is prompted by fears based on the simple arithmetic of nuclear destruction: an attack that kills 50 million people will remove one-fourth of a population of 200 million, one-fifth of a population of 250 million, and "only" one-sixth of a population of 300 million. The use of such a ratio to determine the proportion who would survive overlooks both the nature of the devastation these weapons are capable of and the ecological patterns of the people of the United States. It assumes that the potential of such weapons is to be measured primarily in the *numbers* of people they will destroy rather than in the *area* in which they are lethal. Only if the population of the United States were more or less evenly dispersed throughout the country might a larger population result in a larger number of survivors. The chance of survival would probably be greatest for people living close to the land and away from large cities. Yet, as we have seen, population in the United States is tending toward ever greater concentration in the large metropolitan areas and their surrounding suburbs. The proportion living in rural areas has steadily diminished as our numbers have increased. With a weapon's destructive radius remaining the same, and the number of people within that lethal radius increasing, a larger population may merely succeed in increasing the number who will die, be disabled, or need succor after the blast.

A larger population could, in fact, render a people more vulnerable, and even less capable of recuperation, by making it far more difficult to care for the injured and limit the spread of disease—to say nothing of meeting the need for food, clothing, and shelter. Some difficulties high population density would present to recovery following a nuclear attack are suggested in the estimates made by a group of physicians and physicists associated with the medical schools and universities of the Boston area concerning health problems following a hypothetical 20-megaton attack on Boston. The model adopted for these estimates is the 1446-megaton attack on the continental United States featured in the 1959 civil defense hearings of the Joint Congressional Committee on Atomic Energy, of which Boston's share is 20 megatons. The explosion is assumed to take place at ground level, thus minimizing the effects of blast and fire, though creating severe local fallout.

Somewhere between 739,000 and 2.24 million people have been killed outright. Among the dead are 4,850 physicians. The 640 physicians who have escaped without injury, assisted by the 260 physicians not incapacitated by their injuries, now face the task of caring for between 900,000 and 1.53 million injured. With 1,000 to 1,700 injured persons per doctor, "most of the fatally injured persons will never see a physician, even for the simple administration of narcotics. . . . Many of those injured who might survive with adequate care will also die. . . ." The sorting out of the more "salvageable" injured will be "made even more difficult by the presence of radiation injury. . . ."

In the aftermath of the catastrophe the authors foresee unprecedented public health problems: "It is likely that the vectors of epidemic disease would survive radiation injury

better than the human population. Eastern equine enceph-
alitis, hepatitis, poliomyelitis and other endemic disease
could easily reach epidemic proportions under these circumstances."[11]

The symposium concludes with the recommendation that
physicians explore "a new area of preventive medicine, the
prevention of thermonuclear war."

The idea that greater numbers can give a society a better
chance for survival rests on certain rather dubious assumptions
about the nature of nuclear (gas, biological) war itself: (1) the
governments of the United States, the Soviet Union, or any
other country that gains possession of this weapon would be
willing to sacrifice this many of its citizens in some gamble over
international power (for, if the origin of the attack can be
determined, retaliation is almost sure to follow); (2) the effects
of radiation, loss of oxygen, plague, gas, and so on could be
contained enough to permit the survival of sufficient numbers
from among those not killed outright; (3) enough of the social
fabric could be salvaged to enable the human survivors to meet
their individual needs for biologic maintenance, social order,
and the motivation to survive and do those things necessary for
survival;* and (4) the attacking forces could be prevented or
dissuaded from attacking a second, or third, or fourth, . . . or
nth time.

As Winfield W. Riefler, Chairman at the time of the Social

---

* Herman Kahn (*On Thermonuclear War*. Princeton: Princeton University
Press, 1960) asks, "Will the living envy the dead?" The problem of motivation
should not be minimized, nor should that of maintaining order—as the history
of looting, rapine, and murder in the wake of calamity amply attests. Societies
have survived the loss of substantial proportions of their numbers, as during the
mediaeval plagues, for example. But this was never as sudden as a nuclear
attack and, perhaps far more important, the societies affected were always predominantly rural (in the sense that the overwhelming majority lived on the land)
and, hence, possessed a much readier access to the sources of supply. Moreover,
the soil and other natural resources were left intact: there was no radioactive
fallout.

Science Research Council's Committee on Social and Economic Aspects of Atomic Energy, has pointed out in his preface to a book by Professor Ansley J. Coale of Princeton:

> . . . In contrast to normal divergencies in viewpoint, the scientists who developed the [atomic] bomb have been as one, first, in their warning that there is no defense against its destructive power except widespread decentralization or deep underground shelter, and second, in their admonition that survival depends upon effective international control of this new and terrifying force.[12]

In this book, written in what in our Atomic Age might be described as the Early Mediaeval Period (that is, after Nagasaki, but before Hydrogen), Professor Coale concludes:

> The attempt to reduce casualties and to speed postwar recovery is the most difficult and discouraging aspect of vulnerability reduction in unlimited atomic warfare. . . .
>
> Suppose that, as a protective measure, a wholesale redistribution of population were able to relocate the 50,000,000 at present in the 200 largest cities into more than 1,000 cities, none with a population in excess of 50,000. . . . [A]ssuming that the new urban centers had been planned with a lower density of population, the casualties would be considerably fewer. Unfortunately, however, it seems a plausible conjecture that an increase in number of bombs would be much more easily effected by other nations than a drastic alteration in the distribution of people by this country. The cost of the relocation under consideration has been estimated at $250 billion; at $1 million apiece for atomic bombs and a similar cost for long-range carriers, 10,000 bombs and carriers could be constructed at 8 percent of the cost of relocation. Thus while relocation was being accomplished, other powers might well find it within their capacity to reduce greatly its effectiveness. Deep underground construction of all urban buildings would probably

promise greater reduction in casualties, though it would presumably be even more costly than relocation. The greatest
obstacle—and it seems insurmountable—to the rapid accomplishment of either of the measures is that either would require
a revolutionary interference by the government in individual
choices, a revolution for which popular support can hardly be
envisaged."[13]

[Note: Coale is talking about bombs with destructive capacities only about 4/100 that of bombs tested by the Soviet Union
in November, 1961.]

We cannot mark time while waiting for additions to our
population—even if these additions could be counted on to
make us stronger. The threat of nuclear, or equally annihila-
tive, war is *here now*. To advocate, whether by a change in population or some other means, a society that could be presumed
capable of surviving a nuclear holocaust is the ultimate in
defeatist, chimerical approaches to the realities of international
politics. Modern weapons of mass destruction have rendered
obsolete the idea of "total victory." No nation would benefit
from nuclear (or biological, or gas) war. Whatever the means
necessary to prosecute such a program, the way to national
survival lies not in increasing the potential number of soldiers
and survivors but in the avoidance of military engagements
themselves, particularly those involving the use of weapons of
mass destruction. We cannot rely on human numbers to ensure
either military victory or the survival of our social system against
military attack.

9

The "Selective Control"

Argument

OUR POPULATION DIFFICULTIES (and many others as well) would be solved, according to the "selective control" argument, if we could but change the *distribution* of births. Advocates of this approach to population growth are concerned less with a population's absolute size than with what they define as its quality. Their fear is that a society-wide limitation of births, cutting across all classes, races, income groups, would necessarily lead to a deterioration of the national stock—or, at least, to its failure to improve itself. If population control must come, those of this persuasion would prefer that it be selective: sharp curtailment of parenthood among the inferior or less desirable, with possibly even an encouragement of parenthood among the superior or more desirable. Quite apart from any formal eugenic theory concerning the consequences of extensive birth control for the quality of a population, the feeling seems widespread among the more privileged groups in our society that there must be relatively greater breeding among the socially desirable in order to counteract the supposedly higher natality of social ciphers and liabilities.

Whatever the trait considered desirable—IQ, skin color, income, social class, educational level—there are several difficulties inherent in the "selective control" approach that make it an essentially unsound alternative to general population limitation. There is, first of all, the injustice of demanding unequal sacrifices from the various segments of a society. There is also the obvious problem for a democracy of selecting the traits to be emphasized. Establishing a scale of "socially useful" characteristics would necessarily involve the ranking of all members of the society according to the value preferences of a few. A further difficulty would be determining which individuals actually embodied the desirable traits in proper proportion. And overall, is the question of whether parents with these traits can necessarily be relied upon to transmit them to their progeny.

One of the traits consistently considered most important to the level of population quality has been intelligence—a trait which, incidentally, illustrates most of the difficulties and weaknesses of the "selective control" approach. The conviction that a need exists for a social reallocation of family size is strengthened by studies purporting to show that the differential birth rate of the past several decades must ineluctably have led to a decline in the intelligence of the general population. Three kinds of evidence are offered in support of this conclusion: first, the inverse relationship between family size and social and economic status; second, a supposedly inverse relationship between family size and intelligence; and, third, the assumption of a direct relationship between intelligence and social and economic status. Combining these three has led to fear that the dull were outbreeding the gifted.

Professor Otis Dudley Duncan, sociologist of the University of Chicago, vigorously refutes this hypothesis and offers a more optimistic prognosis for the future intelligence level of our population.[1] Noting that the experts are far from unanimous in their interpretation of the various test results giving rise to this fear, and that the research tool used—the intelligence test—is a highly dubious means for determining actual differences in intellectual capacity, he goes on to point out two other reasons for not taking these test results at face value. The first of these is that trends in various traits one would expect to be correlated with trends in intelligence (if low levels in the latter are, indeed, associated with lower social and economic status and with larger family size), have not only failed to materialize, but have, in fact, shown a persistent movement in a direction opposite to what would be expected from these pessimistic assumptions of a biological Gresham's Law. Life expectancy, stature, general health levels, for instance, each of which is directly correlated with social and economic position, have all risen considerably at precisely the time when higher population increase among the "unfit" ought, instead, to have caused them to decline.

But Duncan's second—and far more telling—reason for rejecting these claims of intellectual deterioration is "the fact that, not only does no direct evidence exist to confirm the existence of such a trend, but what direct evidence there is shows the opposite movement toward a *rise* in the average level of measured intelligence!"[2] So far as population quality is concerned, he writes, "the more important problems at the present time lie in the *known* wastage of *available* ability, rather than in the *hypothetical* loss of *potential* ability."[3]

A variant of this anxiety about deteriorating national intelligence is seen in the notion that a declining or stable population would mean fewer exceptionally gifted individuals—that is, fewer leaders, fewer scientists, fewer inventors, fewer geniuses. In this rather quantitative approach to population quality, a growing population is favored not for itself, but for the increment of creative types it is believed will result from it. The implication is that such persons are born, not made, and that to have more of them there must be more people.

> [E]veryone . . . would take for granted that New York State receives many more patents than Rhode Island, because it has many more people. Thus, when our country is five times as populated as it is today, shall we not be making necessary adaptive inventions fives times as fast (e.g., in hydroponics and synthetic food), other things being equal? To be sure, other things will not be equal, . . . but American inventing, according

to my own measurements, has been increasing rather steadily since 1880 at a rate of 5.8 per cent per year compounded, which makes 110-fold, or 4.14 times faster than the population . . .[4]

No claim is made that mere numerical growth will increase the *proportion* of the population with these "desirable" qualities. Only their *number* will be enlarged. But since, by definition, these "desirable" persons have more social energy—or some other similarly esoteric quality—it is assumed that they will through the products of their creativity and leadership affect the social setting by some variant of the geometric progression, instead of the merely arithmetic progression of everyone else.

Were we to assume this kind of relationship between sheer numbers and various personality and intellectual types, we could just as reasonably claim that population growth would bring us more juvenile delinquents, more criminals, more psychopaths, wife-beaters, uncreative deadweight. It would be hoped, of course, that the social contributions of the leaders and innovators would be enough to outweigh the harmful, antisocial effects of these others. But there might be some anxious moments, nonetheless.

The real weakness of this view, and also of the previous one about declining national intelligence, is that they give primary importance to biological mechanisms in the transmission of characteristics that are incalculably affected by the social and cultural environment. They either underestimate or derogate to a position of only minor significance all those social and cultural conditions which both stimulate behavior and place limits upon it. And this applies to philosophy, art, literature, science, politics, religion—in fact, to every creative activity of man—every bit as much as it does to leadership and technological achievement. How many Italians does it take to produce a Michelangelo or Leonardo? How many Jews a Hillel or Jesus?

How many Indians a Gandhi? How many Japanese an Ito? How many Americans a Jefferson?

In the space of but 50 years, Athens, a little city-state of 120,000 to 180,000 people[5] (less than one-one thousandth of the present population of the United States) produced such men as Pericles, Aeschylus, Sophocles, Euripides, Aristophanes, Socrates, Thucydides, Phidias, and the architects of the Parthenon.[6] With but four million, the United States produced Washington, Jefferson, the Adamses, Franklin, Madison, Monroe, and the rest of that group of statesmen which, in both number and creativity, has probably had no equal since the founding of the Republic. Would there be more people like these if we had a larger population? Or does the explanation for their emergence lie elsewhere—in the "stage" and the "script" they had to work with, for instance?

It is no disparagement of the individual to recognize that his personality is to a very considerable extent a social product: a product, that is, of continual interaction between himself and the others in his society. Parents, siblings, peers, teachers, neighbors, even those with whom he comes in contact only through the media of mass communication, all play their part in molding his personality. The way he acts (or the fact that he fails to act) in any given circumstance is invariably shaped by the combination of what is possible with what is permissible: of the *possible* range of variation with the *allowable* range of variation. The former, though including the universal limitations and possibilities summed up in the laws of physics, chemistry, and biology, is to a considerable extent a social product, too, as it also consists of knowledge, skills, and their material products. The latter, however, is entirely social in origin, being the sum of cultural values and mores (i.e., all the ideas of right and wrong, desirable and undesirable, good and bad, true and false, beautiful and ugly, pleasureful and distressful that one learns as a member of the society). Applying this principle of social determination to invention and discovery leads to a recognition that every inventor not only builds upon the accumulation of things which have gone before, but must also owe to a happy combination of circumstances the opportunity to exercise his special gifts. As the late anthropologist, Ralph Linton, commented, "It is interesting to conjecture what Mr. Edison's contribution to culture would have been if he had been born a serf in central Europe in the twelfth century."[7]

Of course, an inventor or discoverer may seem to be considerably ahead of his culture. The notebooks of Leonardo da Vinci contain a number of completely practicable designs for projects which did not see fruition till much later—aerial bomb, diver's apparatus, helicopter, hydraulic screw, jack, machine gun, military tank, and light projector, for example.[8] But in every instance the materials or ideas out of which these inventions evolved were already a part of the culture. And in every instance whether they were incorporated into the rest of the culture was determined not so much by the specific merits of the proposals themselves as by the interests of the society at the time and the supporting power of the culture base. When in 1765, James Watt invented his steam engine, it was in response to a widely recognized need. Yet he had to wait another ten years to manufacture it because of the insufficient development of mechanical knowledge and skill. Nor is this the only indication that there was more to the invention of the steam engine than can be explained by reference to the fertile mind of James Watt.

> [T]he steam engine too illustrates the law that invention in the last analysis is a social product. There were reasons why it came in the 1760's from the brain of a Scotsman for the service of mines. Science was in the air and had been from the time the Royal Society was founded in 1662. Before 1700 Isaac Newton had elucidated the laws of gravitation and light

and Richard Boyle had demonstrated the relation between the pressure of a gas and its volume. Watt . . . associated on level terms with Priestley and Cavendish, who were revolutionising chemistry, and with his Glasgow friend and adviser Professor John Black, the discoverer of the phenomenon of latent heat . . .[9]

And why should science have been in the air in 18th century England and (more especially) Scotland? For one thing, upward social mobility in these countries had "reached a degree higher than that of any earlier, or perhaps any succeeding, age, thus increasing the availability of tangible rewards for creative efforts."[10] For another, religious dissent took a turn that emphasized education and, what was of particular importance, education not only in theology and literature, but in mathematics, bookkeeping, geography, French, and natural science. Moreover, the universities of Scotland and the nonconformist academies of England were fortunate in having a number of outstanding teacher-scientists, among them Joseph Black, John Dalton, and Joseph Priestley, men whose individual worth to science is perhaps to be gauged as much by the activities of their many outstanding students as it is by their more direct contributions. The exclusion of Dissenters from the English universities, and from office in government and administration, doubtless heightened the attraction of industry and trade as an outlet for their abilities. Add the fact of rapid economic change, which made possible an early assessment of the more "practical" possibilities in any scientific or technological novelty, and we have at least some of the more important conditions underlying this heretofore unprecedented scientific and technological ferment.[11]

During this rich scientific period England had a population of about six million and Scotland, where the scientific output at the time was even greater, a population of less than one million. If we want a faster rate of invention and discovery, a greater literary and artistic outpouring, a higher proportion of genuine statesmen among those who occupy positions of leadership, we should direct our efforts to creating the social environment in which these are most likely to occur, rather than hoping that numerical increase will somehow compensate for the inadequacies of the social and cultural conditions. How many potential Jeffersons do we lose because we calumniate our politicians and give a higher reward to the man who can think up "LS/MFT"; how many Einsteins because our colleges seek the kind of "well-rounded man" who, as one director of admissions at an Ivy League college put it (in describing the type he himself looked for), "will be in charge of the Community Chest drive 15 years after graduation"; how many Newtons because of our fatuous paranoia over "security"?*

But probably the preponderance of those who forward the "selective control" argument are thinking less about the national stock than about maintaining or enlarging the relative size of the groups they prefer. Their aversion to general population limitation springs from the specter of a shrinkage of these groups. Thus, they assert that certain groups in the society are patently superior and should be persuaded to have more children. If the less qualified can at the same time be persuaded to have fewer, then so much the better. This idea is often expressed by members of racial or religious groups who have a preference for their own sort that makes numerical increase seem desirable for its own sake, or who equate increases in size with increases in power. In more recent years it has seemed most convenient when one wished to serve a specific class bias: a preference for the college graduate, the higher income group, the occupants of professional and managerial positions. Increases in these groups are justified by one of two assumptions:

* On the other hand, maybe we should also ask how many Gandhis are we creating in the lunch counter sit-ins and "freedom rides"?

either that the children of the preferred group are inherently superior, or that their parents will offer them a superior environment—however "superior" may happen in the circumstances to be defined. At the moment, the latter assumption seems particularly in vogue, the contention being that, innately superior or not, those who are richer, or have had more schooling, are in a better position to raise socially desirable children. The claim is not that such people are necessarily better parents, but simply that they are better able to provide for their children's development. Whether or not the biological inheritance of these groups is superior, so goes the theory, the social inheritance must surely be. Once this is assumed, it is an easy step to the notion that these privileged groups should—in fact, are almost obligated to—increase the number of their children in order to help counterbalance the effect of excess reproduction on the part of those less privileged and therefore, ostensibly, less qualified.

If these assumptions were valid, then there would indeed be some grounds for maintaining that our national stock could be improved and our population problems lessened by allowing unlimited reproduction to a select few while strictly curtailing the reproduction of everyone else. Obviously, the interests of both children and society are ill served by the birth of children to "unfit" parents. But who is fit and who is unfit is often difficult enough to determine on strictly biological grounds, let alone on the basis of social attributes, such as income, occupation, years of schooling, religion, race, or ethnic group.

What, then, of the first assumption, that some people are innately superior to others? Debate on this question still goes on. Since it is one of the foundation stones of the selective control approach, let us examine in some detail the evidence on which this assumption rests.

That individuals have different physical and mental capacities should be obvious. That certain of these differences rest in part on inherited characteristics is an accepted biological tenet. But to proceed from this to an assumption of innate superiority for certain families, certain racial stocks, or certain social groups is wholly unwarranted by the available evidence. This is despite the fact that two kinds of "evidence" can be cited in support of this claim: cultural differences and differential scores on "intelligence" tests.

Take first the considerable difference between cultures. Can we say that these result from innate differences between peoples—particularly in their intellects, in their inherent capacities to learn and create? Can we say, for example, that the American Indian's technological development failed to attain the metalworking stage of the European because of some genetic difference between the two peoples; that the Spartans and their Athenian neighbors developed along such different political and social lines because of different biological inheritances; that the technologically backward Germans of 150 years ago were a different race from the technologically advanced Germans of the twentieth century? To ask the question is almost to answer it. Nothing we know about either human intelligence or human behavior permits us to draw the conclusion that the members of one society are inherently incapable of learning what is known to the members of another. Nor is there anything to suggest the existence of certain inborn personality or character traits in the members of any group that will manifest themselves irrespective of the cultural setting. The acculturation of immigrants affords ample evidence of this. But the most dramatic examples are probably those in which a child born into one group has been reared to membership in another. One such case is that of a two-year-old girl abandoned by her tribe, the Guayake, of central Paraguay. Discovered by a professor at Lima University, Peru, who happened to be exploring in the region, she was taken back to Lima and there raised as a part of the professor's family. By the age of seventeen this girl had become "a brilliant student of biology, and her teachers and associates were predicting an outstanding career for her in that field of intellectual endeavor." Yet the tribe in which she started life and from which she received her biological inheritance possessed but a Stone Age culture and subsisted on honey and wild beasts![12] The difference between what she became in Lima and what she would have become had she remained with the Guayake was cultural, not biological; learned, not inherited.

If the capacity to learn has no biological referant so far as groups are concerned (it obviously has some bearing on the learning capacity of individuals within these groups), what then of the capacity to *create?* Surely there must be group differences here. Think of all the American inventors—Morse, Bell, Edison, Steinmetz, Westinghouse, Fulton, Pullman, Colt, the Wright Brothers. Where are their counterparts in Africa or India? Or look at the figures in Table 3 on page 32. Those who enjoy the highest material levels of living, the highest rates of productivity, the greatest longevity live in countries settled largely by people of northwestern European, and particularly British, stock. Does not this indicate some kind of innate superiority—if not of intellect, then at least of creativity?

Creativity takes many forms. Every part of culture was at some time the creation of man; and many items have been created and then lost again by peoples whose heredity remained essentially unchanged. What one finds in a list of patents, for example, represents only one part of cultural invention. No one patents a new linguistic form, a new religious belief, a new pedagogical method, mathematical construct, dance form, scientific theory, or agricultural technique.

Can one measure the amount of creativity it takes to invent one or another of these forms? For that matter, who would assert that the development of the reaper was more important than the development of crop agriculture; that the development of the printing press was more important than the development of the alphabet? Material and technological invention lend themselves more readily to evaluation in quantitative terms. Hence, in any comparison between societies, those with the more rapid rates of technological invention will appear at superficial first glance to be the more inventive, while those whose inventiveness takes a more political, social, nonmaterial direction will be statistically relegated to second place. In such fashion do contemporary western European societies take precedence in comparisons with other societies: not because of some special hereditary inventiveness; but because of the cultural materials their members have to work with and the particular kinds of developments they consider necessary and desirable. Just as there is no justification for crediting certain societies with an intellectual level superior to that of certain others, so also is there no justification for believing them superior in creativity.

Further evidence for the cultural basis of creativity can be seen in the numerous instances of simultaneous and independent discovery and invention. These suggest that, given a culture broad enough and a felt need strong enough, the invention or discovery will follow and be adopted by the society. The broader the culture base in any aspect of culture—religion, medicine, textile machinery, for example—the greater the opportunities for additional development in that quarter. If Edison, Marconi, Bell had not done it, somebody else would have. In fact, somebody else often did—the ascription of priority to one or the other indicating more about a people's chauvinism, perhaps, than about their inventiveness.

"Who invented the telegraph?" asks Gilfillan. "Any American who has been through the eighth grade knows that it was Morse and Vail, in 1844. But there was an English commercial line seven years earlier, and the Germans credit the telegraph to Sömmering, of Munich, in 1809, and in Switzerland there was an electric telegraph in 1774, and one was proposed in Scotland in 1753. The matter becomes rather confusing for the eighth grade. . ."[13]

Moreover, most inventive activity is probably unconscious and most certainly piecemeal: a slight change in design here; a slight change in usage there; the different combination of two or more items already in existence.

"A great invention," Gilfillan continues, "is not a completed product, issuing at one time from the brain of one inventor. It is a multitudinous collection of little inventions, and is a growth of centuries. Had a single inventor to make the whole, he would need more hands than a monkey, more lives than a cat and more inventive genius than Pallas, Hermes and Loki combined."[14] Nor has this been altered by the recent bureaucratization of certain developmental processes in technology and medicine—itself a noteworthy invention, by the way (though hardly of the kind for which one secures a patent).

But however important invention and discovery, of far greater import to the development of a culture is *diffusion*—the transfer of culture elements from one society to another. How much borrowing will occur, and the character of the items acquired in this manner, will depend upon the nature and frequency of contact with others and, as with the adoption of inventions and discoveries, upon the culture base of the people doing the borrowing. It is no mere chance that the cities where ancient trade routes crossed were also the sites of the most rapid cultural change. We can never know exactly what proportion of a particular culture is the result of inventions and discoveries made by members of the society possessing it. Professor Linton estimated this to be never more than 10 percent. But there can be little doubt that if each group had had to create every element of its culture—borrowing nothing from other groups—the process of cultural development would probably have been so slow as to permit no people to advance beyond the level of the Old Stone Age.[15] The most primitive peoples of today (judged by Western standards) are those, like the Australian aborigines and the Kalahari bushmen, who for one reason or another have remained largely isolated from contact with other cultures.

To credit one's own society, or race, or ethnic group with a high degree of inventiveness or with a high level of intellect may have its psychic rewards. The imputation of superiority to oneself and one's group, and of inferiority to outsiders, is one of the commonest defenses of man. Some—the Navajo, for example—even use the same word to denote themselves that they use to mean "people," everyone else presumably falling somewhat short of humanity. But whether these ethnocentric ideas are entertained by Americans, Russians, or Navajos, the fact remains that every people has depended greatly upon borrowings from others for the development of its culture.

Quite apart from the terms in which creativity is to be defined, there is another important consideration to any comparison between cultures: time. Those who wish to account for cultural differences by some theory of biological determinism will receive little support from observing the frequency with which societies have undergone extensive cultural change within periods of time far too short to admit of biological change. Witness the differences between the United States of 1915 and that of 1963. At what point in a people's history do we take our developmental soundings? If we elected to compare only contemporaneous peoples we would be comparing not only mid-twentieth century Americans with mid-twentieth century Tanganyikans, mid-twentieth century Patagonians, mid-twentieth century Swedes, but also the Greeks of Periclean Athens with their contemporaries, the wild primitive forebears of today's Britons; the Italians of the early Renaissance with the religious fear-ridden serfs of mediaeval Russia.

Nor can we strengthen the case for racial or ethnic superiority by making our comparisons, instead, only between peoples at the same stage of development; for each culture is unique, as is also the geographic and historical setting specific to it. The Arunta, a tribe of Australian bushmen, may look to us, *using the criteria of our own culture,* like a case of arrested technological and economic development. But though these aboriginal inhabitants of the Australian desert lack clothing and use only the crudest of tools, they "regulate their social relationships within a system of kinship so complex that it required the efforts of two generations of anthropologists to unravel its subtleties. These people have intelligence and use it very well; it is simply that they do not use it in the same ways we do. . ."[16] Some societies show considerable development in technology, others in music, literature, or navigation. With some, development proceeds furthest in religion, government, warfare, kinship structure; while with others, like the Arunta and the Eskimo, it takes the form of an ingenious adaptation to extremely harsh physical conditions.

If the cultural differences between peoples cannot be taken as clear evidence of any group's innate superiority or inferiority, what, then, of that other source of "evidence": differential scores on intelligence tests? Where these tests have been applied, they have shown generally consistent differences between Negroes and whites, Europeans and non-Europeans. Can we assume that these differentials indicate actual differences in intellectual capacity?

Though the word "intelligence" is often used in connection with them, it is quite certain that these tests do not actually measure intelligence. About as much as can be claimed for them is that when applied to some groups of school children and to feeble-minded adults, they probably measure more or less adequately certain important intellectual aptitudes.[17] Whether or not "intelligence" is to be cynically defined as "what intelligence tests test," it is undoubtedly true that what intelligence tests do measure most reliably is an individual's ability (and willingness) to perform those tasks that any particular test consists of: word associations, the learning of nonsense syllables, the backward repetition of a series of numbers, construction with building blocks, and so on. Since "school performance is the criterion to which the great majority of intelligence tests predict and against which they are validated,"[18] it is hardly surprising to learn that they do a remarkably good job of actually predicting "school performance" (i.e., grades) in that kind of school situation against which the tests were validated.

It is essential that we recognize in any interpretation of these scores that the traits thus measured, however adequately, are only a few of the many that comprise what in everyday life we call "intelligence." It is also essential that the persons whose scores are to be compared should have had a similar cultural experience. It is this latter qualification—the importance of similar cultural experiences—that makes essentially meaningless any cross-cultural comparison of scores. No test yet devised is "culture fair." Nor is it likely that any test could be. If they have a certain, though limited, utility in the American school system, intelligence tests surely have none as indicators of relative intellectual prowess between persons reared in different cultural environments. For cultural learning pervades nearly all human mental activity. Substantial differences between cultures exist not only in what one learns, but in how and when one learns it and in the way in which he actually thinks and goes about tackling a problem.

In some cultures abstract thinking (thinking with mathematical symbols, for example) is a commonplace, while in others it may occur but seldom. In some, our Western notion of time, of "beating the clock," does not exist at all. Yet since all intelligence tests stipulate a certain length of time for their completion, differences in the evaluation of speed of performance will invariably be a source of considerable difference in scores. Professor Otto Klineberg of Columbia University, after testing several groups of Indian and Negro children in the United States and comparing their scores with those of white children, concluded, "there is evidence that the superiority of white over Indian and Negro children in preformance tests is largely, if not entirely, a superiority in scores for *time*. There is no superiority, and in some cases an inferiority, in the scores [of white children] for *accuracy* of performance."[19]

Another important cultural difference is motivation. Everyone is motivated to do some things and to refrain from doing others. In some non-Western societies children (or adults, for that matter) may not be motivated to do well those kinds of tasks which comprise an intelligence test. As Professors Leighton and Kluckhohn of Harvard concluded upon finding that Navajo children who had gone to school averaged far higher on a particular test than did those who had not gone to school: "It would be incorrect to claim that schooling makes the children more intelligent: rather it helps them to mobilize their own ability so that they can do well on the Arthur test. . . . [Only in school do they have real experience with pencils and toys and] familiarity with being told by a strange white person to do an apparently senseless task."[20]

Nor does every society put a premium on excelling one's peers, or even on "doing one's best." In fact, in some there are special mechanisms by which the person who happens to find himself in a superior position is enabled to climb gracefully down from it to become once again coequal with his fellows.

Thus, the use of intelligence tests, as now constituted, to indicate intellectual differences between peoples from different cultures must be ruled out on grounds of noncomparability. If the members of certain racial or cultural groups (however defined) are inherently superior to the members of certain other groups, it has yet to be proved. Certainly no proof is to be found in either of the two sets of "evidence"—cultural differences and scores on intelligence tests—from which a scientifically valid proof might most conceivably have been derived.

Recognition of the inadequacies of intelligence testing on the grosser cross-cultural level does not always find its counterpart when it comes to comparisons between members of different groups within the same society. There are still those willing to leap to facile conclusions about inherent superiority of one group over another on the basis of observed differences in test scores between, say, whites and Negroes, rural dwellers and urbanites, children of professional workers and children of manual laborers, when these groups come from the same society.

Yet the same kind of criticism levelled against the comparability of intelligence tests scores as *between* societies can be directed, also, at comparisons *within* societies. For what do differences in income, in father's occupation, in rural versus urban residence, in type of schooling, in race or ethnic group represent if not subcultural differences within the more general culture we label "American"? Can we really say that these will have the same cultural experiences: the white, college-graduated insurance salesman in Chicago and the uneducated Negro sharecropper in Greene County, Alabama; the upper middle class Jewish boy on New York's Central Park West and the son of Puerto Rican immigrants only one block away; the children of an auto worker in Detroit and those of an executive of the same company? Their opportunities in life, their incentives toward school work, the degree of encouragement they receive from family and teachers will all be markedly different.

These subcultural differences—in experience, motivation, rewards, and punishments—will find their way into performance on intelligence tests in exactly the same way as do those grosser differences which separate whole cultures. As long as present social relationships remain relatively unchanged (and

as long as there are no substantial changes, either, in the kinds
of tests administered), we shall continue to find higher average
group scores by the children of white collar and professional
workers as against those of manual workers; by children of college-educated parents; by children from higher income families; by whites as opposed to Negroes (though northern Negroes
often score higher, on the average, than do southern whites);
and by urban dwellers as against rural. We can also expect
the foreign-born to score lower, on the average, than the native-
born; persons of Italian or French-Canadian ancestry lower
than those of Jewish or Greek.

We will continue to find these different group scores not because of any innate biological differences between these groups,
but because the experiences of some will have prepared them
for doing a better job on these particular kinds of tests than
will the experiences of others.

Support for this conclusion is based on three kinds of observations pertaining both to the tests themselves and to the
experiences of different social groups which appear to affect
their skill in taking these tests. First, what the test results themselves show is ambiguous. Though various series of tests consistently turn up the same proportionate differences in group
scores, the scores represent, after all, only averages for the
group. The degree of overlapping is considerable, and the extreme scores in each group approximate those of the others.
Moreover, one's IQ seldom remains constant over time, and the
variations in it follow no "uniformly predictable pattern such
as one would expect of a hereditary characteristic which changed
along with the biological maturation process. In different
individuals the IQ may increase or decrease over time."[21] This
fact of unpredictability is, in itself, an important indication
that what goes into any particular test score derives from much
more than purely hereditary traits—if, indeed, it is affected at
all by hereditary traits, apart from those which find their ex-

pression in the subnormal intellects of idiots and imbeciles. Only here does the hereditary origin of at least some of the causal factors appear to be well established.

Possible sources of bias—even when the comparison is between groups within the same general cultural tradition—are numerous and well-documented. One source is the language used on these tests. The psychologists who devise them are, by definition, among the college-educated, professional minority. Differences in language may be a more obvious source of bias when it comes to the foreign-born and their children, but we should not overlook the substantial regional and class differences which also exist in this country. These represent a potential bias for any comparison between groups, however energetically the creator of a particular test may seek to eliminate it.

Another source of bias is in the kinds of questions asked and the problems presented. There is, for example, a bias against rural dwellers represented by the paucity of test items involving a knowledge of mechanical devices or a skill in handling them, both of which are in our society more prominent among farm and small town residents than among city dwellers. In fact, this is a source of bias, also, against the lower socio-economic groups. One study, in which a large array of intelligence tests was administered to all the available 10-year-olds and 16-year-olds in a Midwestern community, found among the younger group a high intercorrelation between all the tests and a consistent correlation, as well, with socio-economic status, including the results of a mechanical assembly test. But at age 16, though all other test scores correlated significantly with socio-economic status, the mechanical assembly test did not. Why? One explanation is that "mechanical ability is learned as a part of living in the American culture irrespective of school experience, whereas the other tests . . . are increasingly drawing upon the abstraction, judgment, reasoning, and vocabulary learned in school . . ."[22]

In other words, that rare kind of test—one not particularly related to schoolwork—produced no results correlated with socio-economic status when administered to a group of teen-agers, the very group most often differentiated by socio-economic status on the usual IQ test. It would appear from this and similar findings that the generally superior scores of children in the higher socio-economic levels owe less to some kind of innate superiority on their part than they do to the relatively greater success of these children within the school environment.

As we have already noted, intelligence tests are usually standardized on school grades. Items are accepted or rejected for a test largely on the grounds of whether they differentiate persons who get high grades from those who get low. What, then, determines grades? Intellect is one thing, of course, though it is by no means the only. Motivation, self-discipline, interest in the subject matter—all elements which result from the whole environmental situation in which the individual finds himself—invariably bulk large. So also does health, both physical and mental. Over all is the possibility of favoritism, sometimes in terms of grades themselves, but more probably in terms of the teacher's bestowal of personal attention.

The American public school is well known as a middle class institution: in the origins and values of its teachers, in the values it seeks to inculcate in its students, in the criteria for rewards and punishments, in the standards of conduct it requires. As such, it is in many ways a decidedly unreal and unrewarding environment for working-class children, who are, after all, a substantial proportion—if not a majority—of the children who pass through it. Much of what is taught there—mathematics beyond simple arithmetic, English grammar, music, art, geography, languages, history—has little or no apparent relation either to the everyday world of the working-class child or to the world to which he can most reasonably aspire as an adult.

Members of the working class not only tend to put less emphasis on the value of formal education,[23] the working-class parent generally offers his children less encouragement to do well in school. In fact, by stressing the "impracticality" of the curriculum, or by dwelling upon his own dissatisfaction with school, the working-class parent often actually puts a premium on his child's not doing well. The playmates of the working-class child, far more than those of the middle- and upper-class child, reinforce these antischool tendencies by attributing school success to currying favor with the teacher, or by labelling the good student a "sissy." Moreover, the level of aspiration has been found to be generally lower among those reared in lower class environments. The working-class child *expects* to do less well than the middle- or upper-class child, not only occupationally and economically (for which there is considerable supporting evidence, whatever our folklore about equality of opportunity), but also in such minor experimental tasks as dart throwing, which under only the most implausible of assumptions could be presumed to relate to social position.[24]

To do well in school, then, to acquire those skills which ensure higher scores on intelligence tests, the typical working-class boy or girl must overcome obstacles to which the typical middle- or upper-class child is but sparingly exposed. And, at least at the grammar and high school levels, there are generally few attributes of the working-class child's environment capable of exerting a countervailing pressure.

What we have said in explanation of test score differences between income and occupational groups applies, if anything, with even greater force to test score differences in the United States between whites on the one hand and Negroes, Puerto Ricans, Indians on the other. The great majority in each of these latter groups live under physical, economic, social, and psychological conditions no better—and often far worse—than those of the white working class. And the traits of their respective subcultures are even further removed from those of the middle- and upper-class white subculture on which these tests were standardized and to which they predict most accurately. The additional burden of racial discrimination and prejudice merely increases the likelihood of an inferior score by leading the victim to have a lower estimate of his own capacities.

In the face of the evidence of his superior cultural adaptation, the assumption that the middle- or upper-class child is also *biologically* superior to the lower-class child would seem an obvious conclusion. But, as we have seen, this is an erroneous interpretation. Intelligence test results tell us nothing definitive about inherent differences between groups. Until a test has been devised that can screen out the effects of cultural experience, the proponents of selective control will have to look elsewhere for scientifically valid evidence in support of their claims either that group differences in intelligence exist, or that these differences can be biologically transmitted.

However one defines the upper classes—whether on the basis of IQ, occupation, race, ethnic group, wealth, schooling, prestige, or some combination of these—if the children of these groups necessarily have superior intellects it has yet to be proved. Neither cultural differences nor differences between group scores on IQ tests afford this proof. Non-hereditary characteristics are important if not decisive in any test result and in any particular pattern of individual achievement.

More plausible is the contention that, innately superior or not, the better off, better schooled groups of our society are in a better position to raise "superior" children. Now, much sentimentalism exists about the virtues of poverty. Burns exclaims:

> The cottage leaves the Palace far behind;
> What is a lordling's pomp! a cumbrous load,
> Disguising oft the wretch of human kind,
> Studied in arts of Hell, in wickedness refin'd!
> —From "The Cotter's Saturday Night"

But as Galbraith notes, "Wealth is not without its privileges. The case to the contrary, though often made, has never proved widely persuasive." And Sophie Tucker evinces much the same idea with "I've been rich and I've been poor, and believe me, rich is the best."

Certainly the "life chances" of the middle- or upper-class child exceed those of the working-class child. Even while still in the womb he is less subject to malformations and fetal death because of the generally superior prenatal care accorded his mother. Once born, he is more likely to survive the first dangerous months and years of life, less likely to receive debilitating disease and injury as a youth or adult, less likely to die before his time. The ulcers, neuroses, psychoses, heart attacks of the middle and upper classes are amply publicized; but the incidences of these diseases are steadily higher as one goes down the socio-economic scale.[25]

As an adult, the child of upper- or middle-class parents is more likely to start employment at a higher rung on the "achievement" ladder; and he has a readier access to the higher paying, more prestigeful careers.[26] Related to this is the fact that he has a better chance of going further in school, too, regardless of his individual merits as a scholar. Taking the IQ as indicative of ability to do well in school (a valid use for it, since school performance is what IQ tests are standardized on), and father's occupation as the indicator of social position, a study of Boston high school boys found that at each IQ level, the sons of fathers in the top occupational category showed the highest proportion expecting to go to college, those of fathers in the second highest occupational category, the second highest proportion, and so on down through five occupational groupings. Among those boys in the top fifth on the basis of IQ, 89 percent of the sons of "major white collar" workers (the top occupational category) expected to go to college as against 29 percent of the sons of "other labor and service" workers (the lowest occupational category).[27]

Of course, "expecting to go" to college and actually going may be quite different things. Yet a study of Cleveland students, divided into three social classes and three IQ categories, found the same consistent relationship between parental class, IQ, and actual enrollment that the Boston study found between parental class, IQ, and expectations.[28]

But the superior "life chances" of the middle- or upper-class child do not in themselves indicate either that he will be a greater social asset or that he has received a superior upbringing at the hands of his parents. To determine this one would have to assess the importance of differences in values, styles of life, psychic environments. Certainly there are many such differences between individual families and also between various sections of our population. But whether they are so marked as to result in markedly different adult personalities is highly questionable. And even if they were, one can seriously question whether the social benefits to be derived from certain character traits assumed to result more commonly from the family milieu of a particular social group would necessarily be of such importance as to justify allowing that group the privilege of excess reproduction at the expense of the childbearing of others in the society. Are we sure we know what the most desirable character traits are? Even assuming a close correlation between differences in adult personality and differences in social origin, too much of whatever effect an individual has on society would seem to hinge on factors other than his character traits to justify a society's preference for reproduction in one group over that in another. From studies such as those above on college expectations and enrollments we learn far less about the qualifications of parents of different income groups to raise their children than we do about the crippling consequences of an environment of deprivation.

Class differences in, for example, childrearing practices do exist.[29] But no class or social grouping in this country is a homogeneous entity with respect to childrearing — or any other behavior pattern; and the overlap between them is considerable. As long as we maintain a fair amount of social mobility and have communications on a truly mass scale we can expect this intra-class heterogeneity to continue. Each class has been alternately praised and blamed for the childbearing practices assumed to be characteristic of it; and it is axiomatic that every segment of the society has undergone substantial changes in these practices. The scant data we have on adults precludes any systematic appraisal of the consequences of these different practices for behavior. In fact, such a study would be virtually impossible, if only because of the impossibility of separating one set of determinants from another. The family is important. But it is by no means the only agent in a child's development. However readily judges may berate the parents of juvenile delinquents for their offspring's transgressions, a child's misbehavior may owe less to his parents' actions than to some other influence, like the general character of the community, the children with whom he associates, or the spirit of the times.

When it comes to values themselves, we again find a good deal of heterogeneity within classes and considerable overlapping between them—although the differences between class "averages" may be substantial; and we also find occasional uncertainty about what values are really "best." Probably many a parent doubts whether some of the values of persons with whom he would be ranked socially are of the kind he wants to stress in bringing up his own children. One's own values are a consequence of all one's experiences, and they are always best— *by definition*. To choose larger family size as a means of increasing the number of adherents to these values overlooks alternative ways of achieving the same end. It also presumes a closer dependence between family and character than actually exists. The militarist son of a pacifist father, the loose daughter of a virtuous mother, the self-centered children of generous parents, the agnostic son of the manse are not just fictional types.

"You should have no more children than you can afford" is an admirable injunction. But does it follow today that "couples who can afford them should have more"? Does anyone really bear all the costs of supporting his children? Perhaps the taxes paid by a few—a very few—are substantial enough to meet the monetary costs of schooling, public health measures, roads, police and fire protection, and the many other services a community must provide for its citizens.*

But what of the mounting social costs to which we have already referred? The upper income groups may well pay higher taxes. But no group in our society can any longer repay all of the social costs entailed in reproduction in excess of replacement levels—the rich probably least of all; for their style of life, with its extra car, its "second house," larger property, greater amounts of travel, and generally more material possessions, requires a much higher consumption of those very things upon which population increase—in whatever class—places a premium: raw materials and space.

Obviously, in the achievement of overall population stability the most extensive changes in family size will have to come from those groups with the highest natality rates. And—on the average—these higher rates have been associated with the less privileged groups in our society. But must the right to bear children be distributed by the market mechanism? If one must, indeed, be born into a richer or better schooled family in order to have the opportunity to develop his potentialities more fully, or to make the maximum contribution to society, multiplying the children of the more privileged segments of the population is only one way to attain this end—and, we submit, one that is more wasteful of human resources than are the alternatives. Since better food, better health care, better working conditions

* We are not sure about even these few, however, as a sizable amount of the tax burden borne by the citizenry takes the form of taxes on business, which sums are, of course, ultimately paid by the individual through the kind of indirect sales tax consisting of higher prices.

would eliminate many of the *physical* disadvantages of being lower class, and greater educational opportunities, the removal of discrimination on racial and class lines, and the provision of greater economic security would eliminate many of the *social* disadvantages, an obvious alternative would be to work toward this end directly instead of trying to approach it through some kind of flanking movement based on a reallocation of family size.

Thus, the argument for selective control can be challenged not only on grounds of the evidence used to support it, but also on grounds of its actual capacity to achieve its ostensible goal— improvement of the quality of our population. Moreover, by raising the question, however shabbily founded, of the qualifications of different groups for self-perpetuation, it not only accepts the inequities of the *status quo* and sanctions natality increase among the privileged, but it also diverts attention from the real needs: genuine improvement in the lot of the less privileged groups in the United States and society-wide containment of reproduction within replacement levels.

Part IV

Conclusion

Achieving a
Stable Population
in the United States

WE HAVE OBSERVED that population stability must be achieved if any measure of the high quality of life we Americans still enjoy is to be maintained for ourselves and bequeathed to our posterity. None of the four general arguments in support of our continued population growth—singly or in concert—really faces up to the problem of such growth in a finite world. Some of the courses of action that have been proposed could make life more enjoyable. Certain of them—better planned use of land, for instance—are long overdue. But all are short-term measures, at best. They are palliatives, they are not cures.

Our population growth must be curbed or stopped in the very near future. But how? Achievement of population stability on a national—not to mention world-wide—scale will be an exacting challenge, and require a number of changes in our way of life. Yet, none of these changes need be as great as those that would be required to adjust to a vastly larger population. As we shall see presently, there is no dearth of proposals for the attainment of numerical stability which—if put into effect— would involve sweeping changes in our patterns of behavior. But as remedies for present conditions these proposals, though they show an awareness of the components of population change, are so extreme that they are not likely to be taken seriously. They are also, we feel, decidedly premature, since far less drastic approaches have yet to be tried, let alone proved inadequate.

Before reviewing what can be done, however, let us first take a look at two other proposals, both of which are quite frequently mentioned as solutions to population pressures—despite the fact that neither takes into account even the basic facts and components of population growth. The first is redistribution of resources; the second, redistribution of people.

Redistribution: Resources

Massive reallocation of the world's resources is often suggested as a method that would avoid the difficult task of achieving and maintaining numerical stability. This particular "solution" is, in fact, a favorite among those who object to control over conception. By itself, however, it would provide no adjustment to population growth in the United States; for our relative affluence places us at the top of those countries that would be on the giving, and not the receiving, end of any such redistribution of resources. Surely a more equitable distribution of the world's wealth and resources is urgently needed. Upon it depends the economic development of the poorer countries and the improvement of their conditions of life. And more than purely humanitarian considerations support moves to meet this need. As literacy spreads and communications improve, the great international disparities in living conditions are revealed and emphasized. With international rivalries what they are, the peace of a world divided into two such different camps as industrial and non-industrial, rich and poor, will be a precarious one at best. If for no other reason than this, Americans will have to submit to a redistribution of their wealth. But they should be mindful in doing so that, quite apart from substantial amounts of capital (and the various other requisites of economic development), any permanent improvements in levels of living will require in these developing countries the eventual reduction of average family size. Otherwise, population increase itself will consume the gains from higher productivity.

If a redistribution of wealth, however necessary, cannot by itself effectively meet the problems of growth in an economically underdeveloped country, it has even less merit as an adjustment to growth in one that is economically developed. Whether or not it helped to improve our relations with the non-industrialized peoples, such a redistribution would not help us to meet the costs of our own population increase. If anything, it would, in fact, make this task more difficult to the extent that our numbers continued to grow at the same time that we were obliged to make substantial amounts of our wealth available elsewhere.

What then of the possibility of reallocating wealth *within* our own population? If poor people have the largest families, would not raising their levels of living bring a corresponding reduction in their birth rates? Once again, more equitable distribution of wealth—this time in the United States—might have many desirable consequences. But the effect it would have on our population growth is not at all certain. In the past, family size differentials have been closely related to differences in such indicators of relative social position as income, amount of schooling, occupation. On the whole, natality has varied inversely with social position. Families have tended to be larger among rural residents, manual workers, those with lower incomes, and those with lower levels of schooling.

But now, as we have seen, this pattern may be changing. Recent studies point to a narrowing of class differences in family size.[1] Not only are groups that were formerly characterized by higher birth rates now having fewer children; but those with traditionally low birth rates (urban residents, professional and managerial workers, high school and college graduates) are having more.*   In fact, as we have also noted, there is some evidence to suggest that many Americans might want more children if their financial positions improved.   A redistribution of wealth in this country would undoubtedly improve the quality of our population (by raising levels of health, educational achievement, and the like, and by reducing the human wastage originating in substandard conditions of life); but as a solution to the particular difficulties we face as a consequence of our population growth it is simply irrelevant.

If the redistribution of wealth is by itself inadequate to the problem of population increase in the United States, the only remaining alternative must be demographic.   We must look for a solution to the possibilities for changing one or another of those variables that determine a population's size and composition: migration, death, and birth.

Redistribution: People

Migration is frequently offered as a way of meeting population pressure—again most often, it appears, by those who wish to avoid control over births.   In fact, it is the other side of the reallocation formula—but this time it is people, and not resources or capital, who are to undergo redistribution.   Like the reallocation of resources, however, the capacity of migration to deal with problems of international population growth is but

---

* Note that it is groups and not individuals that are being described. Note also that a person may be born into one group (e.g., rural dwellers) and move into another (urban dwellers). If in the process he happened to retain to some extent the family-building patterns of the former position, any differential in rates that might exist between the two groups would be correspondingly reduced. (See David Goldberg, "Another Look at the Indianapolis Fertility Data," *Milbank Memorial Fund Quarterly*, January, 1960.) Much of the recent increase in natality among persons who have attended college, for example, may well be due to the retention of other (non-college) patterns of family building by some of those who helped account for the rapid increase in college attendance since World War II, but who, in prior years, would not have attended college at all. So far as we know, research on this topic has yet to be carried out.

very short term, at best. And it is equally inappropriate to the situation we face today in the United States.

When unclaimed space was still available and extensive land areas were as yet unbounded by national lines, it was possible for large numbers of people to attempt to raise their levels of living through migration to potentially richer regions. Today these conditions no longer prevail. National lines and the absence of unused, unclaimed space strictly curtail migration as a means of distributing masses of people to areas where they can be better supported.* Millions of people still leave their homes: among others, 3.5 million East Germans to West Germany; 1.1 million Chinese fleeing mainland China; 1 million from North Korea; 3 million Pakistanis from India and a similar number of Indians moving out of Pakistan; and in our own hemisphere 100,000 refugees from Cuba, of whom about 75,000 have come to the United States.[2] Ostensibly these people have moved for political reasons. How much of these and other current migratory movements is motivated by the desire for economic advancement is hard to determine. But transfers of this kind often lower rather than raise levels of living. Even leaving aside the social and political problems connected with any redistribution of peoples, migration as a means of adjusting to population pressure could offer only very temporary relief. Unless checked, the rate of natural increase in the evacuated areas would simply reproduce the same conditions of overcrowding.

But the contribution which changes in migration could make to problems of population growth within the United States is not only temporary, it is also negligible. Halting the flow of migrants into this country would help. But such a policy would go counter to much that is important in our heritage. And its

* Current immigration into the United States (apart from that of the Cuban refugees) and into Australia, the second largest immigrant-receiving country in the world, though sizable, is carefully controlled and in no way constitutes a sudden, mass movement.

effect on our numbers would be minimal, for immigration accounts for less than 10 percent of our annual population increase. Even if we halted *all* immigration to this country, we would still have each year over 2½ million additional persons—more than the population of Philadelphia—to find places for.

What, then, of the other side of migration—emigration? Some Americans do, of course, emigrate. But the total is very small, only a fraction of the 2.8 million who would have to emigrate each year if the population of the United States were to be stabilized through this means. Could we get that many to leave each year? Where would they be willing to settle—and what countries would be willing to receive them—year after year after year? Or is the element of choice to be ruled out, replaced by banishment from this country and forced entry into others? Emigration is no solution by itself. Whatever its form, migration can be but a temporary expedient. A reshuffling of peoples, like a redistribution of resources, merely evades and postpones the eventual necessity of halting growth itself.

Increasing the Death Rate

We are left, then, with birth and death. We can alter our rate of growth by either raising the death rate, lowering the birth rate, or effecting some combination of the two. Certainly raising the death rate, although the one means to stability never actually proposed, would be an easy and efficient way to achieve population balance. We could simply withhold the means to save life now at our disposal. Eliminating the use of vaccines and antibiotics would raise the rate somewhat; sending unpurified water through the taps or distributing unpasteurized milk would bring it up a good deal further. Or we could try more direct approaches—infanticide, suicide, homicide, for instance.

Extreme? Of course it is. The whole orientation of our

culture has been in the opposite direction. Our public health and sanitation practices, our medical and welfare programs, our efforts to increase crop yields, control weather and insect pests, farm oceans, take the salt out of sea water—all these represent ways of attempting to master nature in order to lengthen life and increase man's well-being. What a wrench it would be for us to have to abandon such efforts and allow nature to "take its course." If an increase in mortality does eventually halt population growth in the United States, it will not be by our own choice. It will have been forced upon us—through war, for instance, or through reductions in our levels of living as a consequence of the burden of excessive numbers.

Decreasing the Birth Rate

Before we surrender to these gloomy alternatives, what hope is there for achieving stability by a genuine decline in the birth rate? For in the final reckoning, the means of affecting population growth directly narrow down to this irreducible choice: increased mortality or decreased natality. If, for pragmatic as well as ethical reasons, we reject resort to death, then decreasing the birth rate is the only means remaining to us. To be sure, this does not mean we can relax our efforts along other lines. The redistribution of resources as well as the application of science and technology to the welfare of man (not merely to his possible destruction) will have to be enlarged if we are to live decently and preserve the degree of personal freedom we still have. But to continue to evade our responsibilities for achieving population stability out of deference to some religious creed or traditional value, or out of fear of stirring up controversy, is becoming progressively imprudent. It is also increasingly unnecessary, for leading spokesmen of all major religious groups in this country now admit that population increase poses grave difficulties—even if their attention so far has been focussed exclusively on the underdeveloped countries.

Having chosen to decrease natality, the question, then, is how to do this on a scale large enough to bring about population stability. Much of the hesitancy about dealing with the problem resolves itself into finding acceptable means to limit individual family size. Breaking down the barriers to open discussion will help. But we must recognize that attempts to limit family size through widening the availability of contraceptives and contraceptive information represent only part of what is necessary. Such attempts need to be supplemented by a thorough examination of the conditions that promote a favorable predisposition toward family limitation itself. What, for instance, are the types of personal needs being met—or that individual couples think will in the future be met—by the bearing of children in excess of the two (or, at most, three) necessary for replacement? Little is known about this. Yet, without such knowledge, how can we develop alternative methods of fulfilling these needs in order to lessen the inducements to larger families? Short of compelling couples to limit the number of their offspring, a readiness to restrict family size must precede any program of birth limitation that is to be effective.

We cannot rely upon awareness of the facts of population pressure alone to provide the motivation for family limitation sufficient to stabilize our population. Such awareness can be expected to have a certain amount of influence on the decisions of individual couples concerning their own childbearing. And we should hope that this awareness might have quite a lot of influence on those in a position to establish the laws and rulings that serve as guidelines for so much of individual behavior. But if population stability is to be achieved, the most important factors in that achievement will doubtless be changes leading to the development of a social framework in which couples voluntarily decide to limit the number of their children to replacement levels—not so much because of concern with such seemingly remote ends as population stability, as because of concern for more immediate personal needs and aspirations.

Of course, it is only our cultural values that prompt this insistence on voluntary limitation and the absence of repression. Were we to relinquish certain of the freedoms we now possess, there would become available to us a number of means which, if rather arbitrary, and in some instances even tyrannical, would still have the virtue of complete effectiveness. No desires, no whims, no accidental conceptions would prevent the successful attainment of their purpose.

Compulsory sterilization is one such means. Since the number needed for replacement is only slightly more than two children per couple, one way to achieve stability of numbers would be to sterilize every couple after it had borne its quota of two. A few could be allowed a third child to make up for losses through death, celibacy, or involuntary sterility; but their number could be only a fraction of the total. There would be at least one advantage to this method: it would eliminate errors.

Another such means would be to permit childbearing to only a limited number of the adult population. In practice, this is what has happened (though unintentionally) in southern Ireland—the only country, incidentally, to control its population in a way that Malthus, the father of modern population theory, could approve of (i.e., by postponing marriage, rather than by preventing or avoiding conception).[3] In Ireland the average age of brides at first marriage approaches 30 (in contrast to 20 in the United States), while only two-thirds of the women marry before the end of the fecund period.[4] Whether this in any way explains either the continued high rate of emigration from that island, or, as has been implied, the unexpectedly high proportion of its hospital beds that are assigned to mental patients,[5] has yet to be adequately explored. But certainly, what evidence there is on the reasons for the low rate of marriage suggests that the Irish, themselves, would prefer a different pattern.[6]

A slight variation of this would be marriage at the usual time and to the usual proportion—but with procreation permitted to only a certain few. Parenthood would become the monopoly of a specially trained and selected elite. Everyone else would be sterilized.

There are doubtless other variants of these coercive and repressive measures. Yet because of their very nature none can be considered appropriate to any immediate efforts to check American population growth. Adoption of any of them would presuppose a climate of attitudes far different from that current in the United States today. Before such extensive changes could be introduced into our patterns of marriage and family life there would have to be not only a virtually unanimous concern about the relation between population growth and social well-being, but also a virtually unanimous assumption that this relationship called for governmental action of a most drastic nature. Yet, even if a majority were to approve a general check on population, forcing any of these regulations, like sterilization, on an unwilling minority would constitute a type of coercion abhorrent in terms of our present democratic values. Moreover, were such changes adopted through democratic procedures, we submit that the very fact of their adoption would show that they were no longer needed; for their introduction within a context of political democracy could hardly occur short of a profound and essentially unanimous acceptance of the need for stability—in which case population growth would already have been halted by the voluntary action of the aroused population itself. If such extreme measures do come, it will be only after political changes that would, themselves, constitute as great a departure from current practices as would these proposed changes in the family. At least for the time being, therefore, these repressive measures can be regarded solely as intimations of what might eventuate should we fail to come to terms with our excessive reproduction in ways that harmonize with present cultural values.

Discussing some of the less coercive possibilities, Professor Richard L. Meier[7] of the University of Michigan suggests that, although parenthood could be monopolized by a select few, it might not be necessary to sterilize the remainder of the population—if they can be induced to remain childless in response to an environmental context that discourages family building. Some of the forms this context might take would be: greater opportunities for men and (particularly) women in social roles that militate against childbearing, and the development of new kinds of relationships between the sexes that would have as one consequence the inhibition of parenthood. Elaborating on these means, Professor Meier suggests that the state could use its powers to create new social roles, and then induce or persuade people to accept those "which do not require parenthood, and which in effect, discourage it." Many roles of this sort, he notes, already exist in American society—skilled fruit pickers, deep sea fishermen, air pilots and crew, cross-country truck drivers, surveyors, supervisory engineers, travelling salesmen and buyers, newspapermen, on-call medical and nursing staffs, members of the diplomatic service, musicians and entertainers, for example. Traditionally, these occupations have tended to be monopolized by men, but new roles of a sort to discourage parenthood could also be created for women. With increases in pay and responsibility according to experience, they could quite reasonably become lifetime careers.

Meier also cites several possibilities for the development of new kinds of relationships that would restrict parenthood while presenting alternatives to our system of monogamous marriage: acceptance and encouragement of the institution of companionate marriage, including its legal recognition "as a kind of limited liability partnership to which certain tax and inheritance ad-

vantages [would] accrue." This would be tantamount to recog-
nizing two forms of marriage, at least one of which would
anticipate no children. Another possibility he suggests is a
variant of the extended family system: a household with a
multiplicity of adults and but a few children. It might not
afford much privacy, but it would give the childless members
an opportunity to share relations with the children more or less
equally and it would make possible the development of those
close personal ties between several adults that are often so rewarding and yet frequently so difficult to form in the modern
urban setting. Meier points out that prototypes for this ar-
rangement are to be found in some boarding houses, in households that include maiden aunts as members, in the Israeli
kibbutz and in the historical *zadruga* of the Southern Slavs.

A British writer offers still another possibility, which, if nothing else, gives a certain priority to man's physical nature: increased homosexuality. "Perhaps Nature knew exactly what
she was doing when she made mankind sexually polymor-
phous," he writes. [T]he time may yet come when homosexuality is practically compulsory, and not merely fashionable. It
will indeed be a piquant paradox if—in the long run and taking the survival of humanity as a whole as our criterion—this
controversial instinct turns out to have a greater survival value
than the urge to reproduce."[8]

There are others of this genre, but they, too, either partake of
the bizarre—as does Meier's "complex family"—or, like
Clarke's proposed homosexuality, represent such a deviation
from the norms of our society as to be essentially impractical.

Actually, though, we see no necessity to resort to such extreme measures (assuming that they would even work); for the
foundation for population stability in the United States has already been laid. What we must do is extend further the ideal

of the small family. And since the small family system is a part of European culture—in the United States as elsewhere—a far more fruitful course would be to work within that system itself instead of rejecting it out of hand for something less socially palatable, and also, perhaps, less likely to perform adequately the functions currently performed by the family.

Population has already been virtually stabilized through extensive family limitation in such countries as Sweden, France, Hungary, and Austria. It has been almost stabilized in the same way in England and Wales. Control by these means can hardly be considered either alien or unattainable. The practice of family limitation is also widespread in the United States. Private opinion generally favors it, and the means to it are widely known and fairly readily accessible. It is most unlikely that there will be a reversal of this attitude and practice. All indications suggest, in fact, that it will become even more diffused. The wider this diffusion throughout our society, the more sensitively can we expect family size to respond to changes in values, opinion, employment opportunities, international relations. That family size can indeed change in response to such conditions is well illustrated by its sharp fall during the depression of the 1930's and its abrupt rise during the period following World War II.

Herein lies the source of our hope that American population growth can be halted by essentially non-compulsory means; the hope that we can achieve a balance based on individual decisions in response to individual needs—these decisions being, at the same time, influenced by a sense of responsibility for the welfare of the whole society. If in the long run we find that this approach allows the individual couple too much freedom, we in the United States may have to resort to means, like those discussed above, of a more compulsory or bizarre nature. But surely Americans will want to try first to restrict their population to replacement levels by means that do not involve the denial of marriage or parenthood to anyone who wants it.

The problems involved in attaining population stability in a relatively affluent, highly literate country like the United States are obviously quite different from those faced by countries where poverty and illiteracy prevail. Nor is it altogether certain that these problems will be more easily solved in the former than in the latter. There can be impediments to the attainment of population stability in conditions of abundance as well as in want. It is possible, for instance, that voluntary limitation will appear the greater sacrifice to parents who know that their children can be raised in health and material comfort. And certainly in the more affluent countries the opposition to population limitation can be more formidable, less tractable, better organized.

Thus, what we propose below may at first appear all too meager for the task at hand. But in the United States and similarly favored countries we at least have a base upon which to build—the already firmly established tradition of family limitation. It is upon this base that we have formulated our recommendations, purposely keeping them modest in scope, realistic in outline, and attainable within the social context of the present. Whatever the means ultimately used, it is with these, we feel, that the start should be made; but it is also with these, we feel, that the goal of a stable American population can actually be achieved.

In considering our recommendations it should be borne in mind that with the high expectation of life in this country, there would be enough reproduction for replacement purposes if family size averaged only slightly more than two children per couple.* To maintain numerical stability with the average

---

* Under conditions in which 90 percent of a population survives long enough to marry, and succeeds in doing so, an average of 2.3 children per couple will exactly reproduce it. An average of 2.5 will produce an increase of 10 percent in a generation; one of 3.0 children per family, an increase of 31 percent.

number exceeding this figure would require an increase in the proportion who would have to refrain from having any children at all. About 25 percent of all women would need to remain childless if those who became mothers had an average of three children apiece. About 45 percent would need to remain childless if mothers averaged four children apiece; and 65 percent if they averaged six children.[9]

What we propose as the way to avoid such a situation is action along several lines at once directed toward, first, making the control of births even more acceptable and effective than it already is and, second, creating a favorable predisposition toward the limitation of families to no more than replacement size.

Regardless of what individual couples may think they have to offer a child, a large family can no longer in itself be viewed as a social contribution. In fact, children in excess of the number necessary for replacement will increasingly become a liability to our society. If the parents of three children decide to have a fourth, it should be with the full awareness that they are choosing to indulge their personal desires at the expense of the welfare of their society. In short, we must change our ideas about what constitutes social responsibility and what constitutes parental sacrifice. No longer can a parent's contribution be measured in terms of the number of his offspring, however much time, energy, and money he may expend on them. The willingness to keep one's family within an upper limit of three will have to be considered the more socially responsible act; and the couple with but one or two children accorded recognition for the social importance of the sacrifice it makes by not bearing any others.

For with our high levels of living and the widespread ability to plan the number and spacing of children to suit personal desires, childbearing and childrearing now involve fewer hardships, and, perhaps as a consequence, offer more unadulterated satisfactions. That, under such conditions, we should have to curb our personal desire for additional children is certainly one of the more unfortunate consequences of population growth, and one of the more onerous restrictions imposed on our freedom of choice and action. It also makes any attainment of population stability by means of voluntary limitation just that much more difficult.

These, then, are the general lines along which our thinking must be altered in response to changed social conditions. Some more specific proposals follow. Of these proposals none is likely to be in itself adequate to the task of producing a change in behavior sufficient to result in population stability. But together, we feel, they can be enough to create a climate in the United States conducive to the establishment of the two or, at most, three-child family as the normal maximum. And this is essentially all that any set of means need accomplish.

Further Reduction of Infant and Child Mortality

This may, at first, seem an odd provision to head the list of suggestions for a program designed to *reduce* population. But it will be remembered that we reject higher mortality as a means to this end. Moreover, reduction of family size by death represents a kind of coercion, and it is the essence of our proposals that the individual should limit the size of his family voluntarily, rather than have this limitation forced upon him.

In 1958, death occurred to 146,887 children in the United States under the age of 15.[10] For most, it came in the first weeks of life. But for 25,778 it came in the ages from two through fourteen. That this represents a many-fold improvement over conditions of a century or two ago, that the number dying in the first year of life was only 30 per 1000 and that the number dying among those aged 1–14 was fewer than 7 per *10,000*, is of scant comfort to those who lost a child. If we are going to urge couples to limit even further the number of their children, we must be able to guarantee to them that every effort is being made to ensure the health and longevity of those few children they have. This would be justified on humanitarian grounds alone. But it must also be done to forestall any tendency to have additional children as "insurance."

Improvement in Contraceptive Techniques

No contraceptive today is completely foolproof. Quite apart from failures arising from carelessness, conceptions still occasionally occur in spite of the most careful precautions. If only for the maintenance of health and conjugal happiness, surer means of birth control—other than abstinence—must be developed. Whether this would reduce the birth rate is arguable. But it would most certainly help to attain that goal of the completely planned family—the point at which any non-coercive program of population control must begin. Research on methods of birth control is currently limited to the efforts of a relative handful of scientists and receives meager financial support—probably less than $2 million a year from all sources.[11] So far, none of this support comes from the federal government. But it is doubtful whether private sources alone can be found to finance research on a scale necessary to develop the kinds of birth control methods we so urgently need—those that are at once effective and at the same time morally acceptable to the various groups in our society. Along these lines, Episcopal Bishop James A. Pike of California has recently proposed that the National Institutes of Health launch a major research effort to improve all techniques of birth control, including the rhythm method—a suggestion that has been warmly endorsed by some Catholic spokesmen.[12]

The corollary of this is that methods of reducing sterility must also be improved. The inability to bear children is one of the commonest problems brought to gynecologists. To ignore this problem would be akin to forcing into a state of involuntary sterility a certain proportion of those who could, and wanted to, bear children. In an overpopulated and underdeveloped country there may be some merit in not doing anything to counteract sterility—or in, at least, postponing such a program until the birth rate reaches a lower level. But there is, as yet, little to recommend this course in the United States. As we have observed, one of the advantages in being affluent is that our wealth affords us a wider range of alternatives. Not yet are we in the position of having to seize upon *every* available means to the goal of a stable population.

Education in the Need for Family Limitation

People have been educated to the need to brush their teeth, put out campfires, use automobile safety belts, become vaccinated against disease. While family limitation demands personal discipline and personal sacrifice of a far higher order, we suggest that education in the need for voluntary limitation will be an essential ingredient in any concerted effort to lower the birth rate. A rational argument on this subject may not convince very many, but few are likely to be convinced without it. Intellectual awareness of the consequences of growth may in itself be insufficiently strong as a motivating force for limitation, but it is certainly requisite to any extensive public concern about our rapidly increasing numbers. Only in recent years have the facts of population growth begun to be known outside the confines of a few academic and governmental circles. These facts and their implications, which have taken so long to receive attention, must now be widely diffused—in the schools and colleges, in newspapers and magazines, on television and radio, in churches and community groups. And as we emphasize the need for family limitation in a general sense, we must give equal stress to the importance of each couple's making its own decision to limit the number of its children. If population growth is to be halted without resort to coercive measures, it will be up to each individual couple to bear the responsibility for keeping its family within replacement limits. The decision whether or not to practice family limitation is, after all, a uniquely individual affair—even if many of its consequences are not.

Greater Accessibility of Means

If we are to educate individuals to the need for population control, and to the fact that this control must come about through the voluntary action of individual couples, then we must make the means to the attainment of these ends more readily available than they now are. Americans should not be required to confine their family limitation practices to late marriage, abstinence, and *coitus interruptus,* especially when there exist other means that are generally more acceptable. Ideally, a variety of effective, medically sound means (and professional information about their use) should be made accessible in order to satisfy individual differences in needs, values, and tastes.

The restrictions on access to contraceptives that still exist in some of our states must be removed. Contraception is no less a part of the American way of life than is the automobile or the public school. And it should be officially recognized as such— which is not to say that every couple has to make use of this particular technique of birth control. Legislation that restricts accessibility to contraceptive information and appliances may be successfully circumvented by the rich and sophisticated, but it tends to victimize the poor, and those unlikely to avail themselves of the services of a private physician. At the present time, public welfare workers are forbidden to give information on birth control, even when asked; and no government funds can be used for the support of family planning clinics. Unequal treatment in access to the means to family limitation also exists in the case of abortion—a practice fairly widespread in this country, despite the fact that under most conditions it is strictly illegal.* Only the rich woman is likely to be able to procure an abortion in anything approaching a healthful setting.

Increasing the reliability of contraceptives and making them more readily accessible is important, but this is not enough. Contraception must also be made less costly—unless we can find some way to rule out the market altogether. And furthermore, its use must be supported by more adequate medical services. No one should be denied access to these means on monetary grounds, nor should he or she have to rely on word-of-mouth or trial-and-error when becoming initiated into their use. The determination of the number and spacing of one's children is far too important a matter to be left to chance. The most competent professional assistance should be available —as a right.

For the control of family size a variety of means is available to us: late marriage, abstinence, abortion, *coitus interruptus,* contraception, sterilization. Aside from abortion, each is probably fairly acceptable to large numbers of Americans. Contraception appears the most widespread at the present time and probably for most people presents the least psychological hazard. Sterilization may eventually become more common than it is now. But all means, so long as they are effective and do not endanger the well-being of the persons involved, must be considered.

Alter the Image of the "Ideal American Family"

We have already suggested that in a society such as ours, where natality is subject to so much conscious control, there

* In 1957, a group of physicians, statisticians, and demographers estimated the annual frequency of induced abortion in the United States to be no lower than 200,000 and no higher than 1,200,000—or between 50 and 300 per 1000 live-births. See Mary Steichen Calderone (ed.), *Abortion in the United States.* New York: Hoeber-Harper, 1958, chap. 10, "Report of the Statistics Committee," p. 180.

may be fashions in family size much as there are fashions in other social forms: clothing, automobiles, houses, vacations, music, sports. If this is so—and there is a real need to check this hypothesis through sociological and psychological research— then one important way in which to reduce natality would be to work through those channels known to have some influence on people's attitudes and behavior. Movies, radio and television shows, women's magazines, advertisements, biographies of business and political leaders and of movie and sports stars are among the possibilities. There may be some value in a politician's being a family man; but is the point made any more convincingly if the number of his children is five or six instead of one or two? And those daytime television and radio programs —why must the master of ceremonies invariably demand applause for the mother of eight?

The needs of those couples whose ideal of family life simply cannot be satisfied by only two or three children might be met through expanding the possibilities for adoption and making it a much more usual practice. An adopted child may not fulfil completely the urge to achieve immortality through one's children, but he can certainly provide many of the other satisfactions to be derived from having a family. And he can perform the functions of a sibling for a couple's biological offspring. We can also widen the opportunities for adults to participate in activities that bring them into contact with children. Scouting, nursery schools, Sunday schools, day camps, Little Leagues already provide such contacts. The schools could offer many additional possibilities for the effective use of parental energies and skills, such as guidance (particularly vocational guidance), supervision of study halls, coaching of athletic and debating teams, chaperonage of student trips and dances, special programs in art, music, dancing, science. This would lessen somewhat the specialized nature of family life and at the same time return to parents some of the functions they have lost to other groups.

More variety in the age at which couples marry might also be encouraged. Not all children are conceived in marriage, of course, but most are; and as a consequence, any postponement of the age at marriage would have some effect on the number of births. What World War II and the GI Bill did for the American family has never been fully established. The median age of women at first marriage was little affected. But the proportion marrying before they reach their middle and late twenties is far greater today than it was before, particularly among those with more schooling.[13] The married sophomore is now a commonplace on many college campuses. With effective use of contraceptives, this may represent an adjustment to the conflicting pressures that face American young people: on the one hand, a considerable emphasis on sex; and, on the other, a high valuation of premarital chastity. But it undoubtedly enhances the likelihood of parenthood before graduation, as well. It also seems likely to convince many young women (and men) that their marriageable days are numbered: the fad factor again—better marry now while you still have the chance. Everybody else is.

A more flexible attitude toward marriage and its related institution, parenthood, might also contribute to a lower growth rate by removing some of the pressure on Americans to marry. We Americans have one of the highest marriage rates in the world. With us, marriage is considered, certainly by implication and often by word as well, not only as something of a cure-all for one's anxieties, loneliness, frustrations, frictions with parents, but also as the only "natural" state for the adult. This handicaps the unmarried; it also doubtless serves to force into marriage many who might well have made a better adjustment and had a more productive life had they remained single. The same could be said of parenthood. Parenthood is a most desirable state—but is it necessarily desirable for *everyone?* Are individuals so alike that the same status must be expected of them all? We would suggest not.

Alternative Activities for Women

With the shift that has already occurred in the direction of the small family, earlier marriage, and earlier childbearing, American women have come increasingly to realize that most of their married lives will not be taken up with pregnancy and child care. In fact, the average American mother of today can expect only about one-third of it to be so occupied. If we are to encourage women to limit even further the number of their children, we must therefore make available to them alternative activities of generally greater attractiveness than those that now exist. This is even more important for those women who have no particular desire for marriage or, if married, for childbearing. Suitable alternatives must be provided to the social pressure now directed at them to get married and have children.

For the woman who does not have to support herself there are numerous volunteer activities, ranging from hospital work to political lobbying, many of which are very useful to the society. In fact, the unpopular, but important, cause might never have a champion were it not for the volunteer activities of middle-aged housewives and retired career women. For, almost by definition, such a cause will lack the money to hire its representatives. We can think of several—prison reform and workmen's compensation, for example—that have been greatly aided by just this kind of supporter.

A more obvious possibility, however, is employment. This already occupies more than two-fifths of the married women in the United States; one-third of these women being employed full time.[14] It is quite possible that in the United States of fifty years ago, the proportion was even higher than it is today.[15] But the nature of the work situation is now quite different from what it used to be. Today, the employed woman is more likely to work away from home and for someone to whom she is unrelated. The enlargement of these work opportunities, the development of stimulating, rewarding, useful careers for women who elect never to have a family, or who at the age of 35 or 40 no longer find their days taken up with child care, would require no great departure from the past. It would be simply a continuation of prior trends.

Industrial development and labor specialization in this country have increased the number and variety of jobs in categories commonly assigned to women alone, or to men and women on a roughly equal basis. There is every indication this trend will continue. Were we, as part of a general program of conservation, to re-channel more of our productive energies into activities that did not make extensive demands on non-renewable natural resources, the number of job opportunities for women would be even further increased. For this re-channelization would involve a shift away from the manufacture of durable goods, which is a major employer of men, and toward the professions and service industries, where women workers are more numerous. Moreover, as the proportion of women going to college increases, we can expect that an ever larger proportion will want to combine a career of some sort with their familial duties—if not simultaneously, then at least consecutively.

There is still a lot of prejudice against the employment of women (and not just on the part of men, either); and women are customarily discriminated against in both pay and promotion.[16] But at least the general outline of this alternative to multiple childbearing already exists. Its extension and development would represent nothing either very new or very different from what already occurs. But it would be important in any society in which the small family system prevailed.

*   *   *

It is possible that these informal, persausive measures might profitably be supplemented for a time by certain more formal measures, particularly in the area of taxation. As it is now, parents are given a kind of subsidy for each child. That from the Federal government (and some state governments) takes the form of an income tax deduction for dependents. That from state and local governments takes the form of provision of public education, certain health and recreation services, police protection, and so on. An obvious reversal of this policy would be the elimination of such a deduction on the income tax and the imposition of additional taxes upon parents with more than one or two children in school.

But the only benefit we can see in such a program is that it would put the government behind a campaign to reduce natality and might, for that reason, have a certain value as propaganda. Any other benefit from it would most likely be fortuitous. Unless the tax on school children were quite substantial, the difference this program would make in the size of one's tax bill would be relatively minor. Moreover, such a program smacks too much of coercion, and would most certainly be a step in the direction of distributing childbearing by the market mechanism. The most serious defect of such a plan, however, is the risk that children themselves would be made to suffer for the mistakes of their parents. It would be a bit like that formerly widespread practice of punishing the parents of a bastard by marking the child's birth certificate "illegitimate." However true the aim, it was still at the wrong target. Any program of economic sanctions against the perpetrators of excess reproduction runs the risk of ending up with the child, and not the parent, being deprived by the need to meet a higher tax bill.

Besides, sanctions are already imposed on large families in this country. They are not official, and they operate in an indirect, informal way, rather than a direct, formal one. But they are there, nonetheless. One such "sanction"—if that term does not imply too conscious an intent—is the dominant form of the American family itself. The typical family consists solely of the husband, wife, and children—no in-laws, no grandparents, no servants to help with the housework or take care of the children. And this "nuclear" family, as sociologists term it, is more than likely to be "neolocal" as well—that is, to live some remove from relatives, thus making even more difficult a sharing of child care requirements.

But the severest sanction for most American families is probably the expense of raising a child. The fact that so much in this country—recreation, health care, housing, higher education—is distributed by private purchase means that for most families a child represents a very real economic cost. That so many Americans are willing to make this expenditure attests either to our affluence, our love of children, or the social pressures upon us to have them—and probably in some measure to all three at once.

It also suggests how important it is to change our thinking and behavior along the lines suggested above. Large-scale reductions in income, as during the depression of the 1930's, will reduce the birth rate. But when good times return, the rate goes back up, with the result that our schools and the work force are alternately affected by peaks and troughs in the number of persons entering and leaving. This can be a very costly process, and one with potentially serious economic repercussions—as will become increasingly evident as the postwar baby boom generation enters the labor market. If we are to avoid these costly peaks and troughs in our age distribution, the birth rate (and ultimately, therefore, the size of the family) must be fairly uniform from one year to the next.

A state of chronic depression might conceivably lead to greater population stability; but the price seems rather steep (as long as there are alternative means to the same end) and, besides, such a program, even if it could be put into effect, would not be likely to work longer than a generation or so. "Depressed" conditions to the first generation would be defined as "normal" by the next, who would have known no other. It is *change* in the levels of living, not position according to some absolute standard, that most affects the birth rate in countries where family limitation is widely practiced.

To advocate the early achievement of population stability by widespread voluntary effort is not to predict that this is the way it will actually come about. Studies of the factors that determine family size are of such recent origin and are based on such a limited range of experience—only about two generations—that forecasts of future American birth rates really have very little to go on. We can hardly predict natality levels over the next decade, much less over the next half century. Conditions quite different from those we have recommended above might possibly arise to effect a decline in the birth rate sufficient to halt our population growth: severe economic depression (such as occurred in the 1930's) or a feeling of helplessness and pessimism in response to national and international circumstances (as seems to exist today in some of the East European satellite countries), for example. But there is nothing in our present demographic situation to suggest that low natality in a modern industrialized country like ours need occur only as a symptom of social malaise. It can also be a symptom of social health—of a condition in which people were willing to think beyond their own personal interests, and in which they were willing to modify their behavior to meet altered social needs.

Reluctance to undertake limitation for fear that others will outnumber us is only self-defeating. It misinterprets the factors that make for world power, and overlooks the fact that the limits of any population must be defined in the context of its own resources, land area, and way of life. Even if tomorrow we managed somehow to halve our rate of growth we would still be adding each year nearly 1.5 million Americans—as many as there are in the city of Cleveland and its suburbs. There is no chance of keeping our population at 190 million. What we hope to attain with the proposals we have made is a population that does not exceed 210 or 220 million.

In the past, the size of their population and the level of economic development relative to the abundance of land and natural resources permitted Americans a period of essentially unrestricted growth. But such conditions no longer exist. Today, 110 million more of us than at the turn of the century must share what our country has to offer, and we must do so at a time when our way of life places far heavier demands on resources and land area. If our numbers continue to increase, not even the most farsighted of plans will permit coping with the problems entailed. Since eventual population stability is inevitable—if not by reduced natality, then by increased mortality—we submit that the wisest course is reduction by the limitation of births now while we still have something worth preserving.

If we are to retain for ourselves and our posterity much of what is valuable in the American way of life, we must bring our population growth to a halt—and we must do so soon. If we are to emphasize democratic and not totalitarian values, this cessation must be achieved by individual couples acting without coercion. If we are to emphasize the value of parenthood and the dignity and worth of the individual, there must be no greater restriction on the proportion who become parents than there is now.

In short, what we must have—and what our recommendations have been aimed at—is a society in which: (1) no unwanted child is born; (2) the decision to bear or not to bear a child is made solely by the potential parents; and (3), most important of all for the goal of a stable population, this decision is made in a social and cultural context in which a family of three children is considered large.

Notes

Notes

PREFACE

1. Lincoln H. Day, "The American Fertility Cult—Our Irresponsible Birth Rate," *Columbia University Forum,* Summer, 1960. (Published in abridged form in *The Reader's Digest,* November, 1960.)

INTRODUCTION

1. Three notable exceptions are J. J. Spengler, "Does Population Threaten Prosperity?" *Harvard Business Review,* January–February, 1956; Dudley Kirk, "Some Reflections on American Demography in the Nineteen Sixties," *Population Index,* October, 1960; and Kingsley Davis, "Population and Welfare in Industrial Societies," Fourth Annual Dorothy Nyswander Lecture, Berkeley, Calif., April 6, 1960, printed in *Health Education Monographs,* No. 9 (no date).
2. Ronald Freedman, P. K. Whelpton, Arthur Campbell, *Family Planning, Sterility and Population Growth.* New York: McGraw-Hill, 1959.
3. Both examples are quoted in Charles F. Westoff, "The Demographic Variable," Academic Lecture, Twelfth Mental Hospital Institute, Salt Lake City, Utah, October 20, 1960, published by A.P.A. Mental Hospital Service, 1960.
4. Frank W. Notestein, "Problems of Policy in Relation to Areas of Heavy Population Pressure," Milbank Memorial Fund, *Demographic Studies of Selected Areas of Rapid Growth,* New York, 1944, p. 143.

CHAPTER 1
AMERICAN POPULATION GROWTH IN THE WORLD CONTEXT

1. Estimated from data in U.S. Bureau of the Census, *Statistical Abstract of the United States: 1960,* Washington, 1960, Table 25, p. 28.
2. Conrad Taeuber and Irene B. Taeuber, *The Changing Population of*

the United States, Census Monograph Series. New York: John Wiley, 1958, p. 52.

3. *Ibid.,* pp. 53–54.

4. Estimated from data in *Ibid.,* pp. 5, 258, 272, and in Maurice R. Davie, *World Immigration.* New York: Macmillan, 1936, insert between pp. 52 and 53.

5. Calculated from data in Eugene M. Kulischer, "Migration," *Encyclopaedia Britannica.* Chicago: Encyclopedia Britannica, 1952, volume 15, p. 467.

6. A. M. Carr-Saunders, *World Population.* Oxford: Oxford University Press, 1936, p. 42.

7. Figure from *Statistical Abstract of the United States: 1960,* Table 115, together with Hansen's figure of 250,000 for the pre-1820 period (Marcus L. Hansen, *The Atlantic Migration, 1607–1860.* Cambridge: Harvard University Press, 1940, pp. 77–78).

8. Conrad Taeuber and Irene B. Taeuber, *op. cit.,* p. 49.

9. Eugene M. Kulischer, *loc. cit.*

10. Conrad Taeuber and Irene B. Taeuber, *op. cit.,* p. 54.

11. Computed from data in Niles Carpenter, *Immigrants and Their Children: 1920,* Census Monographs VII, Bureau of the Census, Washington, 1927, Table 1, p. 5.

12. *Statistical Abstract of the United States: 1960,* Table 29. When they become available, the 1960 census results will probably show something closer to 19 percent.

13. Thomas R. Malthus, *On the Principle of Population.* Ann Arbor: University of Michigan Press, 1959, p. 37.

14. Louis I. Dublin, "Mortality," *Encyclopaedia of the Social Sciences.* New York: Macmillan, 1933 (1944 printing), volume XI, p. 27. For other data, consult Hornell Hart and Hilda Hertz, "Expectation of Life as an Index of Social Progress," *American Sociological Review,* December, 1944, and A. J. Jaffe and W. I. Lourie, Jr., "An Abridged Life Table for the White Population of the United States in 1830," *Human Biology,* September, 1942.

15. Warren S. Thompson, *Population Problems,* 4th ed. New York: McGraw-Hill, 1953, p. 162.

16. Conrad Taeuber and Irene B. Taeuber, *op. cit.,* p. 249.

17. Alfred J. Lotka, "The Size of American Families in the Eighteenth Century," *Journal of the American Statistical Association,* pp. 154–170, cited by Conrad Taeuber and Irene B. Taeuber, *op. cit.,* p. 249.

18. United Nations, *Demographic Yearbook 1954,* Table 21.

19. *Ibid., loc. cit.*

20. A. M. Carr-Saunders, *op. cit.,* insert between pp. 122 and 123.

21. P. K. Whelpton, "Is Family Size Increasing?" U.S. National Office of Vital Statistics, *Vital Statistics Special Reports,* volume 23, no. 16, August, 1947.

22. Norman B. Ryder, "An Appraisal of Fertility Trends in the United States," Milbank Memorial Fund, *Thirty Years of Research in Human Fertility: Retrospect and Prospect,* New York, 1959, pp. 42–43.

23. Calculated from data in Pascal K. Whelpton, *Cohort Fertility,* Princeton, Princeton University Press, 1954, Table A, and from Lincoln H. Day, *The Age of Women at Completion of Childbearing: Demographic Factors and Possible Social Consequences.* PhD. dissertation, Columbia University, 1957 (microfilmed), Appendix A, pp. 157–161.

24. John Hajnal, "The Marriage Boom," *Population Index,* April, 1953, p. 83, and U.S. Bureau of the Census, *Statistical Abstract of the United States: 1960,* Table 38, p. 40.

25. Computed from data in John Hajnal, "The Marriage Boom," pp. 83 and 85.

26. Computed from data in National Office of Vital Statistics, *Vital Statistics–Special Reports, National Summaries,* volume 50, no. 12, August 26, 1959, Table 7, p. 297.

27. U.S. Bureau of the Census, *U.S. Census of Population: 1950.* Vol. II, *Characteristics of the Population,* Part 1, United States Summary, Table 4, p. 1–5; and *U.S. Census of Population: 1960.* Vol. I, *Characteristics of the Population.* Part A, Number of Inhabitants. Tables Q and 20, pp. XXVI and 1–29.

28. *Ibid.,* Table Q, p. XXVI.

29. Outdoor Recreation Resources Review Commission, *Outdoor Recreation for America,* Washington, U.S. Government Printing Office, 1962, pp. 21–22.

30. U.S. Bureau of the Census, *Sixteenth Census of the United States: 1940. Population.* "Comparative Occupation Statistics for the United States, 1870 to 1940," Washington, 1943, Table XXII, p. 101; and computed from data in *Statistical Abstract of the United States: 1961,* Table 268, p. 203.

31. Philip M. Hauser, "The Census of 1960," *Scientific American,* July, 1961, p. 42.

32. Outdoor Recreation Resources Review Commission, *op. cit.,* p. 83.

33. Rates in the Soviet Union (which seems to be increasing its population about as rapidly as the United States) are not as reliable as those of other industrialized countries, and cannot be considered quite comparable with them, first, because such a large proportion of that country's work force is still employed in agriculture (thus raising a question as to how "industrialized" she can be considered) and, second, because the tremendous losses her people suffered during World War II have had the consequence of leaving a much smaller proportion of her population in those age and sex groups where death rates are higher and birth rates lower. See Warren W. Eason, "The Soviet Population Today," *Foreign Affairs,* July, 1959; John F. Kantner, "Recent Demographic Trends in the USSR," Milbank Memorial

Fund, *Population Trends in Eastern Europe, the USSR and Main-land China,* New York, 1960; and Michael K. Roof, "The Russian Population Enigma Reconsidered," *Population Studies,* July, 1960.

34. Royal Commission on Population, *Report,* London: H. M. Stationery Office, June, 1949, p. 38.

35. A. J. Jaffe, "Urbanization and Fertility," *American Journal of Sociology,* July, 1942, pp. 54, 56. For a fascinating set of statements in opposition to family limitation made by clergymen (both Protestant and Catholic), physicians, government officials, and private citizens in Australia at the turn of the century see New South Wales Legislative Assembly, Second Session, Royal Commission on the Decline of the Birth-Rate and on the Mortality of Infants in New South Wales, *Report,* vol. I, Sydney: William Applegate Gullick, Government Printer, 1904.

36. Quoted in the *New York Times,* November 16, 1960.

CHAPTER 2

TOO MANY OR TOO FEW: THE IDEA OF THE OPTIMUM

1. Aristotle, *Politics,* Book VII, para. 4.

2. Raymond Firth, *We, the Tikopia, A Sociological Study of Kinship in Primitive Polynesia.* 2nd ed. London: Allen and Unwin, 1957, p. 491.

3. In this connection, see Ansley J. Coale and Edgar M. Hoover, *Population Growth and Economic Development in Low-Income Countries.* Princeton: Princeton University Press, 1958, chapters 3, 14, 20, and 23. For an empirical study, see A. J. Jaffe, *People, Jobs, and Economic Development.* Glencoe, Ill.: Free Press, 1959.

4. Frank Lorimer poses a similar question for economic conditions alone in his article, "Issues of Population Policy," *Annals,* January 1945, p. 197.

5. C. P. Snow contributing to a discussion in "What Is the World's Greatest Need?" *New York Times Magazine,* April 2, 1961.

CHAPTER 3

POPULATION GROWTH AND THE AMERICAN WAY OF LIFE

1. C.E.M. Joad, "Introduction" to J. C. Flugel, *Population, Psychology, and Peace.* London: Watts, 1947, p. xiv.

2. U.S. Bureau of the Census, *Statistical Abstract of the United States: 1960,* Table 136, p. 108, Table 740, p. 562, Table 1049, p. 768.

3. *U.S. Census of Population: 1960.* Vol. I, *Characteristics of the Population.* Part A, Number of Inhabitants. Tables Q and 20, pp. XXVI and 1–29.

4. See, for example, Philip M. Hauser, "America's Population Crisis," *Look Magazine,* November 21, 1961, pp. 30–31.

5. John B. Calhoun, "Population Density and Social Pathology," *Scientific American,* February, 1962.

6. Marion Clawson, "The Crisis in Outdoor Recreation," reprinted from *American Forests,* March and April, 1959, Resources for the Future, Inc., Reprint no. 13, p. 5.

7. *Statistical Abstract of the United States: 1962,* Tables 262, 263, 265, 269, and 270, pp. 202–203, 206.

8. Marion Clawson, "The Crisis in Outdoor Recreation," *American Forests,* March, 1959.

9. Outdoor Recreation Resources Review Commission, *Outdoor Recreation for America,* Washington: U.S. Government Printing Office, 1962, p. 51.

10. United States Senate Select Committee on National Water Resources, Committee Print No. 17, "Water Recreation Needs in the United States, 1960–2000," Washington: U.S. Government Printing Office, 1960, p. 1.

11. John R. Vosburgh, Jr., writing in *Audubon Magazine,* as quoted in *New York Times,* February 12, 1959, "Bird Publication Ready to Expand," p. 116.

12. U.S. Senate Select Committee on National Water Resources, Print No. 17, pp. 8–9.

13. Outdoor Recreation Resources Review Commission, *op. cit.,* p. 22.

14. Lewis Mumford, "The Social Function of Open Spaces," *Landscape,* Winter, 1960–61, p. 5.

15. According to Samuel E. Wood, president of Pacific Planning and Research, quoted in *New York Times,* "Recreation Space Said to Disappear," May 13, 1959.

16. Marshall Sprague, "Colorado Ski Rush Will Soon Be On," *New York Times,* December 4, 1960.

17. National Park Service, "Our Fourth Shore," cited in Charles Grutzner, "Park Program for the Great Lakes' Shores," *New York Times,* April 17, 1960, p. X–33.

18. U.S. Senate Select Committee on National Water Resources, Committee Print No. 17, p. 5.

19. Charles Grutzner, "Saturated Parks," *New York Times,* September 13, 1959, p. XX.

20. William H. Whyte, Jr. "Urban Sprawl," in The Editors of Fortune, *The Exploding Metropolis.* New York: Doubleday, 1957, p. 115.

21. See Christopher Tunnard, "America's Super-Cities," *Harper's,* August 1958.

22. Kingsley Davis, "Population and Welfare in Industrial Societies," Fourth Annual Dorothy Nyswander Lecture, Berkeley, California, April 6, 1960, printed in *Health Education Monographs*, Number 9 (no date), p. 15.

23. Merrill Folsom, "Outward Expansion of Industry is Changing Face of Suburbia," *New York Times*, January 29, 1957, p. 22.

24. Edgar M. Hoover, "Comment" on paper by Harold J. Barnett, in National Bureau of Economic Research, *Demographic and Economic Change in Developed Countries*. Princeton: Princeton University Press, 1960, p. 453.

25. Report to the Moore State Commission, quoted in *New York Times*, March 13, 1961, p. 1.

26. Joseph C. Ingraham, "Autos in Urban Regions Rule and Frustrate Living," *New York Times*, January 28, 1957, p. 16.

27. *New York Times*, January 27, 1957.

28. Outdoor Recreation Resources Review Commission, *op. cit.*, p. 9.

29. Robert and Leona Rienow, "The Day the Taps Run Dry," *Harper's*, October, 1958, p. 72.

30. See in this connection Joseph J. Spengler, "Population Threatens Prosperity," *Harvard Business Review*, January–February, 1956.

31. Donald H. McLaughlin, "Man's Selective Attack on Ores and Minerals," in William L. Thomas, Jr. (ed.), *Man's Role in Changing the Face of the Earth*. Chicago: University of Chicago Press, 1956, p. 856.

32. Editorial in the *St. Louis Post-Dispatch*, quoted in *Labor's Economic Review*, vol. 5, no. 10, October, 1961, pp. 61–62.

33. *Labor's Economic Review*, October, 1961, p. 63.

34. Lawrence O'Kane, "Beach Pollution Found the Same," *New York Times*, May 21, 1961, p. 71.

35. *Labor's Economic Review*, October, 1961, p. 63.

36. Walsh McDermott, "Air Pollution and Public Health," *Scientific American*, October, 1961, p. 51.

37. "Air Pollution Rate Dropped 66% Here During Vehicle Ban," *New York Times*, March 13, 1961, p. 31.

38. *New York Times*, July 26, 1960, p. 21, and October 20, 1960, p. 26.

39. *Ibid.*, March 13, 1960, p. 72.

40. Walsh McDermott, *op. cit.*, pp. 54–55.

41. President John F. Kennedy, Special Message to Congress on Natural Resources, February 24, 1961.

42. Charles F. Westoff, "The Demographic Variable," Academic Lecture, Twelfth Mental Hospital Institute, October 20, 1960, published by A.P.A. Mental Hospital Service, 1960, p. 12.

43. Dr. Lindsley Fiske Kimball, treasurer and trustee of the Rockefeller Institute, quoted in *New York Times*, October 3, 1961, p. 24.

44. U.S. Bureau of the Census. *U.S. Census of Population: 1960, General Social and Economic Characteristics, New Jersey*. Final Report PC(1)–

32C. Washington, D.C.: U.S. Government Printing Office, 1962, Table 45, pp. 32–162.

45. *New York Times,* August 13, 1961.

46. Economics Committee, *Report,* Papers of the Royal Commission on Population, vol. iii. London: H.M. Stationery Office, 1950, pp. 48–49.

47. *New York Times,* August 6, 1961.

48. Harrison Brown, *The Challenge of Man's Future.* London: Secker & Warburg, 1954, p. 256.

49. Joseph J. Spengler, "Population Threatens Prosperity," p. 94.

50. Robert A. Dahl, *A Preface to Democratic Theory.* Chicago: University of Chicago Press, 1956, p. 27.

51. Charles Grutzner, "Land Issues Put to 400 at Parley," *New York Times,* December 28, 1960, p. 13.

52. Raleigh Barlowe, "Development of Forest and Water Resources for Recreational Uses," Paper presented at Section O (Agriculture), American Association for the Advancement of Science, New York, N.Y., December 29, 1960.

53. Harrison E. Salisbury, "Study Finds Cars Choking Cities as 'Urban Sprawl' Takes Over," *New York Times,* March 3, 1959, p. 26.

54. *New York Times,* "Expert Predicts Regional Chaos within 25 Years," July 17, 1960, p. 1.

55. Anthony Downs, *An Economic Theory of Democracy.* New York: Harper, 1957, pp. 253–255.

56. Robert Michels, *Political Parties* (first published, 1915). Glencoe, Ill.: Free Press, 1949.

57. J. S. Mill, *Principles of Political Economy.* Book IV, chapter 6, part 2. London: Longmans, Green, 1917, p. 748.

CHAPTER 4

RELIGION

1. Other evidence is to be found in sales of contraceptives, physicians' case histories, public opinion studies. See A. M. Carr-Saunders, *World Population.* Oxford: Oxford University Press, 1936, p. 99.

2. *Ibid.,* p. 102.

3. A. J. Jaffe, "Urbanization and Fertility," *American Journal of Sociology,* July, 1942.

4. Richard M. Fagley, "A Protestant View of Population Control," *Law and Contemporary Problems,* Summer, 1960, p. 472.

5. *Ibid.,* p. 476.

6. Genesis 38: 9–10 (King James Version).

7. Genesis 38: 12–26 (King James Version).

8. Harold Cox, *The Problem of Population*. London: Jonathan Cape, 1922, p. 172.
9. Mark 10: 6–9 (King James Version).
10. Norman St. John-Stevas, *Birth Control and Public Policy*. Santa Barbara, California: Center for the Study of Democratic Institutions, 1960, p. 31.
11. *The Lambeth Conference 1958: The Encyclical Letter from the Bishops together with the Resolutions and Reports,* London and Greenwich, Conn., S.P.C.K., and Seabury Press, 1958, pp. 143 and 147.
12. Leo J. Latz, *The Rhythm of Sterility and Fertility in Women,* 6th rev. ed., 1940, pp. 127–128, as quoted in Alvah W. Sulloway, *Birth Control and Catholic Doctrine*. Boston: Beacon Press, 1959, pp. 117–118.
13. Matthew 10: 35–38 (King James Version).
14. As quoted in Norman St. John-Stevas, "A Roman Catholic View of Population Control," *Law and Contemporary Problems,* Summer, 1960, p. 445.
15. Harold Cox, *op. cit.,* pp. 173–174.
16. William J. Gibbons, S.J., "The Catholic Value System in Relation to Human Fertility," in George F. Mair (ed.), *Studies in Population.* Princeton: Princeton University Press, 1949, p. 112.
17. Pius XI, "Casti Connubii—on Christian Marriage" (Encyclical No. 4, Dec. 31, 1930).
18. Norman St. John-Stevas, "A Roman Catholic View of Population Control," p. 446.
19. Pius XII, as quoted in Richard M. Fagley, *The Population Explosion and Christian Responsibility*. New York: Oxford University Press, 1960, p. 183.
20. Anthony F. Zimmerman, *Overpopulation,* Washington: Catholic University of America Press, 1957, p. 103, as quoted in Richard M. Fagley, *The Population Explosion and Christian Responsibility,* p. 185.
21. William J. Gibbons, S.J., interview in *U.S. News and World Report,* "The Birth-Control Issue—What Both Sides Say," Dec. 21, 1959.
22. William J. Gibbons, S.J., "Responsible Parenthood and the Population Problem," reprinted from *The Paulist Fathers' Monthly Magazine,* New York, N.Y., p. 27 (no date).
23. 1930 statement of the Anglican Bishops of the Lambeth Conference, as quoted in Richard M. Fagley, *The Population Explosion and Christian Responsibility,* p. 194.
24. *The Lambeth Conference: 1958,* p. 169.
25. George Dugan, "National Council of Churches Backs Artificial Birth Control," *New York Times,* February 24, 1961, p. 1. Among the Protestant churches that have endorsed the use of chemical and mechanical contraception are the American Baptist Church, the Methodist Church, the Protestant Episcopal Church, the United

Church in America, and the United Presbyterian Church. (cf. Population Reference Bureau, *Population Bulletin,* November, 1961, p. 130.)

26. Norman St. John-Stevas, *Birth Control and Public Policy,* p. 34.

27. Ronald Freedman, Pascal K. Whelpton, and John W. Smit, "Socio-Economic Factors in Religious Differentials in Fertility," *American Sociological Review,* August, 1961, Table 1, p. 610. Because of the purpose of the inquiry, these couples have more schooling, higher incomes, higher concentration in metropolitan areas, etc., than is the case with the population as a whole. The larger sample of which these are a part was limited to white, married women 18 to 39 years old, living with their husbands or temporarily separated because of his being in the armed forces.

28. P. K. Whelpton and Clyde V. Kiser, "Social and Psychological Factors Affecting Fertility. I. Differential Fertility among 41,498 Native-White Couples in Indianapolis," *Milbank Memorial Fund Quarterly,* July, 1943, p. 229.

29. Samuel A. Stouffer, "Trends in the Fertility of Catholics and Non-Catholics," *American Journal of Sociology,* September, 1935, Tables 1–4. Reprinted in *Social Research to Test Ideas: Selected Writings of Samuel A. Stouffer.* New York: Free Press of Glencoe, 1962.

30. Dudley Kirk, "Recent Trends of Catholic Fertility in the United States," Milbank Memorial Fund, *Current Research in Human Fertility.* New York, 1955, p. 93.

31. Ronald Freedman, Pascal K. Whelpton, Arthur A. Campbell, *Family Planning, Sterility and Population Growth.* New York: McGraw-Hill, 1959, pp. 102, 106–108, 156, 183, 403.

32. Hearings before the Committee on Foreign Relations, United States Senate, 87th Congress, First Session, on S.1983, pp. 472–473, June 9, 1961.

33. Jack Zlotnick, "Population Pressure and Political Indecision," *Foreign Affairs,* July, 1961, pp. 685 and 687.

34. Dr. Sripati Chandrasekhar, Director, Indian Institute for Population Studies, quoted in *New York Times,* November 16, 1958.

35. *New York Times,* May 6, 1959, as quoted in Norman St. John-Stevas, *Birth Control and Public Policy,* p. 24.

36. Rev. John A. O'Brien, "Let's Take Birth Control out of Politics," *Look,* October 10, 1961, as quoted in *Population Bulletin,* Nov., 1961, pp. 134–135.

37. John Rock, M.D., "We Can End the Battle over Birth Control!" *Good Housekeeping,* July, 1961, as quoted in *Population Bulletin,* Nov., 1961, p. 138.

38. Richard M. Fagley, *The Population Explosion and Christian Responsibility,* pp. 8–9.

39. In September, 1961, the Protestant Episcopal Church openly placed itself in the vanguard by approving the dissemination by the United States Government of birth control information to the economically less developed countries. *Population Bulletin,* November, 1961.

CHAPTER 5

ATTITUDES AND VALUES

1. Thomas S. Szasz, "The Ethics of Birth Control, Or: Who Owns Your Body?" *The Humanist,* 1960, No. 6, p. 336.
2. Charles Westoff, Robert G. Potter, Philip G. Sagi, and Elliot G. Mishler, *Family Growth in Metropolitan America.* Princeton: Princeton University Press, 1961, pp. 5–6 and chap. VIII.
3. Robert S. Lynd and Helen Merrell Lynd, *Middletown in Transition.* New York: Harcourt, Brace, 1937, pp. 405 and 408.
4. J. C. Flugel, *Population, Psychology, and Peace.* London: Watts & Co., 1947, p. 35.
5. *The Lambeth Conference: 1958,* p. 147.
6. John Hajnal, "The Marriage Boom," *Population Index,* April, 1953, p. 83, and U.S. Bureau of the Census, *Statistical Abstract of the United States: 1960,* Table 38, p. 40.
7. Public opinion poll data and others are discussed in Lincoln H. Day, *The Age of Women at Completion of Childbearing: Demographic Factors and Possible Social Consequences.* Ph.D. dissertation, Columbia University, 1957 (microfilmed), pp. 82– 88.
8. Computed from U.S. Department of Labor, Bureau of Labor Statistics, *Special Labor Force Reports,* No. 11, December, 1960, Table E, p. A–11.
9. See Jeanne Clare Ridley, "The Number of Children Expected in Relation to Non-Familial Activities of the Wife," *Milbank Memorial Fund Quarterly,* July, 1959.
10. Clyde V. Kiser and P. K. Whelpton, "Social and Psychological Factors Affecting Fertility. XXXIII. Summary of Chief Findings and Implications for Future Studies," *Milbank Memorial Fund Quarterly,* July, 1958, pp. 298–299.
11. See Gerard DeGré, "Freedom and Social Structure," *American Sociological Review,* October, 1946, pp. 529–536.
12. Gary S. Becker, "An Economic Analysis of Fertility," in National Bureau of Economic Research, *Demographic and Economic Change in Developed Countries.* Princeton: Princeton University Press, 1960.
13. James S. Duesenberry, "Comment" on Gary S. Becker, "An Economic Analysis of Fertility," *op. cit.,* p. 234.

14. *Statistical Abstract of the United States: 1961,* Table 1060, p. 761.
15. Clyde V. Kiser and P. K. Whelpton, "Social and Psychological Factors Affecting Fertility," *loc. cit.*

CHAPTER 6

THE ECONOMIC ARGUMENT

1. Frederick Lewis Allen, *Only Yesterday* (first published, 1931), New York: Bantam Books, 1952, p. 74.
2. Colin Clark, "Do Population and Freedom Go Together?" *Fortune,* December, 1960, p. 139.
3. Cf. Bert F. Hoselitz, "Population Pressure, Industrialization and Social Mobility," *Sociological Aspects of Economic Growth.* Glencoe, Ill.: Free Press, 1960, pp. 115–138.
4. Colin Clark, *op. cit.,* pp. 138–139.
5. A. J. Jaffe and Charles D. Stewart, *Manpower Resources and Utilization,* New York: John Wiley, 1951, p. 14.
6. Computed from U.S. Department of Labor, Bureau of Labor Statistics, *Special Labor Force Reports,* No. 11, December, 1960, Table E, p. A–11.
7. The 1960 figures are not yet available. This was the relationship in 1950. See *U.S. Census of Population: 1950,* Vol. IV, *Special Reports,* Part 5, Chapter C, Fertility, 1955, Tables 46 and 47.
8. U.S. Bureau of the Census, *Current Population Reports,* Series P–20, No. 104, September 30, 1960, Table 1, pp. 8–9.
9. *Ibid.,* Table 6, p. 18.
10. U.S. Bureau of the Census, *Current Population Reports,* Series P–20, No. 106, January 9, 1961, Table 5, p. 16.
11. See Kingsley Davis and Jerry W. Combs, Jr., "The Sociology of An Aging Population," *The Social and Biological Challenge of Our Aging Population.* New York: Columbia University Press, 1950.
12. John Kenneth Galbraith, *The Affluent Society.* Boston: Houghton Mifflin, 1958, pp. 161–163.
13. W. D. Borrie, *Population Trends and Policies, a Study in Australian and World Demography.* Sydney: Australasian Pub. Co., 1948, p. 163.
14. See Nathan Albert Pelcovits, *Old China Hands and The Foreign Office.* New York: King's Crown Press, 1948, pp. 4–5, 16–17, 70–71, 102–103. Also see C. F. Remer, *The Foreign Trade of China,* Shanghai, 1926, pp. 231, 233 (cited by Pelcovits).
15. Laurens van der Post, *The Lost World of the Kalahari.* London: Hogarth Press, 1958, pp. 211 ff.
16. David M. Potter, *People of Plenty: Economic Abundance and the*

American Character. Chicago: University of Chicago Press, 1954, pp. 167–168, 177.

17. International Labour Office, Geneva, *International Labour Review, Statistical Supplement,* December, 1961, p. 103.

18. Robert K. Merton, *Social Theory and Social Structure.* Glencoe, Ill.: Free Press, 1949, chap. VII.

19. See for example, Lincoln Clark (ed.), *Consumer Behavior: Research on Consumer Reactions.* New York: Harper, 1958.

20. See A. H. Anderson, "Space as a Social Cost," *Journal of Farm Economics,* August, 1950.

21. W. D. Borrie, *op. cit.,* p. 157.

22. See Talcott Parsons, "Age and Sex in the Social Structure," in Talcott Parsons, *Essays in Sociological Theory Pure and Applied.* Glencoe, Ill.: Free Press, 1949.

23. See, for example, Detroit Area Study, *A Social Profile of Detroit: 1956.* Ann Arbor: University of Michigan Press, 1957, chapter 2.

24. In this connection, see, for example, W. D. Borrie, *op. cit.,* p. 156.

CHAPTER 7

THE "SCIENTIFIC" ARGUMENT

1. Catholic Bishops of the United States, "Explosion or Backfire?" Statement issued November 26, 1959, quoted in *Population Bulletin,* January, 1960.

2. Walter Sullivan, *Assault on the Unknown.* New York: McGraw-Hill, 1961. Quoted by Charles Poore, "Books of the Times," *New York Times,* April 6, 1961, p. 31.

3. Karl E. Meyer, "The Surfeit Society: *Novus Ordo Seclorum,*" *The New Republic,* July 2, 1962, p. 9.

4. R. M. Salter, "World Soil and Fertilizer Resources in Relation to Food Needs." Waltham, Mass.: *Chronica Botanica,* 1948. Quoted in Harrison Brown, James Bonner, and John Weir, *The Next Hundred Years.* New York: Viking, 1957, p. 164.

5. Howard R. Tolley, "Farmers in a Hungry World," *Proceedings of the American Philosophical Society,* vol. 95, no. 1, February 13, 1951, p. 54.

6. Harrison Brown, *et al.,* pp. 57, 65–67.

7. See, for example, Rachel Carson, *Silent Spring.* Boston: Houghton Mifflin, 1962.

8. Joseph J. Shomon, "Do We Need a Geobiotic Ethic?" *Virginia Wildlife,* July, 1960.

9. Harrison Brown, *et al.,* pp. 56–57.

10. *Ibid.*, p. 56.
11. Robert S. Dietz, "The Sea's Deep Scattering Layers," *Scientific American*, August, 1962, p. 50.
12. Harrison Brown, *et al.*, p. 76.
13. See, for example, Alfred J. Stamm, "Production of Nutritive Substances from Inedible Carbohydrates," and H. A. Spoehr, "Chlorella as a Source of Food," both in *Proceedings of the American Philosophical Society*, vol. 95, no. 1, February 13, 1951, and Oswin W. Willcox, "Footnote to Freedom from Want," *Agricultural and Food Chemistry*, vol. 7, no. 12, December, 1959.
14. "How Much and How Clean?—America's Future Water Supply," *Labor's Economic Review*, vol. 5, no. 10, October, 1960, p. 66.
15. Lyndon B. Johnson, "If We Could Take the Salt out of Water——" *New York Times Magazine*, October 30, 1960, p. 17.
16. *Ibid.*
17. Calculated from U.S. Department of Commerce figures quoted in "How Much and How Clean?" *op. cit.*, p. 65.
18. U.S. Senate Select Committee on National Water Resources, Committee Print no. 3, 1960, p. 1.
19. "How Much and How Clean?" *op. cit.*, pp. 64–65.
20. See U.S. Senate Select Committee on National Water Resources, Committee Print no. 32, 1960, Tables 12 and 13, pp. 39 and 40.
21. U.S. Senate Select Committee on National Water Resources, Print No. 32 (quoted in *New York Times*, December 18, 1960, p. 58.)
22. William Petersen, *Planned Migration: The Social Determinants of the Dutch-Canadian Movement*, University of California Publications in Sociology and Social Institutions, vol. 2. Berkeley and Los Angeles: University of California Press, 1955, pp. 56–58.
23. *Ibid.*, p. 197.
24. Sebastian von Hoerner, "The General Limits of Space Travel," *Science*, July 6, 1962, p. 23.
25. Garrett Hardin, "Interstellar Migration and the Population Problem," *Journal of Heredity*, vol. 50, no. 2, March–April, 1959, p. 68.
26. L. R. Shepherd, "The Distant Future," in L. J. Carter (ed.), *Realities of Space Travel*. London: Putnam, 1957.
27. Garrett Hardin, *op. cit.*, pp. 68–70.
28. Waldemar Kaempffert, "Science in Review—Will the World's Population One Day Starve or Simply Cease to Exist?" *New York Times*, July 8, 1956, p. E–11.
29. See, for example, John J. Christian, "Phenomena Associated with Population Density," and Robert L. Snyder, "Evolution and Integration of Mechanisms That Regulate Population Growth," National Academy of Sciences of the U.S.A., *Proceedings*, April 15, 1961.

CHAPTER 8

THE MILITARY ARGUMENT

1. Klaus Knorr, *The War Potential of Nations*. Princeton: Princeton University Press, 1956, p. 41.
2. Linus Pauling, *No More War!* New York: Dodd, Mead, 1958, pp. 29–30. Also, see John W. Finney, "Cheaper A-Bomb Process Is Threat to Arms Control," *New York Times*, Oct. 10, 1960, pp. 1 ff.
3. See Katherine Organski and A. F. K. Organski, *Population and World Power*. New York: Knopf, 1961, pp. 15–21.
4. Kingsley Davis, "The Demographic Foundations of National Power," in Morroe Berger, Theodore Abel, and Charles H. Page (eds.), *Freedom and Control in Modern Society*. Princeton: Van Nostrand, 1954, pp. 222–223.
5. United Nations, *Demographic Yearbook: 1957*, Table 26.
6. Klaus Knorr, *op. cit.*, p. 31. See also Table 1 (p. 34) and the discussion on pp. 32–36.
7. Kingsley Davis, "The Demographic Foundations of National Power," p. 206.
8. *Ibid.*, p. 223.
9. Linus Pauling, *No More War!*, pp. 5–6, 7, 29–31.
10. See, for example, Col. E. B. Crabill, "A Combat Veteran Sounds Off," *Harper's*, April, 1958, p. 13.
11. Symposium on the medical consequences of thermonuclear war in the May 31, 1962, issue of *The New England Journal of Medicine*, quoted in "Science and the Citizen," *Scientific American*, July, 1962, pp. 70–71.
12. Winfield W. Riefler, "Preface" to Ansley J. Coale, *The Problem of Reducing Vulnerability to Atomic Bombs*. Princeton: Princeton University Press, 1947, p. viii.
13. Ansley J. Coale, *The Problem of Reducing Vulnerability to Atomic Bombs*, pp. 60 and 62–63.

CHAPTER 9

THE "SELECTIVE CONTROL" ARGUMENT

1. Otis Dudley Duncan, "Is the Intelligence of the General Population Declining?" *American Sociological Review*, August, 1952.
2. *Ibid.*, p. 406 (italics in original).
3. *Ibid.*, p. 407 (italics added).

4. S. Colum Gilfillan, Letter to the Editor, *Columbia University Forum,* Fall, 1960, p. 50.

5. Kingsley Davis, "The Origin and Growth of Urbanization in the World," *American Journal of Sociology,* March, 1955, p. 432.

6. Herbert J. Muller, *The Uses of the Past: Profiles of Former Societies.* New York: Oxford University Press, 1957, p. 104.

7. Ralph Linton, *The Study of Man.* New York: Appleton-Century, 1936, p. 321.

8. Leonard Broom and Philip Selznick, *Sociology,* 2nd ed. Evanston, Ill.: Row, Peterson, 1958, p. 63.

9. C. R. Fay, *Great Britain from Adam Smith to the Present Day,* 5th ed. London: Longmans, Green, 1950, p. 253.

10. T. S. Ashton, *The Industrial Revolution, 1760–1830.* London: Oxford University Press, 1948, p. 14.

11. *Ibid.,* pp. 14–22. For a detailed discussion of the religious factor, see "Puritanism, Pietism and Science" and for the economic factor, "Science and Economy in 17th Century England," in Robert K. Merton, *Social Theory and Social Structure,* Glencoe, Ill.: Free Press, 1949, chaps. 14 and 15, respectively.

12. Robert Bierstedt, *The Social Order.* New York: McGraw-Hill, 1957, p. 123.

13. S. Colum Gilfillan, "Who Invented It?" *The Scientific Monthly,* December, 1927, p. 529.

14. *Ibid.,* p. 530. See also, S. Colum Gilfillan, *The Sociology of Invention,* Chicago: Follett Pub. Co., pp. 77–78, and 137–139; and William F. Ogburn, *Social Change,* New York: B. W. Huebsch, 1922.

15. Ralph Linton, *op. cit.,* pp. 324–25.

16. Seymour B. Sarason and Thomas Gladwin, "Psychological and Cultural Problems in Mental Subnormality," part II of Richard L. Masland, Seymour B. Sarason, and Thomas Gladwin, *Mental Subnormality.* New York: Basic Books, 1958, p. 302.

17. P. B. Medawar, *The Future of Man* (The BBC Reith Lectures, 1959), London: Methuen, 1960, p. 75.

18. Sarason and Gladwin, *op. cit.,* p. 213.

19. Otto Klineberg, "An Experimental Study of Speed and Other Factors in 'Racial' Differences," *Archives of Psychology,* 1928, vol. 15, no. 93, quoted in Sarason and Gladwin, *op. cit.,* pp. 270–271.

20. Dorothea Leighton and Clyde Kluckhohn, *Children of the People: The Navaho Individual and His Development.* Cambridge: Harvard University Press, p. 153, quoted in Sarason and Gladwin, *op. cit.,* p. 271.

21. Sarason and Gladwin, *op. cit.,* p. 209.

22. *Ibid.,* p. 229. The studies cited are R. J. Havighurst and L. L. Janke, "Relations between Ability and Social Status in a Midwestern Community: I. Ten-Year-Old Children," *Journal of Educational Psychology,*

1944; and L. L. Janke and R. J. Havighurst, "Relations between Ability and Social Status in a Midwestern Community: II. Sixteen-Year-Old Boys and Girls," *Journal of Educational Psychology,* 1945.

23. Herbert H. Hyman, "The Value Systems of Different Classes: A Social Psychological Contribution to the Analysis of Stratification," in Reinhard Bendix and Seymour Martin Lipset (eds.), *Class, Status and Power —A Reader in Social Stratification.* Glencoe, Ill.: Free Press, 1953, pp. 429–432.

24. *Ibid.,* pp. 437–439. Also see Genevieve Knupfer, "Portrait of the Underdog," *Public Opinion Quarterly,* Spring, 1947, reprinted in Bendix and Lipset, *op. cit.,* pp. 255–263.

25. See, for instance, Albert J. Mayer and Philip Hauser, "Class Differentials in Expectation of Life at Birth," *La Revue de L'Institut International de Statistique,* vol. 18 (1950), reprinted in Bendix and Lipset, *op. cit.,* pp. 281–284; Robert E. Clark, "Psychoses, Income, and Occupational Prestige," *American Journal of Sociology,* March, 1949, reprinted in Bendix and Lipset, pp. 333–340; Milton Terris, "Relation of Economic Status to Tuberculosis Mortality," *American Journal of Public Health,* vol. 38, August, 1948, pp. 1061–1070; C. E. A. Winslow, "Poverty and Disease," *American Journal of Public Health,* vol. 38, January, 1948, pp. 173–184; Louis I. Dublin, Alfred J. Lotka, and Mortimer Spiegelman, *Length of Life,* rev. ed., 1949, chaps, 3 and 11; I. M. Moriyama and L. Gualnick, "Occupational and Social Class Differences in Mortality," in Milbank Memorial Fund, *Trends and Differentials in Mortality,* New York: 1956; Jean Daric, "Mortality, Occupation, and Social Status," *Population,* October–December, 1949; U.S. National Office of Vital Statistics, *Vital Statistics—Special Reports,* 33(10), Sept., 1951; August B. Hollingshead and Frederick C. Redlich, "Social Stratification and Schizophrenia," *American Sociological Review,* June, 1954.

26. Seymour Martin Lipset and Reinhard Bendix, *Social Mobility in Industrial Society.* Berkeley and Los Angeles: University of California Press, 1959, chaps. 5–7.

27. Joseph A. Kahl, "Educational and Occupational Aspirations of 'Common Man' Boys," *Harvard Educational Review,* 1953, p. 188.

28. R. C. White, *These Will Go to College.* Cleveland: Western Reserve University Press, 1952, p. 45. Cited in Lipset and Bendix, *Social Mobility in Industrial Society,* p. 229.

29. See, for example, Daniel R. Miller and Guy E. Swanson, *The Changing American Parent.* New York: John Wiley, 1958.

CHAPTER 10

ACHIEVING A STABLE POPULATION IN THE UNITED STATES

1. See, for instance, Clyde V. Kiser, "Changes in Fertility by Socio-Economic Status during 1940–1950," *Milbank Memorial Fund Quarterly,* October, 1956.
2. *New York Times,* "The New Age of Migrations," July 15, 1961, p. 18.
3. See D. V. Glass, "Malthus and the Limitation of Population Growth" in D. V. Glass (ed.), *Introduction to Malthus.* London: Watts, 1953, pp. 30–38.
4. John Hajnal, "The Marriage Boom," *Population Index,* April, 1953, pp. 83–85.
5. Kingsley Davis and Judith Blake, "Social Structure and Fertility: An Analytic Framework," *Economic Development and Cultural Change,* April, 1956, p. 220.
6. See, for example, Conrad Arensberg and Solon T. Kimball, *Family and Community in Ireland.* Cambridge: Harvard University Press, 1940, chapter 6.
7. Richard L. Meier, *Modern Science and the Human Fertility Problem.* New York: John Wiley, 1959, pp. 171–178.
8. Arthur C. Clarke, "Standing Room Only," *Harper's* April, 1958, p. 57.
9. Richard L. Meier, *op. cit.,* p. 172.
10. Computed from National Office of Vital Statistics, *Vital Statistics—Special Reports, National Summaries,* vol. 52, no. 4, August 8, 1960, Table 1, p. 76.
11. See John Rock, M.D., "We Can End the Battle over Birth Control," *Good Housekeeping,* July, 1961.
12. See, for instance, Rev. John A. O'Brien, "Let's Take Birth Control Out of Politics," *Look,* October 10, 1961.
13. See Elbridge Sibley, "Higher Education and Earlier Parenthood: A Changing Cycle of Family Life," *Antioch Review,* Spring, 1957.
14. U.S. Department of Labor, Bureau of Labor Statistics, *Special Labor Force Reports,* No. 11, December, 1960, Table E, p. A–11.
15. See A. J. Jaffe, "Trends in the Participation of Women in the Working Force," *Monthly Labor Review,* May, 1956, pp. 559–565.
16. See, for instance, Theodore Caplow, *The Sociology of Work.* Minneapolis: University of Minnesota Press, 1954, pp. 237–245.

Selected Bibliography
and Suggested Readings

Selected Bibliography and Suggested Readings

The best sources of current statistics on population are the *Demographic Yearbook*, published annually by the Statistical Office of the United Nations, the various publications of the United States Bureau of the Census, particularly the *Current Population Reports*, Series P–20 and P–23, and the following series put out by the National Office of Vital Statistics, United States Public Health Service: *Vital Statistics of the United States* and *Vital Statistics— Special Reports*.

Current discussions of a more analytical sort can be found in *Population Studies*, published by the London School of Economics, the United States Bureau of the Census series, *International Population Reports*, the series of *Population Studies* published by the Population Division of the United Nations, the *Milbank Memorial Fund Quarterly*, and *Population Index*, published by the Office of Population Research, Princeton University. The last is also an essential bibliographical source. A good summary of the preliminary results of the last United States Census of Population (1960) is Philip M. Hauser, "The Census of 1960" (*Scientific American*, July, 1961).

Current economic data are most conveniently found in the *Statistical Yearbook*, also an annual publication of the Statistical office of the United Nations. An excellent summary and discussion of the social and economic gulf currently separating the industrial from the non-industrial countries is A. J. Jaffe, "Population Trends and Controls in Underdeveloped Countries" (*Law and Contemporary Problems*, Summer, 1960).

Good general introductions to the study of population are Warren S. Thompson, *Population Problems* (4th edition, New York: McGraw-Hill, 1953), Dennis Wrong, *Population* (New York: Random House, 1956), and William Petersen, *Population* (New York: Macmillan, 1961). Still one of the best—though possibly a bit outdated in its emphasis—is A. M. Carr-Saunders, *World Population* (London: Oxford University Press, 1936). A more advanced discussion—and one absolutely essential to the serious student of population—is United Nations, Department of Social Affairs, Population Division, *The Determinants and Consequences of Population Trends* (Population Studies, Number 17, 1953). The *Report* of the Royal Commission on Population (London: H.M. Stationery Office, 1949) is a thorough job, and one with wider applicability than might at first be supposed.

Among the best general theoretical discussions of the three demographic variables are: fertility—Kingsley Davis and Judith Blake, "Social Structure and Fertility: An Analytical Framework" (*Economic Development and Cultural Change,* April, 1956); mortality—Louis I. Dublin, Alfred J. Lotka, and Mortimer Spiegelman, *Length of Life* (rev. ed., New York: Ronald Press, 1949); and migration—William Petersen, "A General Typology of Migration" (*American Sociological Review,* June, 1958). The Dublin, Lotka, and Spiegelman work is also an excellent summary of research findings on mortality.

Two good discussions of the implications of world population growth are Harrison Brown, *The Challenge of Man's Future* (New York: Viking, 1954), and Richard L. Meier, *Modern Science and the Human Fertility Problem* (New York: John Wiley, 1959).

A good discussion of population growth in the United States is Conrad Taeuber and Irene B. Taeuber, *The Changing Population of the United States* (Census Monograph Series, New York: John Wiley, 1958). The importance of immigration to the development of the United States is the subject of many studies, among the more general of which are Maurice R. Davie, *World Immigration* (New York: Macmillan, 1936) and Marcus Lee Hansen, *The Atlantic Migration: 1607–1860* (Cambridge: Harvard University Press, 1940).

The most extensive studies of natality in the United States are the Indianapolis Study, the Growth of American Families Study, and the Family Growth in Metropolitan America Study. Interviewing for the first was carried on in 1941, that for the second and third in 1955 and 1957, respectively. Only the Growth of American Families Study covers a nationwide sample, however.

Results of the Indianapolis Study have come out in 32 separate articles published in the *Milbank Memorial Fund Quarterly*. The major findings are summarized in Clyde V. Kiser and P. K. Whelpton, "A Summary of Chief Findings and Implications for Future Studies" *(Milbank Memorial Fund Quarterly,* July, 1958). A reading of this summary should, however, be supplemented by a reading of A. J. Jaffe's review of the final publication in the series *(Eugenics Quarterly,* September, 1960). The Growth of American Families Study is reported on in Ronald Freedman, Pascal K. Whelpton, and Arthur A. Campbell, *Family Planning, Sterility, and Population Growth* (New York: McGraw-Hill, 1959); and the Metropolitan Study in Charles F. Westoff, Robert G. Potter, Jr., Philip C. Sagi, and Elliot G. Mishler, *Family Growth in Metropolitan America* (Princeton: Princeton University Press, 1961).

Another very important study, one based on census materials, is Pascal K. Whelpton, *Cohort Fertility* (Princeton: Princeton University Press, 1954). Among the more thoughtful—and thought-provoking—discussions of present natality patterns in the United States are William Petersen, "The New American Family" *(Commentary,* January, 1956); and Elbridge Sibley, "Higher Education and Earlier Parenthood: A Changing Cycle of Family Life" *(Antioch Review,* Spring, 1957). Excellent examples of the perspective on family life to be gained from an intelligent use of statistics are two articles by Paul C. Glick of the United States Bureau of the Census: "The Family Cycle" *(American Sociological Review,* April, 1947) and "The Life Cycle of the Family" *(Marriage and Family Living,* February, 1955).

Mortality trends in the United States are well covered in the Dublin, Lotka, and Spiegelman work referred to above.

The idea of the optimum population is most thoroughly discussed in Imre Ferenczi, *The Synthetic Optimum of Population* (International Institute of Intellectual Co-operation, League of

Nations, Paris, 1938). Useful, though less general discussions, are to be found in Julius Isaac, *Economics of Migration* (New York: Oxford University Press, 1947), especially chapters 4 and 6, and Joseph J. Spengler, "Population Threatens Prosperity" (*Harvard Business Review*, January–February, 1956). Other discussions are Philip M. Hauser, "The Population Explosion—U.S.A." (Population Reference Bureau, *Population Bulletin*, August, 1960), Henry B. van Loon, "Population, Space, and Human Culture" (*Law and Contemporary Problems*, Summer, 1960), and Lincoln H. Day, "The American Fertility Cult—Our Irresponsible Birth Rate" (*Columbia University Forum*, Summer, 1960).

Religious dogmas concerning population are quite fully discussed in the following: William J. Gibbons, S.J., "The Catholic Value System in Relation to Human Fertility" (in George F. Mair [ed.], *Studies in Population*, Princeton: Princeton University Press, 1949), Alvah W. Sulloway, *Birth Control and Catholic Doctrine* (Boston: Beacon Press, 1959), Richard M. Fagley, *The Population Explosion and Christian Responsibility* (New York: Oxford University Press, 1960), and Norman St. John-Stevas, *Birth Control and Public Policy* (Santa Barbara, Calif.: Center for the Study of Democratic Institutions, 1960). The interested reader is also referred to the articles by Sulloway, St. John-Stevas, and Fagley in the Summer, 1960, issue of *Law and Contemporary Problems*, and, for an earlier view, to Harold Cox, *The Problem of Population* (London: Jonathan Cape, 1922). Another useful work is Glanville Williams, *The Sanctity of Life and the Criminal Law* (New York: Knopf, 1957).

There is little on the nonreligious values surrounding population. J. C. Flugel's excellent little book, *Population, Psychology, and Peace* (London: Watts, 1947), treats the subject to some extent, but his main emphasis is on the psychological factors.

The standard work on the evolution of contraceptive techniques is Norman E. Himes, *A Medical History of Contraception* (Baltimore: Williams and Wilkins, 1936).

There is a growing literature on the relation of population to economic change and development. Part 3 of the United Nations, *Determinants and Consequences of Population Trends*, contains an excellent discussion of a more theoretical nature. Kingsley

Davis, "Population and the Further Spread of Industry Society," and Joseph J. Spengler, "Economic Factors in the Development of Densely Populated Areas" (both of which appear in *Proceedings of the American Philosophical Society,* February 13, 1953), are well worth reading in connection with population in non-industrialized countries. So also are Gunnar Myrdal, *Rich Lands and Poor* (New York: Harper, 1957), and Ansley J. Coale and Edgar M. Hoover, *Population Growth and Economic Development in Low-Income Countries: A Case Study of India's Prospects* (Princeton: Princeton University Press, 1958). Spengler's *Harvard Business Review* article, and chapter 11 of W. D. Borrie, *Population Trends and Policies* (Sydney: Australasian Publishing Co., 1948), discuss population and economic development in industrialized countries.

Unfortunately, there are but few empirical studies of the relationship of population to economic development. A welcome exception is A. J. Jaffe, *People, Jobs, and Economic Development: A Case History of Puerto Rico, Supplemented by Recent Mexican Experiences* (Glencoe, Ill.: Free Press, 1959).

The materials on resources and consumption are usefully summarized in J. Frederic Dewhurst and Associates, *America's Needs and Resources: A New Survey* (New York: Twentieth Century Fund, 1955); Pep (Political and Economic Planning), *World Population and Resources* (London: Allen & Unwin, 1955); United Nations, *Determinants and Consequences of Population Trends,* chapter 10; Harrison Brown, James Bonner, and John Weir, *The Next Hundred Years* (New York: Viking, 1957); Harrison Brown, *The Challenge of Man's Future;* and W. S. and E. S. Woytinsky, *World Population and Production* (New York: Twentieth Century Fund, 1953). A very interesting discussion from the ecological point of view is Lorus J. and Margery Milne, *The Balance of Nature* (New York: Knopf, 1960).

Other, more specific, discussions are the articles by John D. Black and Richard Bradfield in George F. Mair (ed.), *Studies in Population,* and the articles by H. A. Spoehr, Alfred J. Stamm, Lionel A. Walford, and Merle T. Jenkins in *Proceedings of the American Philosophical Society* (February 13, 1951). Additional ones are listed in the bibliography to Harrison Brown, *The Challenge of Man's Future.*

A highly readable and authoritative discussion of human inheritance is L. C. Dunn and Theodosius Dobzhansky, *Heredity, Race, and Society* (New York: Pelican Books, 1946). Another is *The Future of Man,* P. B. Medawar's Reith Lectures delivered in 1959 over the British Broadcasting System (London: Methuen, 1960).

An appreciation of the richness and meaning of man's cultural diversity can be gained from a study of historical changes within various societies and also from a study of current differences. We recommend both approaches. Very interesting accounts are to be found in Ralph Turner, *The Great Cultural Traditions* (Volume I: The Ancient Cities, and Volume II: The Classical Empires) (New York: McGraw-Hill, 1941); V. Gordon Childe, *Man Makes Himself* (London: Watts, 1948); and H. J. Muller, *Uses of the Past* (New York: Oxford University Press, 1952). Studies of the Industrial Revolution as it occurred in Europe are quite numerous. We think one of the best ways to begin is by reading H. L. Beales, *The Industrial Revolution: 1750–1850* (London: Longmans, Green, 1928; new edition with a new bibliographical essay, New York: Kelley & Millman, 1958); and T. S. Ashton, *The Industrial Revolution: 1760–1830* (London: Oxford University Press, 1948). Both of these, but especially the later edition of Beales' work, have excellent bibliographies.

General discussions of social and cultural change are also numerous. Some of the better introductions are: R. M. MacIver and Charles H. Page, *Society* (New York: Rinehart, 1949), chapters 22–29; William F. Ogburn, *Social Change with Respect to Culture and Original Nature* (New York: B. W. Huebsch, 1922), and the same author's article, "Change, Social" (*Encyclopedia of the Social Sciences,* Volume III, New York: Macmillan, 1930); and chapters 18–20 of Ralph Linton, *The Study of Man* (New York: Appleton-Century, 1936).

The student of cultural differences can begin with Hans Ruesch's novel of Eskimo life, *Top of the World* (New York: Permabooks, 1959), and then go on to any of a vast number of anthropological and historical accounts, such as George Peter Murdock, *Our Primitive Contemporaries* (New York: Macmillan, 1934); Book I of William C. Prescott, *The Conquest of Peru* (first published in 1847; currently available from New York: Doubleday, no date); Ruth Benedict, *Patterns of Culture* (Boston: Houghton Mifflin, 1934); and Clyde Kluckhohn and Dorothea Leighton, *The Navaho* (Cambridge: Harvard University Press, 1946).

The social and cultural determination—and definition—of intelligence and personality are well demonstrated in Seymour B. Sarason and Thomas Gladwin, "Psychological and Cultural Problems in Mental Subnormality," Part II of Richard L. Masland, Seymour B. Sarason, and Thomas Gladwin, *Mental Subnormality* (New York: Basic Books, 1958); and also in chapter 10 of Robert Bierstedt, *The Social Order* (New York: McGraw-Hill, 1957); George Herbert Mead, *Mind, Self and Society* (Chicago: University of Chicago Press, 1934); and Ralph Linton, *The Cultural Background of Personality* (New York: Appleton-Century, 1945). The Sarason and Gladwin work is a book-length summary of the findings of nearly 300 research studies. A careful debunking of claims that class differentials in family size have led to declines in national intelligence is Otis Dudley Duncan's "Is the Intelligence of the General Population Declining?" (*American Sociological Review,* August, 1952).

The relation of population to military strength in the modern world has received little consideration. Kingsley Davis' article, "The Demographic Foundations of National Power" (in Morroe Berger, *et al., Freedom and Control in Modern Society,* Princeton: Van Nostrand, 1954) is an excellent introduction to the subject. Conclusions somewhat contrary to those reached by us are ably presented in Katherine and A. F. K. Organski, *Population and World Power,* New York: Knopf, 1961.

Excellent discussions of the role of women in modern industrial societies are to be found in Alva Myrdal and Viola Klein, *Women's Two Roles: Home and Work* (London: Routledge, Kegan Paul, 1956); Theodore Caplow, *The Sociology of Work* (Minneapolis: University of Minnesota Press, 1954), chapters 10 and 11; and Talcott Parsons, "Age and Sex in the Social Structure" in his

Essays in Sociological Theory Pure and Applied (Glencoe, Ill.: Free Press, 1949). Interesting discussions of what *might* be are contained in Richard L. Meier, *Modern Science and the Human Fertility Problem,* chapter 7; Dael L. Wolfle, *America's Resources of Specialized Talent* (New York: Harper, 1954); and William M. Evan, "Recruitment of Women in the Engineering Profession" (*Science,* March 1, 1957).

Index of Names

Index of Names

Abel, Theodore, 176 (n. 4)
Allen, Frederick Lewis, 134 (n. 1)
Anderson, A. H., 149 (n. 20)
Aquinas, Thomas, 84, 85, 89
Arensberg, Conrad, 228 (n. 6)
Aristotle, 35–36, 36 (n. 1)
Ashton, T. S., 195 (n. 10, n. 11), 271
Augustine, Saint, 84

Baldwin, Roger, 121
Barlowe, Raleigh, 69 (n. 52)
Barnett, Harold J., 54 (n. 24)
Beales, H. L., 271
Becker, Gary S., 124, 125 (n. 12)
Bendix, Reinhard, 210 (n. 23), 212
    (n. 26), 213 (n. 28)
Benedict, Ruth, 272
Berger, Morroe, 176 (n. 4)
Bierstedt, Robert, 199 (n. 12), 272
Black, John D., 270
Black, Joseph, 195
Blake, Judith, 227 (n. 5), 267
Bonner, James, 160, 160 (n. 4, n. 6),
    162 (n. 9, n. 10), 163 (n. 12), 270
Borrie, W. D., viii, 143, 143 (n. 13),
    150, 150 (n. 21), 153 (n. 24), 270
Bradfield, Richard, 270
Broom, Leonard, 194 (n. 8)
Brown, Harrison, 66 (n. 48), 160,
    160 (n. 4, n. 6), 162 (n. 9, n. 10),
    163 (n. 12), 267, 270, 271
Brown, Nona B., 54n
Bryson, Gladys, viii
Burns, Robert, 211

Calderone, Mary Steichen, 238n
Calhoun, John B., 48 (n. 5)
Campbell, Arthur, 2 (n. 2), 93
    (n. 31), 268
Caplow, Theodore, 242 (n. 16), 272
Carpenter, Niles, 14 (n. 11)
Carr-Saunders, A. M., 13 (n. 6), 18
    (n. 20), 78 (n. 1), 79 (n. 2), 267
Carson, Rachel, 161 (n. 7)
Carter, L. J., 169 (n. 26)
Chandrasekhar, Sripati, 99 (n. 34)
Childe, V. Gordon, 271
Christian, John J., 171 (n. 29)
Clark, Colin, 134–36, 135 (n. 2),
    136 (n. 4), 171
Clark, Lincoln, 148 (n. 19)
Clark, Robert E., 212 (n. 25)
Clarke, Arthur C., 230, 230 (n. 8)
Clawson, Marion, 48 (n. 6), 49 (n. 8)
Coale, Ansley J., 5, 41 (n. 3), 156,
    187–88, 187 (n. 12), 188 (n. 13),
    270
Coerr, Wymberley DeR., 95–96
Combs, Jerry W., Jr., 141 (n. 11)
Comstock, Anthony, 97, 99
Cox, Harold, 81 (n. 8), 84 (n. 15),
    269
Crabill, E. B., 183 (n. 10)

Da Vinci, Leonardo, 194
Dahl, Robert A., 67 (n. 50)
Dalton, John, 195
Daric, Jean, 212 (n. 25)
Davie, Maurice R., 13 (n. 4), 267

Davis, Kingsley, viii, 1 (n. 1), 53 (n. 22), 141 (n. 11), 176, 176 (n. 4), 179, 179 (n. 7, n. 8), 193 (n. 5), 227 (n. 5), 267, 269–70, 272

Day, Lincoln H., vii (n. 1), 19 (n. 23), 117 (n. 7), 269

DeGré, Gerard, 122 (n. 11)

Dewhurst, J. Frederic, 270

Dietz, Robert S., 163 (n. 11)

Dobzhansky, Theodosius, 271

Douthit, Harold K., Jr., viii

Downs, Anthony, 72 (n. 55)

Dublin, Louis I., 15 (n. 14), 212 (n. 25), 267, 268

Dugan, George, 91 (n. 25)

Dunbar, Leslie W., viii

Duncan, Otis Dudley, 190–91, 190 (n. 1), 191 (n. 2, n. 3), 272

Dunn, L. C., 271

Dusenberry, James S., 125 (n. 13)

Eason, Warren W., 25 (n. 33)

Edison, Thomas, 194, 199

Eisenhower, Dwight D., 58, 88, 101

Evan, William M., 273

Fagley, Richard M., 79 (n. 4, n. 5), 87 (n. 19, n. 20), 90 (n. 23), 100, 101 (n. 38), 269

Fay, C. R., 195 (n. 9)

Ferenczi, Imre, 268

Finney, John W., 175 (n. 2)

Firth, Raymond, 36, 36 (n. 2)

Flugel, J. C., 115 (n. 4), 269

Folsom, Merrill, 53 (n. 23)

Freedman, Ronald, 2 (n. 2), 92 (n. 27), 93 (n. 31), 268

Fulbright, J. William, 95–97

Galbraith, John Kenneth, 141–42, 142 (n. 12), 212

Gibbons, William J., 85 (n. 16), 88 (n. 21), 89, 89 (n. 22), 110n, 113n, 269

Gilfillan, S. Colum, 192 (n. 4), 200–201, 201 (n. 13, n. 14)

Gladwin, Thomas, 203 (n. 16), 204 (n. 18), 205 (n. 19, n. 20), 207 (n. 21), 208 (n. 22), 272

Glass, D. V., 227 (n. 3)

Glick, Paul C., 268

Goldberg, David, 222

Green, Jack, 169n

Grutzner, Charles, 52 (n. 17, n. 19), 68 (n. 51)

Gualnick, L., 212 (n. 25)

Hajnal, John, 21 (n. 24, n. 25), 117 (n. 6), 227 (n. 4)

Hansen, Marcus L., 13 (n. 7), 267

Hardin, Garrett, 168–170, 169 (n. 25), 170 (n. 27)

Hart, Hornell, 15 (n. 14)

Hauser, Philip M., 24 (n. 31), 48 (n. 4), 212 (n. 25), 266, 269

Havighurst, R. J., 208 (n. 22)

Himes, Norman E., 269

Hirtz, Hilda, 15 (n. 13)

Hitler, Adolf, 179

Hobbes, Thomas, 121

Hollingshead, August B., 212 (n. 25)

Hoover, Edgar M., 41 (n. 3), 54 (n. 24), 270

Hoselitz, Bert F., 135 (n. 3)

Hoyle, Fred, 170–71

Hyman, Herbert H., 210 (n. 23, n. 24)

Ingraham, Joseph C., 54 (n. 26)

Isaac, Julius, 269

Jaffe, A. J., viii, 15 (n. 14), 29 (n. 35), 41 (n. 3), 79 (n. 3), 138 (n. 5), 241 (n. 15), 266, 268, 270

Janke, L. L., 208 (n. 22)

Jenkins, Merle T., 270

Jerome, Saint, 84

Jesus, 82, 83

Joad, C. E. M., 46–47, 46 (n. 1)
John XXIII, Pope, 101, 111
Johnson, Lyndon B., 164 (n. 15, n. 16)

Kaempffert, Waldemar, 171 (n. 28)
Kahl, Joseph A., 212 (n. 27)
Kahn, Herman, 186n
Kantner, John F., 25 (n. 33)
Kennedy, John F., 58, 60 (n. 41), 66
Kennedy, Raymond, viii
Kimball, Lindsley Fiske, 62 (n. 43)
Kimball, Solon T., 228 (n. 6)
Kirk, Dudley, 1 (n. 1), 92 (n. 30)
Kiser, Clyde V., 92 (n. 28), 119 (n. 10), 126 (n. 15), 221 (n. 1), 268
Klein, Viola, 272
Klineberg, Otto, 205, 205 (n. 19)
Kluckhohn, Clyde, 205, 205 (n. 20), 272
Knorr, Klaus, 174 (n. 1), 178 (n. 6)
Knupfer, Genevieve, 210 (n. 24)
Kulischer, Eugene M., 13 (n. 5), 14 (n. 9)

Latz, Leo J., 83, 83 (n. 12)
Leighton, Dorothea, 205, 205 (n. 20), 272
Leyburn, James G., viii
Linton, Ralph, 194, 194 (n. 7), 201, 202 (n. 15), 271, 272
Lipset, Seymour Martin, 210 (n. 23), 212 (n. 26), 213 (n. 28)
Lorimer, Frank, 43 (n. 4)
Lotka, Alfred J., 15, 15 (n. 17), 16, 212 (n. 25), 267, 268
Lourie, W. I., Jr., 15 (n. 14)
Lynd, Helen Merrell, 112, 112 (n. 3)
Lynd, Robert S., viii, 112, 112 (n. 3)

McDermott, Walsh, 58 (n. 37), 60 (n. 40)
MacIver, R. M., 271

McLaughlin, Donald H., 56, 56 (n. 31)
Mair, George F., 85 (n. 16), 110n
Malthus, Thomas R., 15, 15 (n. 13), 227
Masland, Richard L., 203 (n. 16)
Mayer, Albert J., 212 (n. 25)
Mead, George Herbert, 272
Medawar, P. B., 203 (n. 17), 271
Meier, Richard L., 229–30, 229 (n. 7), 233 (n. 9), 267, 273
Merton, Robert K., 148, 148 (n. 18), 195 (n. 11)
Meyer, Karl E., 159 (n. 3)
Michels, Robert, 72, 72 (n. 56)
Mill, John Stuart, 73–74, 74 (n. 57)
Miller, Daniel R., 213 (n. 29)
Milne, Lorus J., 270
Milne, Margery, 270
Mishler, Elliot G., 106 (n. 2), 268
Mitchell, Joseph McD., 115
Moriyama, I. M., 212 (n. 25)
Muller, Herbert J., 193 (n. 6), 271
Mumford, Lewis, 51, 51 (n. 14)
Murdock, George Peter, 272
Myrdal, Alva, 272
Myrdal, Gunnar, 270

Northrop, Robert M., viii
Notestein, Frank W., 6, 6 (n. 4)

O'Brien, John A., 100 (n. 36), 235 (n. 12)
Ogburn, William F., 201 (n. 14), 271
O'Kane, Lawrence, 57 (n. 34)
Organski, A. F. K., 175 (n. 3), 272
Organski, Katherine, 175 (n. 3), 272

Page, Charles H., viii, 176 (n. 4), 271
Parkinson, C. Northcote, 54n
Parsons, Talcott, 151 (n. 22), 272
Paul, the Apostle, 82, 83, 84

Pauling, Linus, 175 (n. 2), 182 (n. 9)
Pelcovits, Nathan Albert, 145 (n. 14)
Petersen, William, 167 (n. 22), 168 (n. 23), 267, 268
Pike, James A., 235
Pius XI, 86 (n. 17)
Pius XII, 87, 87 (n. 19)
Poore, Charles, 155 (n. 2)
Potter, David M., 146–47, 147 (n. 16)
Potter, Robert G., 106 (n. 2), 268
Prescott, William C., 272
Priestley, Joseph, 195

Redlich, Frederick C., 212 (n. 25)
Reed, Stephen W., viii
Remer, C. F., 145 (n. 14)
Ridley, Jeanne Clare, 118 (n. 9)
Riefler, Winfield W., 186–87, 187 (n. 12)
Rienow, Leona, 56 (n. 29)
Rienow, Robert, 56 (n. 29)
Rock, John, 100 (n. 37), 235 (n. 11)
Roof, Michael K., 25 (n. 33)
Ruesch, Hans, 271
Ryder, Norman B., 19 (n. 22)

Sagi, Philip, 106 (n. 2), 268
St. John-Stevas, Norman, 82 (n. 10), 84 (n. 14), 86 (n. 18), 91 (n. 26), 99 (n. 35), 269
Salisbury, Harrison E., 70 (n. 53)
Salter, R. M., 160 (n. 4)
Sarason, Seymour B., 203 (n. 16), 204 (n. 18), 205 (n. 19, n. 20), 207 (n. 21), 208 (n. 22), 272
Selznick, Philip, 194 (n. 8)
Shepherd, L. R., 169, 169 (n. 26)
Shomon, Joseph J., 162 (n. 8)
Sibley, Elbridge, 240 (n. 13), 268
Smit, John W., 92 (n. 27)
Smith, Curtis, viii
Smith, Elaine, viii

Snow, C. P., 43, 43 (n. 5)
Snyder, Robert L., 171 (n. 29)
Spengler, Joseph J., 1 (n. 1), 56 (n. 30), 66 (n. 49), 269, 270
Spiegelman, Mortimer, 212 (n. 25), 267, 268
Spoehr, H. A., 163 (n. 13), 270
Sprague, Marshall, 51 (n. 16)
Stamm, Alfred J., 163 (n. 13), 270
Stewart, Charles D., 138 (n. 5)
Stouffer, Samuel A., 92 (n. 29)
Sullivan, Walter, 155 (n. 2)
Sulloway, Alvah W., 269
Swanson, Guy E., 213 (n. 29)
Szasz, Thomas S., 105, 105 (n. 1)

Taeuber, Conrad, 12 (n. 2), 13 (n. 3, n. 4, n. 8), 14 (n. 10), 15 (n. 16, n. 17), 267
Taeuber, Irene B., 12 (n. 2), 13 (n. 3, n. 4, n. 8), 14 (n. 10), 15 (n. 16, n. 17), 267
Terris, Milton, 212 (n. 25)
Thomas, William L., Jr., 56 (n. 31)
Thompson, Warren S., 15 (n. 15), 267
Tolley, Howard R., 160 (n. 5)
Tucker, Sophie, 212
Tunnard, Christopher, 52 (n. 21)
Turner, Ralph, 271

van der Post, Laurens, 145 (n. 15)
van Loon, Henry B., 269
von Hoerner, Sebastian, 168, 168 (n. 24)
Vosburgh, John R., Jr., 50 (n. 11)

Walford, Lionel A., 270
Watt, James, 194–95
Weems, Constance Dulles, viii
Weir, John, 160, 160 (n. 4, n. 6), 162 (n. 9, n. 10), 163 (n. 12), 270
Wensberg, Erik, viii

Westoff, Charles F., 5, 5 (n. 3), 61, 61 (n. 42), 106 (n. 2), 268
Whelpton, P. K., 2 (n. 2), 18 (n. 21), 19 (n. 23), 92 (n. 27, n. 28), 93 (n. 31), 119 (n. 10), 126 (n. 15), 268
White, R. C., 213 (n. 28)
Whyte, William H., Jr., 52, 52 (n. 20)
Willcox, Oswin W., 163 (n. 13)
Williams, Glanville, 269

Williams, Robin M., Jr., 113n
Wilson, Woodrow, 179
Winslow, C. E. A., 212 (n. 25)
Wolfle, Dael L., 273
Wood, Samuel E., 51 (n. 15)
Woytinsky, E. S., 270
Woytinsky, W. S., 270
Wrong, Dennis, 267

Zimmerman, Anthony F., 87 (n. 20)
Zlotnick, Jack, 97 (n. 33)

Index of Subjects

Index of Subjects

Abortion: condemned by churches, 87; as means of family limitation, 238; practice of, in U.S., 238, 238n

Abstinence: as means of family limitation, 79, 238; religious support for, 79, 91

Adoption, extension of, as means to population stability, 239

Advertising, 146–47

Africa, 13, 29–30, 32–33

Age structure: origin of changes in, 12, 62; consequences of changes in, 62–65, 244; effect on supply of professional personel, 62–63

Anglican Church: approval of family planning, 82, 89–90; Lambeth Conferences, 82, 90; condemnation of birth control, 90; attitude toward sex, 116

Apathy, in face of population growth, vii–viii, 75

Argentina, 30, 40

Asceticism: of early Christianity, 83–84; and attitude toward birth control, 84–85; and attitude toward sex, 84–85

Asia, 18, 29–30, 32–33

Aspirations, level of: in nonindustrialized countries, 33; class differences in, in U.S., 210

Athens, 36, 193, 198

Attitudes: 103–30; of Americans toward U.S. population growth, vii–viii, 1; relevance to demographic conditions, 103, 107; specific to given culture, 103; as indicators of values, 107; Roman Catholic in U.S., 108n; congruent with opposition to population control, 109; congruent with support for population control, 109; of U.S. working class toward school, 210

Australia: 71; demographic conditions, 18, 29–30, 32; economic and social conditions, 32; population and economic conditions, 40, 143–144; aborigines in, 202, 203; migration to, 223n

Austria: net reproduction rate, 18; population density, 23; stabilization of population in, 231

Balance of Nature, 2, 161–62

Belgium: population density in, 22, 23; economic development in, 40

Biological weapons, 180, 181; as "equalizers" of military strengths, 183; need for controls over, 183–84

Birth control (*also see* Contraception *and* Family planning): 2–3, 25–27, 78; methods of, 36, 86–87, 238; religious argument against, 86–89, 105; religious argument for, 87–88, 90–91; humanist view of, 105; effect on family size, 127–28

Birth rate (*also see* Natality): decreases in as means to population stability, 2, 6, 225–34; defined, 12; in Europe, 15; in U.S., 15, 17, 18, 25, 26, 79; in industrialized countries, 18, 25, 26, 32; declines in, 25–26, 79; and demographic transition, 26–29; supports for high birth rate, 28; statistics, 32, 79; economic conditions and, 171

Black Death, 135

Brazil: effect of population on military strength of, 176, 179; relative size of population, 176

Bushmen of Kalahari Desert, 145, 202

Businessmen: beliefs of, 146–48; fear of depression, 147

California, overuse of parks in, 51

Canada, 18, 29, 40, 149

Capacities, individual and group, 198–216

Capitalization, as means to higher economic productivity, 40, 144–45

Celibacy, highly regarded by early churchmen, 84

Centralization, in response to population increase, 70

Ceylon: demographic conditions, 23, 30, 32; economic and social conditions, 32; effect of population on military strength of, 176

Change, social: relation to declines in natality, 27; and problem of determining "overpopulation," 38; economic consequences of, 153–54

Childlessness, 19, 21

Childrearing, effect on women, 119; differences in methods of, 213–14

Children, feeling of responsibility to: as inducement to lower natal-

ity, 126; as inducement to higher natality, 126–27

Children, liking for: as inducement to higher natality, 124–26; as inducement to lower natality, 125–26

China: migration to U.S. from, 13; and demographic transition, 30; population growth in, 30, 173; lack of markets for European goods, 145; effect of population on military strength of, 176, 179

Christianity: development of doctrine concerning contraception, 82–83; attitude toward sex, 84–85, 114–16

Church of England. *See* Anglican Church

Coercion: means of avoiding in achieving population stability, 103, 230–42, 245–46; types of for achieving population stability, 227–30, 242–43

Coitus interruptus: as means of birth control, 36, 238; Biblical reference to, 80

Cold war, effect on individual freedom in U.S., 67

Colorado, overuse of parks in, 51

Columbia University Forum, vii (n. 1), ix

Communist bloc, population of, 173

Comstock Acts, 97–99

Conception, involuntary, 21

Congestion, in U.S., 53

Connecticut, population density of, 23; prohibition on use of contraception, 98, 99

Consumption, economic: factors determining rate of, 137, 139, 145–50; population and, 137, 139, 145–50

Contraception (*also see* Birth control): practice of, 28–29, 92, 238;

laws concerning, in U.S., 29n, 97–100, 122; Biblical reference to, 80; changes in Roman Catholic position on, 86–88; approved by Protestant churches, 91 (n. 25); information on, defined as obscene, 97–98, 122; effect on family size, 127–28; need for improvements in techniques of, 235; need for greater access to, 237–38; unequal access to, in U.S., 237–38

Controls over individual behavior: in response to population growth, 66–74; in response to urbanization, 69

Costs of population increase in U.S., 45–74

Creativity: and population size, 191–93; determinants of, 193, 199–203

Crime, population increase and, 48

Culture: as determinant of optimum population, 35–37, 47, 49–74; as determinant of levels of economic consumption, 137, 139, 142, 145–46; as determinant of levels of economic productivity, 137–45; importance of, to invention, discovery, and diffusion, 193–96, 199–203

Culture differences: and problem of determining "overpopulation," 38, 46–48; assumed indicative of innate superiority and inferiority, 198–203; effect of, on intelligence test scores, 204–7

Dallas, Texas, water shortage in, 56, 164

Death rate (also see Mortality): increases in, as means to population stability, 6, 224–25; defined, 12; in U.S., 15, 17; declines in, during demographic transition, 25–28; statistics, 32

Defense against military attack: relevance of population to, 184–88; difficulties of, in age of weapons of mass destruction, 185–88; economic factors in, 187

Delaware, population density of, 23

Democratic party, statement on pollution, 58–59

Demographic transition: 25–32; and population increase in Europe, 28; reasons for, 28–29; defined and redefined, 29

Denmark: population density of, 23; economic development in, 40

Denver, Colorado, 51, 56

Depression, economic: effect on population growth in U.S., 18, 19; fear of, by businessmen, 147; as means to population stability, 244–45

De-salinization, 165–66

Dietary levels. See Food

Diffusion: defined, 201; importance of, 201–2; social and cultural determinants of, 201–2

Discovery, social and cultural determinants of, 193–96, 199–203

Disease, 27–28, 57, 135

Dissenters, religious, and industrialization in Britain, 195

Divine Plan, belief in and attitude toward population control, 112

Donora, Pennsylvania, air pollution in, 59–60

Draper Committee. See President's Committee to Study the United States Military Assistance Program

Eastern Orthodox churches, opposition to family planning, 91

Economic argument against population control: 133–54; noneconomic foundations of, 150–53; as support for religious opposition, 153

Economic conditions: effect on population, 18, 19, 137, 244–45; affected by population, 40, 137–41, 150, 153–54

Economic development: in various countries, 40, 135; and composition of work force, 117–18, 138, 242; and population, 135–36

Educational levels: statistics, 32; and crowding in schools, 47

Egypt: demographic conditions, 32, 37; economic and social conditions 32; effect of population on military strength of, 176

Employment of women: in U.S., 117–18, 241–42; relation to family size, 118; as means to reduction of family size, 241–42

Energy, consumption of, 32

England. See United Kingdom

Eskimo, 203

Ethnocentrism: and desire for population increase, 196–97; and ascription of priorities in invention and discovery, 200–2

Eugenic argument against population control. See "Selective control" argument against population control

Europe, 13, 29, 136

European Economic Community, 136

Expectation of Life, 15, 32

Fad: and family size in U.S., 128–30, 238–39, 240; and marriage patterns in U.S., 240

Family, American: changes in size of, 12, 19–21, 78–79; narrowing range of size of, 12, 19–21; child-

lessness, 19, 21; size of, today, 19–20; functions of, 123–24; possible effect of fads on, 128–30, 238–39, 240; patterns of childrearing, 213–14; need to alter ideal of, 238–40; dominant form of, 243–44

Family planning: attitude of Roman Catholics toward, 85–89, 91, 92; Anglican approval of, 89–90; attitude of Protestants toward, 89–91, 92, 94; attitude of Jews toward, 92, 94; clinics in U.S., 99; need for education in, 236–37; methods of, 238

Famine, 13, 27–28, 40–41

Fatalism, in face of population growth, 75

Fecundity, declines in with age, 21

Fertility. See Natality

Finland, 40

Food: consumption of, 32; surpluses of in U.S., 159; possibilities for increasing production of, 159–64; effect of population growth on types of, 160–64

Foreign aid, U.S., 33–34

France: demographic conditions, 18, 23, 26, 135, 180; economic development, 135; less affected by depression, 150; as nuclear power, 180; stabilization of population, 231

Freedom: origin of decreases of in U.S., 66–74; origin of increases of in U.S., 67

Germany: net reproduction rate, 18; population density, 23; birth rate, 26; natural increase, 26; experiences during wartime, 141–42, 173n, 174; technological development, 198

Gifted individuals, assumptions concerning relation of population size to number of, 191–96

Great Plains of U.S., 149–50

Gross national product: as indicator of level of living, 41; calculation of, 42

Guatemala: demographic conditions, 32; economic and social conditions, 32

Haiti: population density, 23; effect of population on military strength of, 176

Hamburg, Germany, 141–42

Hiroshima, Japan, 182

Home ownership: increase of in U.S., 125; possible effect on natality in U.S., 125

Homosexuality, as means to population stability, 230

Housing: effect of population on, 47, 53, 69, 152; possible effect on population, 129

Hungary, stabilization of population in, 231

Illiteracy, in nonindustrialized countries, 30, 32

Immigration. See Migration

Immortality, belief in and attitude toward population control, 109, 110–11

Income, per capita: statistics, 32; as indicator of material level of living, 37, 42–43; as indicator of quality of life, 41–43

India: population growth in, 15, 30–31, 96; population density, 23; and demographic transition, 30; birth rate, 32; death rate, 32; energy consumption, 32; food consumption, 32, 160; infant mortality rate, 32; level of living, 32; life expectancy, 32, 176–77; per capita income, 32; population in agriculture, 32; urban population, 32; overpopulation in, 37; economic development, 96, 136; effect of population on military strength of, 176, 179

Indianapolis, Indiana, survey of natality in, 92, 118, 119, 126

Indians, American: number, 12; Guayake of Paraguay, 198–99; limited technological development, 198; Navajo, 202; scores of on intelligence tests, 205

Individual rights, attitude toward: and attitude toward population control, 109, 119–22; and attitude toward government, 120–22

Indonesia: and Demographic Transition, 30; population growth in, 30; effect of population on military strength of, 176, 179

Industrial Revolution. See Industrialization

Industrialization: defined, 25n; and population, 25–32; and development of public health programs, 27; and development of scientific medicine, 27; and levels of living, 27, 32–34; and pressures for reduction of family size, 27, 78; social changes during, 27, 78; effect on employment of women, 117, 242; effect on military conditions, 178–79

Infant mortality, 30, 32

Institute of Judicial Administration, 65

Intelligence: as criterion in "selective control" of population, 190–91; assumptions of declines in, 190–91; difficulty of assessing, 190; difficulty of defining, 190, 203–4

Intelligence tests: ambiguity in re-

sults of, 190–91, 207–8; assumed
indicative of innate superiority
and inferiority, 198; usefulness
of, 203–4; construction of, 204–5,
209; meaningless for cross-cultural
comparisons, 204–7; scores of different groups on, 205–7, 208;
sources of bias in, 208–11; sources
of group differences in scores on,
210–11
Invention: social and cultural determinants of, 192–96, 199–203;
adoption of, 194; bureaucratization of, 201; often unconscious,
201; piecemeal character of, 201
Inventiveness, social and cultural
determination of, 192–96
IQ tests. *See* Intelligence tests
Ireland: emigration from, 13; famines, 13; control of population in,
227–28; marriage patterns in,
227–28
Israel, women soldiers in, 174; effect
of population on military strength
of, 176
Italy: population density, 23; effect
of population on military strength
of, 176

Japan: demographic conditions, 23,
26, 29, 32, 52; economic and social conditions, 32; economic development of, 136; effect of population on military strength of,
176, 179; atomic bombing of, 182
Java, overpopulation in, 37
Judaism: pro-natalist doctrines, 78;
attitude of Jews toward family
limitation in U.S., 92, 94; number of children expected by U.S.
Jews, 92
Juvenile delinquency, population
increase and, 48

Keene, New Hampshire, 57
Korea, population density, 23

Labor force. *See* Work force
Lambeth Conference. *See under*
Anglican Church
Land, competition for, 53–54, 68–
69
Latin America: population growth
in, 18, 30, 96; and demographic
transition, 29–30; inequality of
incomes in, 41 (*also see* under individual country headings)
Level of living, material: relevance
of population to, 7, 53–56; differences between industrialized and
nonindustrialized countries, 30–
34; per capita income as indicator
of, 41–43; and pollution of air
and water, 57–60
Level of living, nonmaterial: differences between industrialized and
nonindustrialized countries, 30–
34, 176–77; relevance of population to, 45–52, 57–74
"Life chances," different levels of
in U.S., 212–14
Life Magazine, 134
Lobbying: in response to population increase, 70–72; inequality
in, 71–73
London, England, air pollution in,
59
Luxembourg, economic development in, 40

Marriage: in U.S., 20–21, 117; age
at, 21, 227; in England and
Wales, 21; in Ireland, 21, 227–28;
proportions marrying, 21, 117,
227; Roman Catholic view of, 85–
86, 91; economic consequences of,
138–39; changes in types of as
means to population stability,

227–30; postponement of as means to population stability, 227, 240

Maryland, population density, 23

Mass transportation, 69–70

Massachusetts: population density, 23; laws against contraceptives, 99

"Mater et Magister," 101

Medicine, 27

Mental Illness, population and, 48

Mexico: demographic conditions, 32; economic and social conditions, 32; effect of population on military strength of, 176

Miami, Florida, 50

Michigan, overuse of parks in, 51–52

Migration: as solution for population pressure, 2, 14–15, 136, 167–68, 222–24; and U.S. population growth, 12–13, 13–15; determinant of population growth, 12; quotas in U.S., 12; determinants of, 14, 223; interplanetary, 136, 168–70; contemporary movements, 223

Military argument against population control, 173–88

Military strength, national: determinants of, 173–74, 181; relevance of population to, 173–88; economic cost of, 175; effect of population on, in various countries, 176

Mississippi, 56

Mortality (also see Death rate): control over, 2, 15–16, 27–29; determinant of population growth, 2, 6, 12, 30; in U.S., 2, 15–17; increases in, as means to population stability, 6–7, 154, 224–25; factors in reduction of, 15–16, 25, 27–29; infant and child, 30, 234–35;

decreases in, as means to population stability, 234–35

Muncie, Indiana, 112–13

Nagasaki, Japan, 182

Natality (also see Birth rate): control over, 2, 25–29; determinant of population growth, 2, 12; in nonindustrialized countries, 3, 15, 32; decreases in as means to population stability, 7, 154, 225–34; in U.S., 2, 15–21, 221–22, 222n; factors in reduction of, 25–29; in industrialized countries, 25–29; values and level of, 28–29; religious differentials in, in U.S., 92–95

National Council of Churches, approval of family planning, 90–91

Nationalism, 32–33

Natural increase: defined, 12; in U.S., 12, 13, 15–18, 25; in various countries, 13, 26; in world, 26

"Natural law," 85–87, 91

Near East, 29–30, 33

Net reproduction rate: as predictor of population growth, 16; defined, 16; in various countries, 16, 18

Netherlands: population density, 22, 23; economic development, 40; population pressure, 135; encouragement of emigration from, 167–68; shortage of space, 167

New Jersey: population density, 22, 23; water pollution, 57; overcrowded schools, 64–65; water shortages, 164

New York: population density, 23; air pollution, 59

New York City: traffic, 54; water shortages, 56, 164; water pollution, 57; air pollution, 58

New Zealand, 18, 29, 40

Newburgh, New York, 115

Nonindustrialized societies: population growth in, 3, 15, 30–31; mortality in, 28; conditions of life in, 30–34, 176–77; economic conditions, 32; natality in, 32

Norway, economic development, 40

Nuclear weapons, 180; as "equalizers" of military strengths, 183; need for controls over, 183–84

Old Testament: support for pronatalism, 79–81; and high evaluation of children, 81; support for conjugal affection and companionship, 81

Onan, Biblical story of, 80–81, 84

Optimum population: 35–44; and goals, 35–37; and values, 35–37; definitions of 35, 37, 39, 42, 43; criteria of, 36–41, 43; economic criterion of, 39–41

Oregon, water pollution in, 57

Outdoor Recreation Resources Review Commission, 54–55

Overcrowding: in U.S., 50–52; and mortality levels, 171

Overpopulation: extent of related to culture, 35–37, 47, 49–74; difficulty of measuring, 37; noneconomic criteria of, 37, 43, 73–74; economic criterion of, 40–41; in U.S., 45

Pakistan: population growth in, 30, 96; effect of population on military strength of, 176, 179

Parks, national and state in U.S., 48–52, 53

Pennsylvania, population density of, 23

Personality, individual, social and cultural determinants of, 193

Pesticides, 161–62

Planned Parenthood Federation, 99

Planning, social: difficulties of, without population stability, 61, 66; Kennedy Administration and, 66; need for, 66, 68, 70

Poison gas weapons: 180, 181; as "equalizers" of military strengths, 183; need for controls over, 183–84

Pollution: 56–60; water, 56–57; air, 57–60; causes of, 57–58; dangers of, 59–60

Population control, arguments against: economic, 133–54; "scientific," 155–72; military, 173–88; "selective control," 189–216

Population control, arguments for, 6–7, 43–74, 219

Population density: 22–24; assumed effects on individual and social well-being, 48; effect on behavior of rats, 48; costs of low density, 149–50

Population distribution, in U.S., 21–24

Population stability: need for, in U.S., 6–7, 45–46, 62–66, 219; in nonindustrialized countries, 30; redistribution of people as means to, 222–24; compulsory means to attainment of, 227–30, 242–43; voluntary means to attainment of, 230–42, 245–46

Population, U.S.: attitudes of Americans toward, vii–viii, 1; confusion and misinformation about, vii–viii, 3; reporting about, in media of mass communication, vii–viii; growth of, 1, 3–5, 11, 12, 13–21, 25, 30–31, 173; projected growth, 4–6, 7, 45; Colonial period, 11, 14; depression and, 14, 18, 19, 244–45; foreign-born, 14; birth rate, 15, 17, 18, 25, 26, 79; distribution of, 21–24; urbanization, 21–22, 23–24; density of settlement, 22–24; rural population, 22; suburbanization, 22, 24; and demographic transition, 29–30

Population, U.S.: consequences of, 7, 31, 45–74; creation of new needs, 24; less open space, 24, 46, 48–52; limitations on recreation, 24, 46, 48–52; effect on social relationships, 46, 123–24; increased costs, 53–56, 73; limitations on personal freedom, 66–74

Population, World: confusion and misinformation about, vii–viii; rapid growth, 1, 11, 18, 24–25; affects social conditions, 6, 7, 45; cessation of growth inevitable, 6; determinants of, 6, 12; projected growth, 11; expansion of European peoples, 13; growth in western Europe, 13, 18; growth in Asia, 18; growth in English-speaking countries, 18; growth in Latin America, 18; growth of, as great achievement of mankind, 27

President's Commission on National Goals, 97

President's Committee to Study the United States Military Assistance Program, 88, 97, 101

Production, economic, factors determining rate of, 137–45

Productivity, economic: differences between industrialized and nonindustrialized economies, 29–30; methods of increasing, 144–45

Protestant churches: pro-natalist doctrines of, 78; support for family limitation, 79, 82, 89–91; lack of unity concerning family limitation, 85, 89, 90–91, 101; failure to take stand on population, 89; attitude of Protestants toward family limitation, in U.S., 92, 94; number of children expected by U.S. Protestants, 92; and enactment of Comstock laws, 99

Public health, 27

Puerto Ricans, 210

Quality of life: definition in terms of values, 35, 38–39; difficulty of defining, 35–44, 47–48; relation of population to, 35, 45–52, 56–74; declines in, as consequence of population growth, 45–47, 50–52, 58–74

Racial antagonism, population increase and, 48

Racial prejudice and discrimination, effect of, on intelligence test scores, 210–11

Recreation: effect of population growth on, 49–52, 69; need for, 49–50; statistics of in U.S., 49–50; estimates of future needs, 50

Religion: importance of, in limiting discussion of population, 3, 95–97, 101–2; and aversion to controlling population, 77; and failure to think about population, 77; medieval theological doctrines, 78; pro-natalist doctrines, 78; pro-natalist heritage, 79–81; and approval of family limitation, 81, 105, 114; and opposition to family limitation, 81; importance of, in determining family size in U.S., 93–95

Republican party, statement on pollution, 58

Resources: consumption of, in industrial societies, 33, 53, 55–56, 164–65, 177; possibility of increasing supplies of, 155, 157, 158, 165–67; redistribution of, as adjustment to population growth, 220–22

Response, desire for, as inducement to higher natality, 123–24

Rhode Island, population density, 22, 23

Rhythm method of birth control: justification for, 83, 86–88; history of, 86–88; determinants of success of, 115

Roman Catholic Church: use of non-religious arguments against population control, 75; pro-natalist doctrines, 78; evolution of doctrine on family, 83; lack of unity concerning family limitation, 85–89, 100; approval of "rhythm" method of birth control, 86–88; statement of American bishops on population, 88, 101; attitudes of Catholics toward family limitation in U.S., 92, 94; number of children expected by U.S. Catholics, 92; influence on government policy in U.S., 95–97, 100–101; and retention of Comstock laws, 99; attitudes toward sex, 115–16

Royal Commission on Population, 26, 65

Russia: population increase in, 25 (n. 33), 30, 173; and demographic transition, 30; inequality of incomes in, 41; experiences during wartime, 173n, 174; population and military strength of, 176, 179; as major military power, 184; nuclear tests by, 188

Sacrifice: inevitable in attaining population stability, 2, 107; on part of parents with few children, 233

"Safe" period. See Rhythm method of birth control

School: percentage of adults with no schooling, 32; effect of population growth on provision of, 64–65; as middle-class institution in U.S., 209; working class attitudes toward, in U.S., 210

"Scientific" argument against population control: 155–72; as cover for other forms of opposition, 155; used by Catholic bishops, 155; utopian nature of, 156; underlying assumptions of, 157; danger of accepting, 158; based on studies of nonhumans, 170–71

Scientists, number of, determined by social and cultural conditions, 192–96

Scotland. See United Kingdom

Security, desire for, as inducement to higher natality, 123–24

"Selective control" argument against population control: 189–216; class bias in, 189; difficulties of determining criteria to be used, 189–90; injustice of, 189; racism in, 189; difficulties of determining which individuals meet criteria, 190; intelligence as desirable trait, 190–91

Sex, attitudes toward: of medieval Christianity, 84–85, 114–15; and attitude toward population control, 109, 114–16; of Roman Catholic Church, 115–16

Sex ratio, origin of changes in, 12, 20–21

Slavery, importation of slaves into U.S., 13

Social change, attitude toward man as an agent of, and attitude toward population control, 109, 111–14

Social classes, in U.S.: and scores on intelligence tests, 206–11; different attitudes toward school, 209–10; different school experiences, 209–10; differences in levels of health, 212; different "life chances," 212–14

Social obligations, attitude toward: and attitude toward population control, 109, 119–22; and attitude toward government, 120–22

Social services: 60–66; housing, 47, 53, 69, 152; recreation facilities, 49–52, 69; effect of population growth on, 53, 60–70; factors affecting demand for, 53, 61, 66–70; custodial care, 61; lag between needs and provision, 61–65; police and fire protection, 61; professional services, 61–63; roads, 61; sanitation, 61; schooling, 64–65; administration of justice, 65; zoning, 68–69; mass transportation, 69–70; pollution abatement, 70; traffic control, 70; sewage disposal, 70; water, 70

Society, feeling of responsibility to: as incentive to higher natality, 127–28, 197; as incentive to lower natality, 127–28, 231, 233

Space, possibilities for increasing amount of for settlement, 136, 166–68

Space travel: as solution to overpopulation, 136, 168–70; possibilities for, 168–70

Spartans, 198

Specialization, economic, 40

Steam engine, invention of, 194–95

Sterility: involuntary, 21; need for improvement in methods of reducing, 235–36

Sterilization: condemned by churches, 87; as means to attainment of population stability, 227; as means of family limitation, 238

Sweden: demographic conditions, 26, 32; economic and social conditions, 32; less affected by depression, 150; stabilization of population in, 231

Switzerland, economic development in, 40

Taxation, as means to population stability, 242–43

Telegraph, invention of, 200–1

Tikopia, and optimum population, 36–37

Traffic congestion: in Europe, 47; in U.S., 51; cost of, in U.S., 54

Underdeveloped countries. See nonindustrialized countries

Underpopulation: economic criterion of, 39–40; in various countries, 40

Union of Soviet Socialist Republics. See Russia

United Kingdom: birth rate, 15, 26, 32; net reproduction rate, 18; natural increase, 26; death rate, 32; economic and social conditions, 32; infant mortality rate, 32; life expectancy, 32; inequality of incomes in, 41; as nuclear power, 180; population of, 180; as major military power, 184; development of science and technology in, 194–96; Dissenters, 195; population of, during period of rapid industrial and scientific development, 195–96; stabilization of population in, 231

United States: population increase in, 1, 3, 5, 11, 12, 13–21, 30; birth rate, 15, 18, 25, 26, 32, 79; death rate, 15, 32; life expectancy, 15, 32, 177; natural increase, 15, 25, 26; urban population, 21–22, 22, 24, 32; population engaged in agriculture, 24, 32; and demographic transition, 29–30; consumption of nonrenewable resources, 31, 34; adults with no schooling, 32; energy consumption, 32; food consumption, 32; infant mortality rate, 32; level of living, 32; per capita income, 32; population and military strength of, 176, 177, 179; military activities of, since World War II, 180; monopoly of nuclear weapons, 181; as major military power, 184; family limitation in, 231; impediments to attainment of population stability in, 232, 233–34

United States Department of Health, Education, and Welfare, 97

United States Department of State, report on world population, 97

United States Supreme Court, ruling on Connecticut birth control law, 98

United States vs. one obscene book entitled "Married Love," 97–98

Urbanization: in U.S., 21–22, 24–25, 47, 52; differences between industrialized and nonindustrialized countries, 29–30, 32; population in cities (statistics), 32; and increased needs, 57, 70; and defense, 184–85

Uruguay, and demographic transition, 29–30

Utah, water pollution in, 57

Values: 103–30; and idea of optimum population, 35; as determinants of demographic conditions, 103; in definition of a

"problem," 103–4; specific to given culture, 103; absence of empirical evidence on, 104–5; influence of on behavior, 104; in U.S., 106; indicated by specific attitudes, 107–8; Roman Catholic, 110–11n; group differences in, 214

Venezuela: demographic conditions, 32; economic and social conditions, 32

War: effect on population, 18, 19, 141; World War II, 18, 141–42, 180; effect on work force, 141–42; Korean War, 174, 180–81; "conventional" war, 180–82; manpower requirements of, 182–84

Water: increased use of, 55–56, 164–65; pollution, 56–57; shortages of, in U.S., 56, 164; increasing demands for, 164–65; consumers of, 165; determinants of consumption, 165; possibilities of increasing supply, 165–66; and settlement of empty spaces, 167

Westchester County, New York, 53

Women: attitude toward, related to attitude toward population control, 109, 117–19; employment of, 117–18, 241–42; need for activities alternative to childrearing, 241–42

Work force: in agriculture, 24, 32; size of in underpopulated country, 40; factors determining composition of, 138–43; effect of mass death on, during World War II, 141–42; means to increase size of, in U.S., 143; increase in types of jobs commonly assigned to women, 242; effects on, of changes in birth rate, 244

Zoning: urban, 67–68, rural, 68–69